PRAISE FOR *THE PO*

'Simon Fanshawe has written the n ~~p~~ ...~~ng~~ book on diversity I've ever read. Beautifully written and full of narrative power, *The Power of Difference* weaves together the author's personal experiences, insights from research and remarkable stories of others' journeys to show both how to build genuine inclusion and why it matters so very much in our multi-cultural world and to the success of organizations.'
Amy C Edmondson, Professor, Harvard Business School and author of
The Fearless Organization

'*The Power of Difference* reminds us that no company can afford to let diversity and inclusion slip down the priority list. With wit and clarity, it lays out practical ways for all of us in business to attract and engage the widest range of talent in these uncertain times, in order to make our companies more innovative and profitable. I urge leaders to read it and act on its solutions.'
Lord Karan Bilimoria CBE, President of the CBI and Founder and Chairman of Cobra Beer

'*The Power of Difference* is incredibly timely. Simon Fanshawe brings wit, wisdom and challenge to pointing a way forward and how inclusion must embrace all voices. This is a call to action for every one of us to play our part in using our difference to power a better future for companies.'
Peter Cheese, CEO, Chartered Institute of Personnel and Development (CIPD)

'With insight, great stories and wonderful language, *The Power of Difference* helps all of us – managers, teachers, citizens – listen, truly listen, so that we can redesign how we live and work and discover the enjoyment of managing diversity along the way.'
Iris Bohnet, Academic Dean of Harvard Kennedy School and author of
What Works: Gender equality by design

'Diversity is the life-blood of innovation. What is often missing are the practical ways to create the culture for teams to thrive, where everyone has the confidence to contribute. This is an essential part of the environment for discovery, research and implementation to flourish safely. *The Power of Difference* provides managers and entrepreneurs with practical insights to drive innovation, while having the rigorous discussions that engage everyone's voice in assessing and taking risks.'

David Gann CBE, Professor of Innovation and Entrepreneurship, Saïd Business School and Chairman of the UK Atomic Energy Authority

'*The Power of Difference* is wonderful, a remarkably enjoyable and immensely helpful read for any one in a leadership position or indeed anyone who feels the huge responsibility of improving the experience of their colleagues. The practical but powerful examples and illustrations peppered throughout the book contain the dilemmas and opportunities faced by a wide range of individuals and institutions. The golden thread was yes, the complexity but also the huge potential that exists for individuals and organizations.'

Stephen Posey, CEO, The Royal Papworth NHS Trust

'At the beginning and end of his wide-ranging book on "the power of difference", Simon Fanshawe underscores that safe spaces should offer safety for disagreement, not from disagreement. That bracing insight is the calling card of this worthy work. In a warm and accessible manner, the book opens space to rethink diversity and inclusion efforts from first principles, including asking if diversity really is good for business, if the promises made for implicit bias can be fulfilled, and if the "tone at the top" matters as much as many say. I predict readers will find themselves in equally vehement agreement and disagreement with different parts of this work, but ultimately emerge feeling enriched by its many provocations.'

Kenji Yoshino, Chief Justice Earl Warren Professor of Constitutional Law, NYU School of Law and Faculty Director, Center for Diversity, Inclusion, and Belonging

'*The Power of Difference* both acknowledges the complexity in working on diversity and inclusion and then suggests really practical ways through. I simply loved it and the way it was written.'

Geeta Nanda OBE, CEO, Metropolitan Thames Valley Housing

The Power of Difference

Where the complexities of diversity and inclusion meet practical solutions

Simon Fanshawe

KoganPage

First published in Great Britain and the United States in 2022 by Kogan Page Limited

2nd Floor, 45 Gee Street
London
EC1V 3RS
United Kingdom
www.koganpage.com

8 W 38th Street, Suite 902
New York, NY 10018
USA

4737/23 Ansari Road
Daryaganj
New Delhi 110002
India

Kogan Page books are printed on paper from sustainable forests.

© Simon Fanshawe, 2022

The right of Simon Fanshawe to be identified as the author of this work has been asserted by him in accordance with the Copyright, Designs and Patents Act 1988.

Hardback   978 1 3986 0156 7
Paperback   978 1 3986 0154 3
eBook   978 1 3986 0155 0

British Library Cataloguing-in-Publication Data
A CIP record for this book is available from the British Library.

Library of Congress Cataloging-in-Publication Data
Names: Fanshawe, Simon, author.
Title: The power of difference : where the complexities of diversity and inclusion meet practical solutions / Simon Fanshawe.
Description: London ; New York, NY : Kogan Page, 2022. | Includes
    bibliographical references and index. |
Identifiers: LCCN 2021021289 (print) | LCCN 2021021290 (ebook) | ISBN
    9781398601543 (paperback) | ISBN 9781398601567 (hardback) | ISBN
    9781398601550 (ebook)
Subjects: LCSH: Diversity in the workplace. | Multiculturalism. | Personnel
    management. | BISAC: BUSINESS & ECONOMICS / Human Resources & Personnel
    Management | BUSINESS & ECONOMICS / Workplace Culture
Classification: LCC HF5549.5.M5 F36 2022 (print) | LCC HF5549.5.M5
    (ebook) | DDC 658.3008–dc23

Typeset by Hong Kong FIVE Workshop, Hong Kong
Print production managed by Jellyfish
Printed and bound by CPI Group (UK) Ltd, Croydon CR0 4YY

CONTENTS

SOME THANKS

This book wouldn't have happened were it not for several groups of people.

The women, the lesbians and gays and the friends from wholly different social backgrounds who I met through university and community politics and who generously gave me a really hard time about class and feminism and, frequently to my great discomfort, opened my eyes to their life experience.

The writers and doers whose rigour and research have so inspired material progress on diversity and the transformation of organizations: Iris Bohnet, Chris Brink, Jim Collins, Jennifer Eberhardt, Amy C Edmondson, Martin N Davidson, Scott E Page and the late Katherine Phillips.

The writers whose clarity always shines a light and raises the challenging questions: Ta-Nehisi Coates, Caroline Criado Perez, Atul Gawande, Doris Kearns Goodwin, Adam Kingl, Kenan Malik, Adolph Reed, Adam Rutherford, Sathnam Sanghera, Matthew Syed and Kenji Yoshino.

The friends and colleagues who read and commented on parts of the text, giving it direction as it blundered through its various iterations: Rantimi Ayodele, Kate Dodsworth, Jilly Forster, Hannah Jordan, Bryony Mortimer, Holly Phillips, Jesse Singal, Kathleen Stock and Kate Varah.

To Jo Berry and Jacqui Gavin whose choices and the way they live them out in the world inspire.

And particularly to my old university friend, Frances Howie, my one-time history teacher and remarkable expert on conflict resolution, Oliver Ramsbotham, and my partner in business, long-standing friend, fellow performer and ever gentle challenger, Roy Hutchins. Each of them showed me how to open up the text to transform assertions with which to disagree into invitations to debate and discuss.

And to my husband, to whom I dedicate the book, whose encouragement is constant, whose belief in my possibility is disarmingly certain and who is the power of difference in my life.

To my lovely husband, who is the power of difference in my life

It is hardly possible to overrate the value... of placing human beings in contact with persons dissimilar to themselves, and with modes of thought and action unlike those with which they are familiar... Such communication has always been... one of the primary sources of progress.

John Stuart Mill in *Principles of Political Economy*
(Mill 1846, vol 2, book 3, chapter 7, section 5)

Introduction

Who am I and why this book?

Before we start, I feel the need to explain what this book is. And what it isn't.

It's written by a diversity professional – me – aimed at people whose work or curiosity – intellectual, personal or political – draws them into thinking about diversity. That's you. But it's not Ten Easy Steps to Diversity in Business. It's not Inclusion Made Easy. In fact, rather the opposite. If anything, it's about pointing out just how incredibly difficult the whole field of diversity and inclusion is. But there's optimism in here because, no matter how difficult, there is nothing more satisfying than making honest interaction between people and their differences flourish in order to achieve great things. Which is ultimately the point.

What I have written largely comes from my own experience over four decades of trying to work out how a middle-class, public school educated, White bloke, who happens to be gay, can find a role in the pursuit of social and organizational change. Often when that change is a challenge to the advantages of my own privileged start in life. So, as well as drawing on that journey and a range of current research, the book is told through stories – often quite personal ones – experiences of working with movements of social change and also with clients through my company Diversity by Design. The purpose of all of that is to engage you in the profoundly rich experience of increasing the diversity of your colleagues and to engage you in thinking in fresh ways about diversity's relevance more broadly to society.

It's about the power of seeing difference, valuing it and combining it in those you manage and work with to increase the effectiveness of what you are attempting to do together. I am struck by what people often say when they first meet each other socially. Understandably they exclaim with great enthusiasm: 'We had so much in common!' But I always find myself thinking. How dull is that? What you have in common can only be a starting point. The excitement really kicks off when you begin to discover each other's differences.

One of the first times I became aware of the significance of difference was a day when I was walking to the train station in my last year at university in 1978 in Brighton. I had been studying law for almost three years at Sussex, where I had found a whole host of clues to who I might be in the rest of my life. A year or so before that I had come out. To my friends, who all appeared to know already. To my parents, who wonderfully reassured me of their continuing love. And to the rest of the world, or at least as much of it with which I had so far communicated, who mainly reacted with supreme indifference, occasionally peppered with bursts of hostility.

These were the student days when badges were worn. If you didn't have a badge or a t-shirt with a slogan in condemnation of apartheid in South Africa or in support of A Women's Right to Choose, you really were thought to have no opinions at all and absolutely nothing to say. Our political stances were emblazoned on cotton and tin staking our claims to virtue and our constant preparedness for verbal fisticuffs 'on the side of right'.

That day I was wearing a badge that said something charmingly inviting to the outside, largely heterosexual, world like 'Scr*w You I'm Gay'. I was getting predictably hostile looks. On reflection over 40 years later, they were probably as much for my aggressive tone that early in the morning as for any kind of antipathy to me being gay. But the stares irked me. Even though I was brimming with the zeal of the newly liberated, they fanned my insecurities. I reached up to unpin the badge from my lapel. At the exact same moment, I glanced over to the other side of the street. A young Black woman was walking in the opposite direction. My hand dropped. I left the badge where it was. It was my naïve tribute to the fact that she couldn't hide. However proud or not she felt of being Black, she couldn't pop back into a temporary closet and conceal her colour. Even though the looks she would receive pretty much every moment of every day would mark her out as different in a majority White country that, as many people of colour have written, might well have made her shiver inside with discomfort.

That moment has stayed with me. That tiny unspoken moment. Because it was a realization of what can happen when you encounter difference. I saw diversity and realized how it could enrich my understanding of life. Finding my way through the world didn't mean wearing badges announcing what I thought. It meant living my values openly, embracing difference and through it finding common cause with others. I am not Black. Who knows if she was a lesbian. But what I saw in the difference between us was where I thought that we might have something in common. We might both understand the feeling of being observed as different.

Creating alliances through difference

Six years later, on 10 December 1984, my father died of cancer. By then I was a comedian. Apparently, the UK's 'first openly gay comedian', although that fact rather passed me by in the frenetic swirl of myriad other new voices emerging in what was then called 'alternative comedy'. The Miners' Strike was going full pelt. Despite serious doubts about their leader Arthur Scargill and his refusal to hold a ballot, many of us still gave full throttled support. Among the hundreds of 'X, Y or Z Support the Miners' groups was the most unlikely alliance between the pitmen and their defenders: Lesbians and Gays Support the Miners (LGSM). If you've seen the film *Pride* you will have witnessed how this glorious mismatch somehow flourished. The miners came to London (and Brighton, where I still live) and uncomplainingly ate their way through vegan stews and LGSM members happily consumed spam fritters and bacon rolls when they took cash and supplies down to the pit village in the Dulais Valley in South Wales. The differences between us were cultural, in many cases our vastly different class backgrounds and certainly our life opportunities. To be blunt, had we ever met any miners and had they ever met any lesbians?

I had called my mother for news in the afternoon that day and she told me that my father had finally gone. 'Go and do your gig, darling', she said. 'Come home in the morning.' What she didn't know, and I never told her – middle-class army widow that she now was – was that the 'gig' was 'Pits and Perverts', an LGSM fundraiser for the striking miners (1). It had been named after *The Sun* newspaper's story about the group that had appeared under the headline: 'Perverts support the pits' (2). Top of the bill was Jimmy Somerville (then in the band Bronski Beat) with a bunch of comics supporting. The highlight though was when a miner called David Donovan spoke to the audience on behalf of the Dulais mining community. He said, 'You have worn our badge "Coal Not Dole" and you know what harassment means, as we do. Now we will support you. It won't change overnight, but now 140,000 miners know... about Blacks and gays... and we will never be the same.'

He didn't say we will all wear the same badge. He said you wore our badge, now we will wear yours. Two more different groups it would be hard to imagine, but we were able to recognize our differences and, through them, link arms towards a common objective.

Forget the specifics of the politics – you may or may not be the kind of person who would have agreed with or supported a national strike – but I can only hope that David Donovan's words resonate with you wherever you work. The heart of what he said is that only by recognizing their differences can people really find the way to collaborate. That is as true in the office as it is on the picket line. Because understanding that we are different is at the core of our relationships with one another.

The value of conflict: turning it positive

I remember as an impressionable teenager reading RD Laing, of whom his son said, 'It was ironic that my father became well-known as a family psychiatrist when, in the meantime, he had nothing to do with his own family' (3). Laing was alcoholic and depressive, so perhaps I shouldn't have been surprised by the bleakness of his writing. There was something, on the face of it, very disheartening about his assertion that, 'I cannot experience your experience. You cannot experience my experience. We are both invisible men' (4). I found the whole sentiment thoroughly dispiriting until I caught on that it was the *attempt* to understand each other's experiences that yielded the richness. He was just stating our profound separateness. Once we all recognize that, then we've got a journey to go on together. The truth about humans is that maybe the only thing that we have in common is that we are all completely different. And we can never properly know one another. We can never see the world through another's eyes, filter it through another's experience. We will always be approximating, in the hope that we get closer to some kind of truth over time. While we can never know each other, it can be a great joy to go on the journey in order to try. And if we go on that journey, we must do so in the certain knowledge that it will never end. To seek to understand each other's differences is an essential human challenge. To know that we never will is the human condition. At its heart, that is all diversity is. To appreciate the power of difference.

My parents argued. A lot. About money mainly. It's not that they didn't have any. It was just that they had very different attitudes to the money they did have. My mother always said, 'buy the best you can afford'. My father, who was as emotionally generous as he was financially cautious, always tried to spend less. Money was a proxy. They were really fighting for control. But, ferocious as their arguments felt, they always made up. And they always reassured me that not only did they love each other, which they did, but they also loved me. So I grew up in the vortex of, what at radical refectory-occupying Sussex I would later find out Marxists called, dialectic. Stanford University's *Encyclopaedia of Philosophy* now tells me that it means 'a method of philosophical argument that involves some sort of contradictory process between opposing sides' (5). This is a more genteel and rather academic way of describing my mother and father's irregular but furious barneys. In other words, I inherited an emotional landscape from my parents in which life is lived through the conflict of opposites.

However, it wasn't until I was in my forties that I started to meet people who were making sense of that in a deep, personal and constructive way. They accept that conflict is a given. Whether large or small, it's an inevitable part of human relationships and life. More often than not, it can't be prevented or resolved. It can only be faced and managed. But the best thing they showed me was that sometimes, against every expectation, managing it can produce remarkable and optimistic results. Conflict comes in many forms: casual rudeness, language that offends, relationships that damage us, and friends or family who turn their back on us. For most of us, most of the time, it's at a fairly low level – families, neighbours, colleagues – but at its most heinous it escalates to violence, assault, torture, even murder. It can happen to us or to our most dear. In one way or another it will always feature in our lives, so the question is how will we respond? What choices will we make?

Some people – and I may be talking about you and your family or you and your colleagues at work here – hold on to the hurt done to them and metaphorically take it out regularly and burnish it. I've certainly done that! They may even get an amount of perverse energy from doing so. I've done that too! Others, and these are the ones who began to fascinate me, handle it in such a way that it brings significant rewards and motivation to their lives. These people have decided that if they cling fast to the injury done to them, they will probably be trapped. But by exploring it, understanding it, reaching out across it, they can find a way forward. They have had to respond to the most catastrophic kinds of event possible, but the more I heard their stories, the more I realized that there were lessons for everybody in dealing with the much smaller things that happen in our personal lives and at work.

In 2001, I had lunch in South Africa with Peter and Linda Biehl, a well-off couple from the United States. I was talking to them for a piece I was writing for a magazine. There were five of us at the table. The other two were a young South African guy and his girlfriend. The Americans raise several million dollars a year in the United States to support community projects in The Cape through the Amy Biehl Foundation, named after their daughter. The young man was one of the employees of the charity. The two couples saw a fair amount of each other. This lunch in Franschhoek, one of the smartest addresses in the wine district and renowned for its restaurants, was a bit of a treat. A day out. Some time off. Even though the young man had murdered Amy.

In 1993 Amy had spent a year in South Africa, where she went to study and work with women in the transition to democracy at a crucial time at the end of apartheid. It was a very volatile moment in the country between Nelson Mandela's release and the first free elections. She got caught up in a school student riot on the edge of Guguletu township in Cape Town and was attacked and killed. Four activists were convicted. One of whom, Ntombeki Ambrose Peni, was the young man at lunch. His childhood friend, Mzikhona Easi Nofemela, was one of the others gaoled. He also now worked for the Foundation. The four had each been sentenced to 18 years in prison. However, in 1995 Archbishop Desmond Tutu led the establishment of the Truth and Reconciliation Commission (TRC). For him it was a tool of national healing and the Act that established it was called The Promotion of National Unity and Reconciliation Act. The Head of Research at the TRC until it ended, Charles Villa-Vicencio, now a senior research fellow at the Institute of Justice and Reconciliation in Cape Town, told me, 'It was a compromise. But those who suffered are cursed with good memory and the TRC created the time and space for South Africans to come to terms with their past and their consciences. It thrust into the public consciousness the idea of dealing with the past and wrestling with the idea of reconciliation.'

The story that Easi and Peni and Peter and Linda Biehl told is a compelling description of the anatomy of that process. When the criminal trial ran, Linda only went for a week to support the witnesses but mainly to see the four accused. Her experience of the proceedings was not so much as a victim than as a parent. She told me that she:

> wanted to get a sense of who they were. My first inclination was to know the families. Easi's dad was at the trial. He was always looking at me, kind of wanting to say hello, but also 'I'm here for my son'. It wasn't appropriate to

speak to him there because there were all the newspapers and cameras. But I knew someday I would speak to him.

Peter was totally uninterested in the trial:

> At first the whole thing was a kind of abstraction. I felt really empty with the loss and had no real thought of meeting anyone involved in Amy's death. I am not interested in punitive justice generally speaking. But when the Truth and Reconciliation Commission offered the possibility of an Amnesty hearing I was very interested indeed. Restorative justice presented me and everybody with something.

What they saw in the TRC was the opportunity, in reaching out to the young men, to come to terms with what had happened and more importantly to celebrate their daughter and from that create a future for her and themselves. Peter was adamant that he and Linda could not forgive. This was not from bitterness, but because they believed that forgiveness was not in their gift.

> Typically in the Christian tradition forgiveness is reserved to a man and his God. And we are not God. We feel awkward about the idea of dispensing forgiveness. Forgiveness is an unfortunate term. The end game for us is reconciliation. There are three things. If you can understand why someone wronged you, then you can accept that person and then you can reconcile. The real effort comes from building that relationship.

As Linda said, there was promise even in their grief. 'A death can create a new sense of energy. I mean who wants "closure"? That ends the energy. Death doesn't have to do that. Death can be an inspiration.' Later she added, 'I raised Amy to be the person she was. I fought for that kid, so I will continue to fight for her. And when you look at Peni, I think he's my baby. I think that Amy's spirit is totally in him.'

Two days later I met Easi and Peni at Peni's home. We talked for a long time as they generously let me explore their lives. I asked Easi why they had agreed to seek amnesty. He said:

> I went to the TRC because I had killed somebody and I wanted to just go and speak and take it out of my heart. Peter and Linda helped us to speak out, to take this thing out of our heart. They had come to South Africa with the vision already to forgive us. They understood the situation in South Africa.

Then he became agitated as he spoke about the proceedings: 'I was beginning to get a picture of myself... "you are a killer, you are a killer, you are a killer". But Peter and Linda didn't come and say, "you are a killer". They know that I did this but their way to treat others is to forgive. They gave me direction.'

Peni also talked about how the dynamic of reconciliation had helped him to balance his responsibility with his future:

> They have never asked us exactly about that day. They are more concerned about our personal lives. Their forgiveness has had a major role in helping me to bridge over the trauma of being involved in their daughter's murder. It is not easy at home to come to terms with what you have done. You can come to terms with it if you view it politically, but if you view it personally you feel very difficult.

He told me that when Peter and Linda were on television, his friends shouted, 'Your mum and dad are on the telly.' Because I saw it in his eyes, I asked him whether he loved them? Very shyly he simply replied, 'a lot'.

It wouldn't be an exaggeration to say that meeting the Biehls and Easi and Peni changed my way of looking at life very profoundly. The story I wrote became part of something in the UK called The Forgiveness Project, started by a journalist, Marina Cantacuzino. On days when I am driven low by anxiety or feeling overpowered by life, I go to the website and read the stories. Click on the photos and there you will find tales of how people have found their way through the most dire events: loved ones murdered or violated in political conflicts in Ireland, South Africa, Sierra Leone, Chechnya; Black and Asian people racially abused in Britain; partners killed by drunk drivers; women raped; a teenage daughter stabbed at a party; killings that were part of a robbery; parents of children whose organs were removed for research without consent; kids sexually abused by their relatives; fascists and White supremacists who have renounced their former lives and work to tackle radicalization and extremism.

On the face of it they are horror stories. Conflict, aggression and violence are threaded through every narrative. Yet, however ghastly the impact on their lives and whatever different routes these people have found through what has happened to them, reading their stories is always uplifting. Many of them have met the people who killed or hurt their loved ones or their own abusers and aggressors. A great number of those who were perpetrators have met those they attacked. All the stories are complicated. Not one of them has an easy solution. None of them involves the concept of 'should' or 'ought'. There is no obligation to follow this path. In some cases that's just not possible, as they don't know the identity of the perpetrator. I have always thought that the 'Forgiveness' in the title of the project should have a question mark after it. Marina, playing with the word's contentiousness, called the Project's first photo exhibition 'The F Word'. The stories are all just humanly muddled, individual approximations at finding a way to a future rather than remaining in the past. The choices these people have made show the possibility and value of reaching out and bridging divides. They offer hope and a better future through the exploration of difference. My experience has revealed this to be one of the most compelling impulses to pursue diversity.

Many of them, I discovered, were motivated by their faith. An atheist myself (or if I am unsure about being that definite, does that make me an agnostic?), I have met very many people whose desire to create significant social change has been inspired by their religion. When I was younger that troubled me. I even felt slightly hostile to the idea, thinking religion was somehow more appropriately engaged with the mythical rather than material. For my part, I was motivated by what I thought was the rational idea that one of the points of life was, in the face of inequality and injustice, to get stuck in and improve the world for my family, friends and fellow beings. Growing up deeply middle class I had inherited from my mother her rather patrician sounding advice that 'the very least one can do, darling, is to make marmalade for the fête'. This I took to be a metaphorical exhortation towards social responsibility. But I came to see that the same obligation to engage with what needs to change in the world is expressed and explained in many different personal ways. The religious and the non-religious can happily co-habit in a joint effort.

The complexity of our differences

In 1993 the nun Sister Helen Prejean published her book *Dead Man Walking: The eyewitness account of the death penalty that sparked a national debate* (6). It was subsequently made into an Oscar-winning film and an opera. She summed up why she opposes the death penalty in a statement of brevity and power that has always resonated with me as an expression of deep compassion: 'People are more than the worst thing they have ever done in their lives' (7). Each of us is not, in our best or poorest moment, just one thing.

We are formed by the criss-crossing of our actions, experiences, backgrounds and origins. Recognizing the multifarious nature of who we are, what has made us, how we behave, how each of us has many streams of character that inhabit our one person, seems to me to be fundamental to the practice of valuing diversity.

In 2020, just over 30 years after she coined the term 'intersectionality', Professor Kimberlé Crenshaw from Columbia Law School described it as:

> a lens, a prism, for seeing the way in which various forms of inequality
> often operate together and exacerbate each other. We tend to talk about race
> inequality as separate from inequality based on gender, class, sexuality or
> immigrant status. What's often missing is how some people are subject to all of
> these, and the experience is not just the sum of its parts.

But she added to this explanation a serious warning. When asked what intersectionality is, she says: 'These days, I start with what it's not, because there has been distortion. It's not identity politics on steroids' (8).

Where her caution is so important is that it serves notice on the easy arithmetic that reduces the complexity of her idea to a Venn diagram of rigid categories. Those intersecting circles supposedly show how lives are affected by the overlapping designations of sex, race, sexual orientation, disability and so on. But that maths fails to take account not only of her reminder that 'the experience is not just the sum of its parts' but also that the experience of life inside each of those categories is not singular. As Sister Prejean says, we are more than a single word or deed, name or label.

There is a complexity to this that needs to be explored. We experience life both as individuals and also as members of groups. A vital characteristic of the equality movements that gave rise to the tick box of labels, which appear in every diversity strategy in the known world, is that in their early days of their struggle for equality the bond of common purpose and experience serves each group very well. It makes absolute sense in the beginning to submerge differences in the face of the provocation of a shared offence to liberty and rights. At the start there is a clarity about who the group is, the discrimination they are suffering and what they want done about it. You can reasonably apply its label to all in the group to describe at that point their most salient experience of life.

I was one of the six people who started Stonewall, the lesbian gay equality lobby in the UK, in the late eighties. We were able to be quite clear about who we were and what we wanted. We were lesbians and gays and we wanted equality. Just equal treatment under the law along with everyone else. Pure and simple. Having established that, it was a fairly easy task to locate the group and mobilize the vast majority of them towards that goal.

However, as we fought these battles something happened to disturb that simplicity. We started to win. First with public opinion and then in Parliament. Our coherence as a group, forged by the prejudice and the secrecy forced upon us in the past, gave way to a diversity among us that grew from our new freedom. Progress brought the liberty for lesbian and gay people to follow their aspirations and develop their private and public lives and their social and political views as individuals in any way they wanted. The solidarity in the face of discrimination didn't entirely disappear, because the problem hasn't completely disappeared. But the assumption of a single group experience could no longer capture the diversity of needs, wants, ambitions and politics of the individuals within it. The rigidity of any identity category needs to flex to encompass the increasing differences in people's public and private lives and in their divergent opinions.

This arc is followed by all of those groups that fight for rights and in whose campaigns lie the origins of the work you do on diversity in your organizations. The four women of the Pankhurst family were the leaders of the movement for women's equal suffrage in Britain. In 1903 the mother and her daughters, Emmeline and Christabel, founded the Women's Social and Political Union. Sylvia the second and Adela the youngest sister worked with them until the two pairs fell out irretrievably with each other. All four of them remained utterly loyal to their commitment to the struggle for women's rights. But after 1918, following the partial victory of securing votes for women over 30, they took off in wildly different political directions: Emmeline became a Conservative MP, Christabel a born-again Christian, Sylvia a Communist and Adela a Fascist (9). Women may have forged a single-minded alliance to get the vote. But once they had it, they didn't necessarily cast it in the same direction, which reveals for me one of the key outcomes of progress on diversity. It produces a flowering of variation. Labels shouldn't contain people. They should be enablers of difference, not prisons of sameness.

Why inclusion needs to include all voices

This raises two of the great challenges for those who are engaged in diversity. You are often asked to privilege one voice from a community as the single voice of that group. Also, if you are not a member of that group it can be expected of you that you accept without question the subjective voice of someone who is. But, while it is vitally important to acknowledge the validity of personal experience, giving sole credibility to the single voice or the subjective voice can present considerable difficulties in developing a trusted approach in either business or politics. It can put uniformity at the heart of inclusion rather than diversity. If all your people are to feel heard and motivated in working on diversity, the processes in your organization, and you personally, need to develop the confidence to take into account the variety of views within social categories, what the Equality Act calls the 'protected characteristics'.

In recent years #MeToo and #BlackLivesMatter have become ever present in the workplace and in work on diversity. They have ignited a much-needed urgency and added momentum to vital issues that affect people's lives in intense and personal ways. They represent the strongest feeling that society, official bodies and companies have simply not given the prominence that they should have to stamping out racism and sexism, and thus to creating environments in which people can live and work free from discrimination. Campaigners have pointed with justification to the inadequacy of the response to the disadvantage – and often harassment – to which women and people of colour can give testament from their everyday lives. However, the nobility of those causes has sometimes given rise to mantras that mask the complexity that needs to be understood to significantly improve those responses.

When I was a comic a semi-rule emerged on the 'alternative' comedy scene that only gays could tell gay jokes, or only Jews Jewish jokes and so on. This always seemed to me to miss the real challenge. It wasn't who told the joke that mattered. It was what joke they told. What always counted for me was the warmth of the gag and how the performer's empathy shone through. I once saw Billy Connolly do 15 minutes on his huge discomfort at having a male doctor do a prostate exam. This was to an almost entirely gay male audience. We found it absolutely hilarious.

There is an ever-present danger in the way that diversity is often framed and pursued at the moment that we reinforce and perpetuate the idea that *who* says something and *who* can challenge becomes way more important than *what* they are saying and the *content* of their challenge. The claim for the legitimacy of this way of thinking is rooted in current identity politics. It appears that on the Left and the Right not only is there increasingly a prohibition on disagreement and discussion, an intolerance of differences, but it's being dictated by identity rather than by substance. My personal and professional experience has convinced me, however, that discussions should be about views, vision and values. Not about who you are, but about what you think. If discussions are framed as being between people of immutable identities, that pre-empts the movement and change, the tolerance and the acceptance of difference, that is essential to how we find common ground, and the collaborations in organizations and in wider society to bring about change. As long as disagreement is pitched as a face-off between enemies, each of whom is decrying the legitimacy of the other, rather than as differences to be explored in the pursuit of co-existence, compromise will be seen as betrayal. Diversity is not the clashing of two opposing sides. It is the interaction between varying life experiences, perspectives, cultures, origins and identities that, only when they are able to combine through recognizing those differences, can potentially produce results far greater than we can on our own. Interaction based entirely on rigid ideas of identity produces little more than animosity and gridlock. Instead of diversity engaging our differences positively, when it is pursued through this form of identity politics it solidifies them to the point where they become irreconcilable. One of the main purposes of this book is to show how to find our way out of that cul-de-sac and situate having those difficult discussions in a positive way at the heart of the definition of true diversity and inclusion.

Of course, this way of behaving has been fanned, more often than not over-dramatically and destructively, on social media. But the result is that people in offices and with their friends are becoming over-anxious about saying what they think, of asking questions in case they offend, or challenging in case they are attacked. Whenever I've seen people walking on eggshells it has restricted their curiosity. Relishing difference requires an ever-respectful and constant inquisitiveness.

Tricky situations are personal

When we pursue this curiosity either as leaders, managers or as colleagues, are there any questions that we cannot or should not ask? Are there questions that are just so sensitive or are so capable of falling insensitively on the listener that we must just keep them to ourselves? In general, I'd say no. What matters far more than the question is your sensitivity to its impact and learning more about that every day from people who are not like you and with whom it might fall differently.

If I had a pound for every time I have been asked, 'When did you first know you were gay?', I'd have a tidy pile in the bank. I always answer it now in the same way, 'When did you first know you weren't?' To be honest the question bores me. But behind it maybe lies a certain nervousness about how to approach the issue on the part of someone to whom it is personally relatively unfamiliar. Maybe it's just a slightly clumsy way of opening up the subject. Maybe it's genuine curiosity about my story. Whatever its intention, it's an opening and, however jaded I am with being asked it, I shouldn't get miffed, but rather make the conversation more interesting. Try and move it on to where there might be similarities between 'coming out as gay' and facing up to any hidden realization that they might have experienced in their life.

Once I had an amazing conversation with a client after he winced with pain as he walked down the stairs to the front door of his building. Asking if he was ok led to the story about his 20 years of pain from a rugby injury as a young man that persisted all the way through his very successful career in finance and had finally brought him to a minor breakdown. He'd had to go to his boss and ask for time off. In a very competitive (pretty masculine) environment he had to own up to the stress he has been hiding all those years. I had always wondered why he, a classic public-school-educated-two-kids-and-wife-at-home-living-in-Kensington banker, was such a supporter of lesbian and gay issues. No reason that he shouldn't have been, but I just wondered where his passion for it came from. I always assumed he had a family member or a great friend who was gay. When he told me the story of his breakdown, I realized it was him. He had 'come out' not about being gay, but about his mental health.

Along the same lines, the question that really bugs so many of my Black and Brown friends and colleagues is, 'Where do you come from?' It is so loaded with the implication that they do not belong here, that they do not have the legitimacy of being 'properly' British, that there is a misplaced audacity to their assumption of equality. Again there are many reasons for the question to be asked. It is more than likely that if you are Black or Brown, your family will have come to Britain since the Second World War. The question might genuinely come from a place of curiosity, albeit clumsily expressed. While intention is significant – in law it is after all the difference between murder and manslaughter – it is not the main issue here. However the question started out in the person's mind, if they're White and didn't show any sensitivity to how it might be received, how it might feel to the Black or Brown person being asked, it will merely add to the incessant reinforcement of the idea that they are not really rightful citizens of the country. Curiosity will transform into another everyday harm. So, if what the White person asking really does want to understand is something of the Black or Brown person's history and that of their family, they need to find a more careful way of asking that question. And so it goes for asking women about 'managing' to look after their children and also working, and disabled people why they use a wheelchair. In all these potentially awkward situations, don't stop asking the questions. Instead, think about how to ask them well. Think about how to discover people's stories with genuine interest rather than implied judgement. Inquisitiveness is best rewarded when pursued with thoughtfulness. The more aware we are of how our questions feel to others, the more those questions will open doors rather than put up defences.

These situations are tricky at work. They're tricky for men to know how to react to women's experiences, for White people to Black and Asian experience, for straights and gays, for disabled people and those without disabilities. I have had to unpick this working with clients and also personally because I am White and I am married to a man who is Black. He is Nigerian, so he grew up in a Black country. His experience of race there is wholly different from his experience of race in the UK, and to the experience of someone who grew up as a person of colour in Britain. Every day through him I watch and hear the experience of being Black, in Africa and in the UK. Lots of it is great. Some of it, not so much. Ten years of knowing each other has had a deep effect on how I think about and encounter debates about race. An example: I no longer would second guess his personal experience. By that I mean that in the past when he said something had happened that he felt was racist, from the best of motives and hoping probably to reassure him and me that he hadn't had a horrible experience, I might have wondered, 'Are you sure?' But I have come to understand how that intended comfort can too easily strike him as undermining and disbelieving. My work in progress is to listen to hear rather than listening to respond.

But I wouldn't, and my husband wouldn't let me, surrender my opinions to him on an issue because he's Black and I am White. Or vice versa. Even on race. We have found there has to be respectful listening and deep curiosity about experience. That should be as true around the kitchen table as it is at work. Experience of working with clients shows that, after proper hearing comes discussion through which, collectively, colleagues need to decide on what to do. On what is the best way forward, what are the smartest strategies and plans to tackle racism or sexual harassment or discrimination against gay people in your workplace? For that, all voices need at some stage to 'be in the room', even though they will have different relationships to the issue at hand, and that will affect how they listen to each other and will give different weight to what each person contributes. To create the best solutions, views have to matter more than viewpoints, opinions more than identity, what you say more than who you are.

One of the main strands that runs through this book is that realizing the power of difference, the creation and leveraging of diversity, by definition is about the creative tension in discussion. Diversity is not safe. Safe spaces don't offer safety *from* disagreement, they offer safety *for* disagreement. From all our work it is clear that it's not whether you disagree, it's how you disagree. Only through constructive dissent can you find the route to consensus and alliances, to the support of the majority of your people.

In the courts, the cases that Stonewall brought on the age of consent and the other key issues, the argument had to be on narrow legal grounds. Outside, though, wider coalitions had to be forged. Something particular always stood out to me in the way that Stonewall went about gathering that support. While there were egregious wrongs to be righted, the focus was not just on what lesbians and gays wanted from society. Wider than that, Stonewall created a platform from which lesbians and gays could make their contribution to a country in which everybody wanted to live. The success came from winning mothers, fathers, brothers, sisters, cousins, aunts, uncles, friends, neighbours and colleagues round to a vision of a country where equal treatment under the law and fairness for them too was reinforced as a fundamental right. So they had a personal interest. Stonewall was helping to create not a gay world, no longer just a straight world, but a country in which equality could flourish for all.

In 2011 a legal case was finally won that gave the surviving member of a gay couple the right to inherit a tenancy in the way that one half of a heterosexual couple would do in the same circumstances. Antonio Mendoza and Hugh Wallwyn-James had shared their flat for 19 years when Wallwyn-James died from cancer in 2001. Their landlord had promptly served a repossession notice. Antonio refused to accept it saying that he should inherit the tenancy rights from his partner. He won. The House of Lords, then the highest court in the land, rejected the landlord's claim. The basis of the ruling by Lady Hale, the presiding judge, was highly significant. She said the guarantee of equal treatment was 'essential to democracy' (10). The importance of the case spoke beyond the couple to the values of the whole of society.

The connections that Stonewall was able to build around a shared objective of equality were the most powerful fuel in the success of the campaigns. In the same way, to win support for diversity at work, companies need to win over their employees. For all that championing diversity, particularly in the corporate world, has gained broad support from senior executives and management, there are still many in and outside of your organizations who need to be convinced. In the public sphere, the likes of Fox News in the United States or *The Daily Mail* in the UK and other similar outlets, often present a caricature of diversity that allows them to dismiss it as 'political correctness gone mad'. Inside your organization there will be those that object or don't see it as important. But looking back to the 1980s, I am struck by how diversity is far more broadly supported now than gay equality in Britain was then. But we argued for it. And built the alliances. And it worked.

A way you can change minds

You may not remember what it was like. But in 1986 *The Sun* railed against a rather innocuous little book called *Jenny lives with Eric and Martin* – about a gay couple bringing up the daughter of one of them, with her mother living nearby. 'Vile book in school!' screamed a front-page headline (11): 'perverted' and 'a direct threat to the children of Britain' cried another (12). 'Pulpit poofters' in 1987 was another headline in the same paper describing gay priests. Ray Mills the *Daily Star*'s new columnist was introduced to its readers in 1986 under the heading 'The Angry Voice' promising he would rail against 'wooftahs, pooftahs, nancy boys, queers, lezzies – the perverts whose moral sin is to so abuse the delightful word "gay" as to render it unfit for human consumption' (13). These were not untypical views. In that atmosphere Stonewall had to win the public round. Not all at once, but bit by bit. The experience taught me that there are four conditions required to change people's minds. They need to:

- be convinced of the central principle (in that case equality under the law and fairness);
- see that it benefits society (it speaks to something beyond the minority's own self-interest);
- know and mind about someone who is affected by the inequality (have an emotional connection);

- be reassured that they aren't going to lose out personally (in the end we do all look out for ourselves as well).

These conditions hold for companies and organizations too.

My contention is that there are wider lessons to be drawn for work on diversity, that are not confined to their specific issue, from the campaign to change Britain for the better for gays and lesbians or from the Forgiveness Project and other movements for social transformation. These lessons can contribute significantly to helping create success in enhancing the diversity of your company. In particular because your diversity proposition has to be one that all your employees can embrace and ultimately act on. While there will be many of your colleagues who support it, there will also be a proportion who do not. Their reasons may not be negative, they may just come from inertia. They might feel it's a threat to them or they might even just think that it's not where the energy of the employees and company should be spent.

Consequently, in the book, there will be examples and understanding that I have drawn from my experience of Stonewall's campaigns and The Forgiveness Project, from my own life and from our work with clients over the last ten years. As a result of my age and the generation I belong to, I happened to have participated in these movements and they have had enormous influence on how I see diversity. I have found that many of the lessons from them successfully read across into wider work on diversity in companies and organizations. The experience has particularly showed me how perspectives from a minority can illuminate much wider issues for society and, in the focus of this book, companies and organizations.

These examples are not designed to suggest that there is anything particularly special about being gay or Black or female or disabled, in and of itself. But, in a phrase you will read here often, it's not *who* you are that matters in generating the benefits from diversity, it's what you can bring '*through* who you are'. Given your individual talents and skills, it's then what you can also contribute through your life experience. And how you can combine that with others. Difference is an asset and the book will explore ways in which companies can value in all their people a combination of expertise, skill and, importantly, life experience to achieve their goals. Pursuing diversity is a choice. It's not about who you are, it's about what you've decided to do, what you value in others, and what kind of company and organization you want to be part of.

The book is full of questions – as many challenges as there are answers. There are many examples of, and suggestions for, effective action, but its main purpose is to provoke you to think differently about the best way to increase diversity in your organization and in society, and how you can interrogate some of the assumptions that are too often made about how to do that. The intention is to encourage you to think and act in new ways about the field of diversity.

Through the six chapters you'll be able to explore how to tackle the diversity deficits and realize the diversity dividends by harnessing the power of difference to:

- develop a specific rationale for diversity in your company;
- create real inclusion so all employees' voices are heard;
- ensure that the perspectives from minorities enhance the effectiveness of the whole organization;
- honestly confront bias and equip employees to overcome it effectively;
- redesign your recruitment and promotion to create the most effective teams;
- enjoy managing diversity.

01

What is diversity for?

What Abraham Lincoln can teach us about achieving diversity

Abraham Lincoln said at the start of his second Senatorial campaign in 1858: 'If we could first know where we are and whither we are tending, we could better judge what to do and how to do it.' Doris Kearns Goodwin, the renowned biographer of US presidents, in her book *Leadership in Turbulent Times*, comments that:

> this opening campaign statement offers a clear glimpse into his general blueprint for orienting his followers by gentle education and persuasion... With this simple statement he launched upon a communal storytelling voyage with his audience so that they might collectively address a problem and together set about to forge a solution (1).

If you can really investigate and answer the question: 'What is something *for?*', that will decisively set your approach. It will define how to achieve your goal. It will tell you *where, whither, what* and *how.*

Personally, Lincoln thought slavery morally abhorrent and he had a deep sense of its illogical inequity. In notes from the period he wrote:

> If A can prove... that he may, of right, enslave B, why may not B snatch the same argument, and prove equally, that he may enslave A? You say A is white, and B is black. It is color, then; the lighter having the right to enslave the darker? Take care. By this rule, you are to be slave to the first man you meet, with a fairer skin than your own.

However, alongside his personal revulsion for slavery, Lincoln also had an overwhelming 'devotion to the Union'. As Doris points out, Lincoln's public position 'was no abolitionist credo'. He was, in many ways, a single-issue politician. But a pragmatist rather than a purist. In relation to slavery his aim was abolition. But he was a man of his time. In the debates with the racist senator Stephen Douglas in 1858, he argued, 'I do not understand that because I do not want a negro woman for a slave I must necessarily want her for a wife.'

But he also maintained quite emphatically, 'there is no reason in the world why the negro is not entitled to all the natural rights enumerated in the Declaration of Independence – the right to life, liberty, and the pursuit of happiness. I hold that he is as much entitled to these as the white man.'

Frederick Douglass the abolitionist and former slave, and an orator every bit as compelling as Lincoln, summed up the complications of the man and his time: 'We were able to take a comprehensive view of Lincoln, and to make reasonable allowance for the circumstances of his position… we came to the conclusion that the hour and the man of our redemption had some-how met in the person of Abraham Lincoln' (2).

Hard as it is to hear, from someone we have so many reasons to admire, the contradictions in his views reflected the time. Not only was it arguable that slavery was protected by the Constitution but also, at first, popular opinion didn't support abolition.

In 1862, a year into his presidency, the Northern Armies suffered an almost catastrophic defeat by General Robert E Lee. It was the catalyst for a change in Lincoln's position. Within one month he had drafted the execu-tive order that was his Emancipation Proclamation. Within six months he had presented it to his Cabinet, discussed every objection and angle with them and finally signed it into activation. Lincoln didn't change his personal opinion about slavery. He changed his approach. After the defeats he went to visit the troops. He intended, as Doris recounts, 'to comfort the wounded, talk with them in small groups, bolster their morale and sustain his own spirits. The stimulant of the president's unexpected visit on the enervated regiments was instantaneous'.

These conversations cemented in his mind the connection he could now make between the civil war and, not just the Union, but the cause of aboli-tion. He reflected – as always by turning over all possibilities in his mind – and realized that by freeing the slaves in the South he could gain a military advantage for the North and for the Union. He could not previously have taken a *political* decision to free the slaves but, as Commander-in-Chief, he could take a *military* decision to liberate them. If the Southern slaves could be free to join the Union army and to fight for the North it would make it more difficult for Southern soldiers to leave home to fight for the Confederacy. That was a military advantage for the Union.

This careful change in his line of attack, his finding the right argument at the right time and within his own power to enact, set off the train of events that lead to the 13th Amendment ending the iniquity of legal human slavery in America. By the time of his assassination Lincoln had also brought to an end the civil war. His careful and effective politics in linking the question of abolition to the maintenance of the Union was combined with his considerable personal empathy and ability to engage those who disagreed with him, reflected in his calculated move to create what Doris called his 'Team of rivals'.

There are two striking insights illuminated by his approach. The first is that he was more concerned with the achievement of his ultimate goal than he was with parading his own passion for it. He made his position clear only when he knew he could pursue it, win the votes and make it tell to effect fundamental change. The second was that he was always clear in his own mind about that ultimate goal and through the precision of his interrogation and understanding of the issues, he created clarity about how to put into action the most effective strategy towards it. The accuracy with which he articulated and pursued his objectives contributed hugely to his success in achieving them.

Passion can be your worst enemy

Passion is seen as a great quality. Even in business, leaders exhort their people to be 'passionate' about what they do. Steve Jobs said to employees when he returned in 1997 to the company he had co-founded, which was now running out of cash and close to bankruptcy, that Apple's 'core value is that we believe that people with passion can change the world for the better' (3). Jobs with his colleagues did reignite Apple. But Lincoln's political brilliance should caution us about the efficacy of passion. Counterintuitive as it may sound, in most arguments, passion can actually be your worst enemy. Because who cares what you are passionate about when you are trying to convince others? Your passion can mean little to their scepticism or indifference. Communicating your passion means that you might not listen to theirs. You might not find the common ground. Instead you could just widen the differences by perfectly demonstrating the distance between your passion and them. In the end it can simply create barriers to working out where you could meet.

People can confuse passion with enthusiasm. Without enthusiasm you can never convince anyone else. But if all you have in business or politics is passion, you may find yourself metaphorically shouting alone in the desert or, as Macbeth says of life, your efforts will be 'a tale told by an idiot, full of sound and fury, signifying nothing' (4). This is not to decry feelings of passion in the face of injustice or, in the field of this book, at the lack of diversity in your organization or business. But it is to sound an alert to the dangers of passion on its own.

In business it can verge on indulgence. Or these days worse, as the passion frequently isn't designed to convince others or change the business. More often it is just designed to signal what a right-thinking business yours is or what a social conscience it possesses. Most of what is said about diversity still sadly fulfils that function. It's corporate virtue signalling. Plucked at random from corporate reports: 'We are passionate about diversity.' 'We want to ensure that we have a workforce as diverse as the communities in which we operate.' 'A diverse workforce is integral [to our business].' And so on and so forth. Look at my company, look at our brand. Come work for us, come buy from us. We really care!

But brand activism is dangerous territory for a company if the values it espouses are not evidenced by its behaviour. If a gap emerges between them the business puts itself at risk. In 2018, H&M Group ended up appointing a leader for diversity and inclusiveness because of the global backlash it had received from its completely tone-deaf use of a Black child to advertise a hoodie with the slogan 'Coolest Monkey in the Jungle' (5). Two years later in 2020 CNN Business obtained a photo of possible products for one of H&M's sub-brands '& Other Stories', one of which was captioned 'Nigga Lab Beanie' (6). The Inclusion and Diversity page on the H&M website, ironically in the circumstances, maintains that, 'Diversity boosts our creativity and gives us the ability to make truly innovative business decisions.'

If you're confident that behaviour and values do match in your organization, there's nothing wrong with virtue signalling as a first step. It does change the tone. But it rarely changes the numbers. It rarely changes people's lives. What Lincoln understood above all was the pointlessness of just boasting about his own feelings and views on slavery rather than listening in order to determine the right approach and finding the language that would bring other people with him. He strived to be clear in his own mind about the goal and to be specific about the route to achieve it. To create greater diversity companies need to do the same.

Why we need to do more than make gestures

A wide response to the killing of George Floyd in Minneapolis in 2020 was an extraordinary eruption of anger and criticism at the police, the state and their effect on the lives of Black and Brown people. To many in the United States and the UK it felt different in character to previous reactions to such tragedies. The Covid-19 pandemic lockdowns in both countries had largely produced extraordinary initial self-discipline and sacrifice among people and a sweeping outbreak of personal solidarity as people took care of each other. Simultaneously they viewed the actions – or inaction – of their governments on halting the pandemic with increasing suspicion. The People appeared to trust each other inversely to trusting their governments. George Floyd's murder seemed to bring to life those feelings of solidarity between people and enact their hostility towards government and its agencies. The crowds who took to the streets looked different this time. They were Black, Brown and White, melded together demanding change. A new solidarity seemed to flower.

Even though #BlackLivesMatter is far more a child of the distinctly business-unfriendly, and in many eyes way too extreme, Extinction Rebellion or Occupy than it is of the Civil Rights Movement, businesses felt the need to respond. Many of them were swift to reassure the world that they 'stand with Black people'. Technology and social media companies, which had powered the exposure of the crimes against those more recently killed and underpinned the ability of people to organize about them, were at the forefront of the reaction. Snapchat stated, 'Racial violence and injustice have no place in our society and we stand together with all who seek peace, love, equality, and justice in America' (7). The CEO of Microsoft, Satya Nadella, said to his employees, 'We all have a role to play. I will do the work. The company will do the work. I am asking each of you to do the work' (8).

Tim Cook, the CEO of Apple, wrote an eloquent letter to all his people on 31 May 2020 in which he said:

> Our mission has and always will be to create technology that empowers people to change the world for the better. We've always drawn strength from our diversity, welcomed people from every walk of life to our stores around the world, and strived to build an Apple that is inclusive of everyone... To our colleagues in the Black community – we see you. You matter, your lives matter, and you are valued here at Apple. But together, we must do more (9).

His personal conviction shines through the letter. But the share of Apple's technical workers who are Black remained flat at 6 per cent from the end of 2013 through to the end of 2017, the last year the company published diversity data (10). This drops to 3 per cent in leadership roles, which compares with 13 per cent of the US population overall who are African American (11). It's not unfair to underline Cook's last line – 'we must do more' – and ask, 'what will you do?' Otherwise he is merely virtue signalling.

The broadcaster CNBC in June 2020 did a roundup of what tech companies, from Airbnb to Uber, have pledged to do 'to fight racial injustice' (12). They reported that Airbnb, Alphabet, Amazon, Box, Cisco, Comcast, Facebook, Intel, Lyft, Microsoft, Netflix, Peloton, Shopify, Slack, Softbank, TikTok, Twitter and Uber between them pledged to donate over $150m to organizations who variously 'address social injustice and anti-racism', 'fight injustice and inequality' or 'work on racial justice'. Among those organizations were the NAACP (The National Association for the Advancement of Coloured People), the Black Lives Matter Foundation and NFL player Colin Kaepernick's organization 'Know Your Rights Camp'.

Without significant change in the policies and, more importantly, the practices of these businesses there is a certain irony here. In effect these behemoths of Silicon Valley are giving money to those organizations to increase their ability and capacity to campaign to put pressure on those same companies giving the money to change and do better for Black and Brown people. What is needed is not just philanthropic donations but also change. As Brian Chesky, the CEO of Airbnb, told CNN, he and too many other executives are 'now realizing we could have done so much more... There's not been enough action. I think the time for boldness is now, and we've got to take significantly more action' (13).

But as the Philadelphia writer Tre Johnson put it with a degree of scepticism, 'is this the racial ouroboros our country finds itself locked in, as Black Americans relive an endless loop of injustice and White Americans keep revisiting the same performance, a Broadway show that never closes, just goes on hiatus now and then?'

In order for it not to be, he continued, 'the right acknowledgment of black justice... won't be found in your protest signs... or organizational statements. It will be found in your earnest willingness to dismantle systems that stand in our way... It's not just about amplifying our voices, it's about investing in them and in our businesses [and] education' (14).

He might also have added that not only did the companies need to do something rather than just say something, but #BlackLivesMatter itself needed not just passion on the streets but also to build on that with clear aims and embracing objectives that would be able to gain support from and unite the widest range of people to enable lasting change.

One of the more striking examples of corporate transformation actually happening rather than just being talked about was when the cofounder of the social news website, Reddit, Alexis Ohanian, resigned from his company's board and urged them to replace him with a Black candidate (15). Almost immediately they did. They recruited Michael Seibel, the CEO of the tech start-up funder Y Combinator, as the first Black board member in the company's history (16). It may not be insignificant to Ohanian's close personal understanding of the issues and his reaction to #BlackLivesMatter that he is married to the champion tennis player, Serena Williams.

His gesture appears so far to have been exceptional. As Shaun R Harper, executive director of the University of Southern California's Race and Equity Center, wrote with some resignation in *The Washington Post*:

> the goal, of course, is for customers and others outside those companies to find all these gestures compelling and believable. But many Black employees find them confusing, at times even laughable, because such pronouncements and headline-garnering investments are so terribly inconsistent with their first-hand experiences in workplaces that have long devalued their lives and professional contributions (17).

Good intentions only get you so far

This is not to knock good intentions. Without them, without the statements of intent, without sincere aspiration, nothing would even get to the starting blocks of the race for more diversity. But to achieve significant change, even though such announcements are ubiquitous in the field of diversity and quite sincere, good intentions truly are not enough. Until they lead to action and measurable change.

There is a set of diversity commitments signed up to by an alliance of companies in one sector of British business (18). That may sound coy, but identifying who they are is not the point. The point is to show you something else. Here are public pledges on diversity from four of those companies (articulated by their CEOs or company statements):

- 'We want to ensure that we have a workforce as diverse as the communities in which we operate. A diverse workforce is integral [to our business].'

- 'We strongly believe that attracting, supporting and retaining a diverse workforce and being an organization which is truly inclusive for all is essential for us to achieve the ambitious goals we have set ourselves for the next few years.'

- 'It's true to say that D&I has a pivotal role to play in our success as an organization. After all, it's only if our people understand the diversity of our customers and the communities we operate in, that we can hope to meet their ever-changing needs.'

- 'As our business grows we want to attract people with new ideas, perspectives and experiences which will enrich our culture. Everyone should have the opportunity to reach their potential and have their contribution recognized.'

Despite these warming words, it turns out that 'reaching their potential' and getting to the top of these companies is a rather more feasible ambition for the members of one group than for any other. Between them they have 26 people on their Boards and 34 on their executive committees. However, despite affirming that 'D&I has a pivotal role to play in our success as an organization' and so on, of those 60 senior people, 54 are White men, just 6 are women and none at all is Black or Asian. And one of the companies has a Board of seven White men and an Exec of 10 of the same. It would seem that in reality homogeneity has a more pivotal role to play. It's not that these companies don't mean what they say. It's not that they don't want it to be true. It's not that they don't want it to happen one day. You can be quite sure that they hope that it will. But saying it doesn't make it so.

To be fair to that group of companies – and we can admire them for at least putting down a public marker on the issue – they are not isolated in their lack of diversity. Take the FTSE 100. In 2016 I researched the people in the top three jobs in each of the listed companies, looking at their company website photos and noting their names. This revealed that there were more White men called John, David or Andrew who were Chair, Chief Executive or Chief Finance Officer of the 100 companies than there were women or people from Black or Asian backgrounds. To get it on the record my MP asked a question about it in the House of Commons on 14 April of that year. I've just done the research again. There's progress. Although it's not much of a cause for celebration. To make the comparison work this time round, I've had to add the Michaels. There are now more White men called John, David, Andrew *or Michael* than there are women or people from Black and Asian backgrounds in the top 300 jobs of the FTSE 100.

Why is this still the case? Business must be doing something wrong or not doing something right. Because, as you know from seeing thousands of similar pledges to those above, making diversity commitments these days is obligatory for every business in town. The problem is partly the way they are expressed. They are almost always far too generalized. Those of you who work professionally in the field of diversity will know what I mean. You can spend hours at events that never seem to be just called 'meetings' these days, but 'hackathons' or 'summits' or 'symposiums'. Presumably to make them sound worth the usually enormous entry fee. But actually they still involve a bunch of people trapped in a darkened hotel function room all day being drowned in PowerPoint and pelted with digestible bullets for business by a diversity pro wearing a rainbow lanyard. Who then almost always concludes, with a sweeping sense of certainty, that 'diversity is not just the right thing to do, it's good for business'.

Except that it isn't. It certainly can be. In the best circumstances, with the right design and focus it will be. When the right mix of people is combined to solve the right kinds of problems. When it's a conscious talent strategy to achieve what your organization is there for. Then it is good for business. But not always and not in relation to every kind of problem or challenge. Or business. Stating that it is, is a duck-billed platitude that is neither true nor effective. It is just a generalization, tinged with lazy self-congratulation, albeit driven by a desire for a nice outcome. The truth is that you need to be much more accurate. What do you mean by diversity? When does it deliver a bonus? When does it deliver that bonus specifically to your company or department, and how? When should it be seen as a business benefit and when is it a corrective to decades, centuries even, of group disadvantage? And when doesn't it really have any significant effect at all?

Diversity deficits and dividends aren't the same thing

The first useful move towards clarity is to make a sharp distinction between the two different facets of diversity: the diversity deficits and the diversity dividends. Clearly they are related. But they need separate focus. The deficits can be ascertained through data. You should be transparent about the numbers. In doing so, it's also very important to remain alert to the danger that averages are the enemy of action. It is far more important and illuminating to understand where the women (or people in any other minority-status group) are in your organization, at what grades and what seniority, in what positions of influence and what are their prospects for promotion, than simply to show an overall percentage of women among your employees. 'Eliminating the deficits in your business', is what people often mean when they say, 'it's the right thing to do'. Because it is the right thing to do if that means your organization making sure that opportunities really are open to all. Or if your organization is attempting to change the fact that being disabled or Black or female, for instance, means that you are several times less likely to get the job or the promotion. Opening up prospects by eliminating discrimination so people can be judged on their talent and contribution must be the right thing to do.

The next stage, as you start to remove those deficits and allow talent to flourish and employees to move up the organization, is to work out how to realize the dividends. Solving the deficits is hard. Realizing the dividends is even harder.

Eliminating the deficits has been met with stubborn resistance for years. Movement in a positive direction has been partial and glacial. Even though the data is unequivocal, it's always surprising when people argue with it. But they do. They tend to fall into two groups: the polite and the offensive. The latter is a group that includes the kind of men who happily describe themselves as 'patriarchs' and tell us that women working brings down civilizations, that certain jobs are not for girls, that Black people are just not as intelligent as White people, that there is no gender pay gap, that gays shouldn't be allowed to be teachers in order to protect children, and so on. Intellectual plankton, if you like, festering in, among other places, the Twitter swamp. They need not detain us at any great length. Years ago, I asked my late friend the theatre critic, Jack Tinker, what was the worst play he'd ever seen. He said, 'I can only ever remember the last worst. Because if you keep all the worst ones in your brain, it just makes you ugly.' The same is true of the Twittersaurus. They are recalcitrant proof by a happily dwindling, although loud, section of the population that enough progress has been made for them to feel they need to react against it and push back with their very angry rhetorical fists.

The others – the polite – are much more important because they are far larger in number and because they are your colleagues at work and you might bump into them every day. They are the soggy marsh through which progress inevitably has to stagger. They are not so much actively resistant as often just captured by inertia – sometimes benign in intent but never in effect – and they get security and comfort from the traditional. They are at ease with the way things are. Mainly because they benefit from it. So they experience change as a disadvantage to themselves.

Whatever people's reaction to them, diversity deficits are weeds in the garden of work. They are perennial, pervasive and persevering. It doesn't matter where you look, there they are. Here are some of them.

In the NHS (to many people's surprise):

- 14 per cent of England's population and 19.7 per cent of all NHS employees are from a Black and minority ethnic background, yet only 8.4 per cent of board members in NHS trusts and only 143 very senior managers are (19).

- 77 per cent of NHS employees are women, yet they make up only 46 per cent of very senior managers, 41 per cent of chairs and non-execs of NHS trusts, 42 per cent of chief executives, 26 per cent of finance directors and 24 per cent of medical directors (20).

In tech, the big tech companies have finally started to publish their stats in recent years (21):

- Facebook says just 23 per cent of its tech employees globally are female, Google is similar.

- The proportion who are Black or of Latin American descent at Google and Microsoft has risen by only about one percentage point since 2014.

- The share of Black technical workers at Apple is less than half the proportion of African Americans in the US population. And at Google it is even lower at only 2 per cent.

In universities:

- Across England of all the students who enter with the same A level tariff, those who are Black, Asian or from minority ethnic backgrounds get 13 per cent fewer firsts and 2:1 degrees compared with their White friends (22).

- In recent years at entry level, academics are 50:50 men and women, but only 25 per cent of professors are female (23).

- There were just 140 Black men and women among 21,000 professors in UK universities, which is just 0.7 per cent (24).

- Universities had more Black employees who were cleaners, receptionists or porters than lecturers or professors in 2015–16 (25).

In financial services:

- At the end of 2000, 14 per cent of fund managers were women.
- At the end of 2019, still 14 per cent of fund managers were women, while just under 50 per cent of employees in the sector are women (26).
- Financial services in North America had a 24 per cent gap between the rates of first promotions (from entry-level to manager) of women and men, despite them asking for promotions at comparable rates (27).
- The first-promotion gap is even greater between women of colour and their male peers at 34 per cent (28).

The list could go on. If you're in one of those groups of people you experience these deficits every day in personal ways that are acute, frustrating and, at worst, hostile. If you aren't in one of those groups you might want to know how it feels. So, when you next go into work, before a meeting starts, ask your colleagues to do this short exercise. Each of you turn to a person next to you, look them straight in the eye and say to them slowly and deliberately, 'This is as far as you are going in your career.' Whenever I have asked audiences to do this, they've clearly felt uncomfortable. Often responding with laughter, possibly from embarrassment. Sometimes individuals have just exclaimed 'No!' It feels intolerable, if you have any sense of fairness and any degree of empathy, to look someone in the eye and say that. But that is exactly what organizations are doing to certain groups of employees. Everyday.

However, as egregious as the assault of these deficits on people's potential may be, is it the role, and is it in the interests, of businesses to do something about them? Is tackling the diversity deficits 'good for business'? It is certainly the right thing to do in the world. But that is not the same as saying that it should be a priority for any particular business, in terms of their strategic goals, profit, viability, success, innovation, supply chain or return to shareholders.

There is much research on the relationship between diversity and organizational performance. This was given an early rocket boost by McKinsey's first report, *Women Matter*, published in 2007, that 'identified a positive relationship between corporate performance and elevated presence of women in the workplace in several Western European countries' (29). But that report did both a great service and a great disservice to the pursuit of diversity. It equipped advocates, for pretty much the first time, with some extensive research that showed the link between diversity and company performance. Unfortunately, it also gave permission to the laxness with which people then deployed that connection. No one, not that report nor anyone since, who has properly researched the field, has ever claimed that eradicating diversity deficits is *always and automatically* good for business and *inevitably* causes a diversity dividend. At best all that kind of wide-ranging general research proves is not causation but only a correlation between diversity and performance.

This is what Professor Scott E Page, in *The Diversity Bonus* calls the 'causality conundrum' (30). In 2007 he set out to prove that 'diversity trumps ability' in a book called *The Difference* (31). He's a mathematician, so he uses formulas, algorithms and logic. He combines them with clarity for a lay reader and a commitment to the value of diversity to making a better world. In *The Diversity Bonus*, published 10 years after *The Difference*, he cited a number of diversity studies. In 2014 a Credit Suisse analysis of 27,000 senior managers at 3,000 large firms revealed 'positive correlations between the percentage of women in leadership roles and firm performance' (32). McKinsey in 2015 found a 'positive linear relationship between diversity and financial performance' (33). But Scott warns, 'As powerful as they may seem, all of these studies can be challenged on the grounds that they only report correlations.'

This is one of the great challenges of working on diversity. When studies find a correlation between the diversity of Executive teams and the performance of that company, did the diversity cause the high performance? Or are companies that have greater diversity at senior levels the kind of organizations that have put in the effort, taken the time and made the investment to develop people from groups whose talent too often remains untended? And if those organizations care about talent in that way, and develop it right to the top, they might just be the kind of business whose culture and management ethos inspire greater performance in their people. McKinsey's 2018 *Delivering through Diversity* report concluded that their most recent research 'support(ed) their earlier perspective on what likely drives the relationship with performance: that more diverse companies are better able to attract top talent... improve their customer orientation, employee satisfaction and decision making; and to secure their license to operate' (34).

If there is no provable causative relationship between diversity and performance, and neither simply demonstrating passion nor making sweeping generalizations is effective in getting real traction for change in the numbers and in delivering a real dividend from greater diversity, what is? What does work? How can companies follow Old Abe's guidance to go from *where* and *whither* to *what* and *how* so that their statements of intent are both accurate to their specific context and produce results? How can a company frame its pursuit of diversity by articulating clearly *what diversity is for* and so start to realize the dividends?

There are broadly three main reasons that businesses rely on to pursue diversity:

- the right thing to do;
- the representative thing to do;
- the smart business thing to do.

How effective is each of them?

The right thing to do

For some organizations 'the right thing to do' can indeed be a relevant business priority. My company Diversity by Design worked with an NHS hospital trust that a recent merger had made the largest employer in the area. As a result, its primary purpose was not just to make patients better and ensure the wellbeing of its people but also to be an accessible, attractive and responsible employer in the region. The conclusion to our first bit of work was a Rationale for Diversity, developed through facilitating discussions with a wide range of their people, which we organized into nine bullet points across three sections: Patients, People and Place. They listed the following as their reasons for pursuing diversity under Place:

- show, through Board membership, that X Trust, as one of the region's biggest employers, belongs to the whole community we serve;
- plant the seeds of aspiration and so inspire the widest range of people in our area and in our fields of operation to want to work in the NHS at X Trust;
- be a beacon for society, locally and nationally.

This particular commitment to diversity was a result of their obligations as an employer, rather than as a hospital. They saw their value relying in part on making themselves an employer of choice. This would both contribute to the region and also help them tackle the near crippling shortages of people wanting to work in the NHS, which results not just from the failure to train enough future employees but also because, rather surprisingly, the NHS doesn't always have a great reputation as an employer. This trust is determined, as are many others, to make sure that all sections of the community – 'the widest range of people in our area' – see it as a welcoming place to work. Added to which the non-White population of the UK is growing and so it makes sense to ensure that, as an employer, you are appealing to the whole population. The right thing to do – ensuring that you reach and offer opportunity to potential employees from Black and Asian backgrounds as well as White people – in that case coincided with the talent needs of the trust, and so met one of its main strategic imperatives.

Enhancing diversity will also be the 'right thing to do' for organizations in situations where it directly affects the ambitions and prospects for the talent of its people. Eradicating the diversity deficits sends a powerful message. If you look to the top of your organization and see no one who looks like you, it just saps energy and reinforces the impact of organizational and pervasive disadvantage. If you are in one of those groups of people outside the status quo in a business, all the research suggests that you simply have to work harder and make more of an effort to get into and then rise up the business. Moreover, your likelihood of then succeeding, even with all that extra effort, is still considerably smaller than your mainstream colleagues. Reducing the diversity deficits raises morale, when it is successful, and opens up routes for talent – to whatever level.

One of the 'Magic Circle' law firms recently showed how it matters. They discovered that they had more partners called David than they did women – 14 per cent were called David and 11 per cent were women. (Now you know what inspired me to count the top three roles in the FTSE 100.) They had an idea that part of the problem might be that there was a fixed idea in the firm of what a good partner 'looked like'. And it wasn't female. To find out, they asked all the partnership board to nominate three 'great' partners. They were right. All the male partners nominated themselves. But only 3 per cent of the women partners did.

Then the firm analysed the level of ambition of those applying to be partners, who were pretty much 50:50 men and women. Ambition to run the firm, rather than simply be a lawyer, is pretty much what marks out a partner from the layer below. So they set a simple test to measure it. The women turned out to be less ambitious than the men. What was happening? They identified two possible reasons why this might be the case. The first was that women lawyers as a group are just less ambitious than male ones, which doesn't seem very likely. The second was that the ambitious women had left early. What they discovered on further inquiry was that it was the second. These women were looking up at the partners and seeing no one like themselves. The deficit in women at the top was creating a failure of morale, a recognition of their lack of opportunity for promotion and was resulting in a very expensive flood of talent to other firms that offered women more role models and better prospects. The firm was losing talent in whom they had made a considerable investment.

To women who experience this kind of imbalance in leadership, it operates as a block to their career ambitions in that company, not to mention making a dent in their self-esteem and being an unjust failure to offer reward for their skill and hard work. To employees in companies, whether you're a lawyer, a fund manager or have some influence or you don't have any pulling power in the world or in your organization, these deficits are soul and career destroying. [Businesses have very good reason to develop the talents and prospects of their people without prejudice and without preconception in order to open up the pool and the flow of talent, to create a positive atmosphere in the workplace, to enhance the reputation of the business and to demonstrate their responsibility to the community where it is based.]

But, despite all those reasons, simply saying to your people that enhancing diversity is 'the right thing to do' does not always inspire them. Because they might not agree with you. The managing director of a company with whom we were working said it to us recently. So we tested it. When we looked at the employee survey it turned out that 70 per cent of his workforce didn't think it was. They either thought diversity wasn't about them, it was irrelevant to their work or they were actively hostile. The business was in a pretty traditional sector for diversity – transport – and our experience indicated that often the longer serving men were hostile to diversity when it was framed simply as a numbers game. That made them anxious that diversity would simply be a barrier to their promotion or prospects as those opportunities in future would only go to women. What that example shows is, in order to make real advances in increasing diversity and having them stick, you have to try to make those efforts mean something to those who find it difficult as much as to those who are full blown advocates – to the 'polite' resisters as well as the enthusiastic adopters. Unless you can convince colleagues that there is a core business reason for it being the right thing to do, you risk being drawn into the trade-off argument.

Diversity by Design was the critical voice in the recruitment of a UK university vice chancellor (VC). We took the selection group through the rigour of deciding exactly what they needed in their new VC. They looked at the internal and external challenges the university was facing. Then they evaluated its existing strategy, assessing the tools the leadership already had to meet those challenges and those they didn't. It was the latter that they wanted the new VC to bring to them. All of which discussion led them to listing the qualities they were looking to add through this critical appointment. They included: the ability to challenge, push back and bring a new perspective; to demonstrate difference in how they see the world; and to understand and build the combination of differences into leadership – bringing in different skills and ideas to create something new.

Through this process they had reached a clear agreement that the lens of difference, of diversity, was an enormously helpful way of looking at whom they needed to recruit. They used it to describe a new VC who might just not be like the people they already had in their leadership. In other words, someone who might, alongside their skill and experience and any other personal qualities, conceivably be female or Black or Asian. Then one of the Board members involved in the process said, 'But we wouldn't want to appoint someone just for the sake of diversity.'

There were three senior women in the chairs closest to me. From where he was sitting, he didn't see their eyes roll. 'Surely', I said, 'you're not suggesting that appointing a woman or someone who is Black or Asian would be appointing someone who wasn't as good as a man?' He retreated. While the process we had taken them through had guided the others to realizing and expressing the value that diversity in the appointment could bring to the institution, we had failed to take him along. He was still thinking that this way of approaching the appointment was just 'doing the right thing' rather than appointing the person they really needed and wanted for the job because they could bring something new, something different to what the senior leadership team already had. He still saw diversity as a trade-off with excellence.

The main pitfall of framing diversity as the 'right thing to do' – even though it might be – is that it looks like you're reducing diversity to a numbers game. Righting the wrong of under-representation can be seen by those who have been privileged by over-representation as taking something away from them. If they think they have got there solely through their own talent, rather than through a combination of ability and advantage, then appointing someone who brings a whole quiver of difference not only risks quality in their eyes, it certainly makes competition stiffer for them. But aiming to diversify your senior team by opening up more opportunities for women, as Andrew Stevens former MD of IBM Australia put it, '[doesn't] guarantee a woman a job or a promotion. What [it does] is increase the probability that a talented woman will be considered alongside a talented man' (35). No business would ever sensibly, or with any respect for the talent of that individual, just appoint someone 'because they were Black or female'. If they didn't have the skill to do the job it would give them a considerable handicap with their colleagues and negatively affect the business. But how many times have you heard it said that someone 'only got the job because...'?

The mindset that thinks reducing the diversity deficits poses a trade-off with quality, sees it therefore as a cost to business rather than a dividend. If your aim is just 'we should get more women', 'we should get more Black people', without understanding specifically why that will benefit the business, you risk building resentment rather than progress. You also run the risk of the person appointed firstly feeling patronized and, secondly, that you've put them in a difficult position with colleagues because they have to make double the effort to prove to them that they were indeed the right hire. If you want to improve the numbers of people unrepresented at different levels of the organization, you have to know why. Don't stop asking yourself and your colleagues that question, until you are satisfied that you can answer clearly what they will specifically bring to your organization.

Actively bringing on and developing capable people who belong to groups that typically experience disadvantage has to be based on recognizing their abilities and be a core part of your talent strategy, of your values, and has to be embraced by your people as part of their collective endeavour. Or it will be dismissed as compliance or politically driven conformity and you will end up defending diversity against quality, which is a false dichotomy because, as in all good appointments and promotions, you will have set clear quality thresholds.

The representative thing to do

The second justification, the 'representative thing to do' can also get you into trouble. Companies often express their commitment to diversity with variations of the statement: 'We want our employees to represent the diversity of our customers and the communities we operate in.' This does have an apparent logic. If the diversity of your employees matches that of your customers, suppliers and the community, surely your business will necessarily benefit from understanding, communication, sales insight and so on? Well, as with this whole argument, it only might do. That's because it's not simple to define what you mean by 'representative' when it comes to your community or your customers.

The 2011 Census revealed that there are over 100 languages spoken in the boroughs of London. Some 78 per cent of Londoners speak English as their main language at the same time as belonging to many different cultural traditions. The remaining 22 per cent – just over 1.7 million people – have another first language. The Office for National Statistics discovered that overall there are 53 'main' languages in the capital spoken by at least 0.1 per cent of residents and there are another 54 that include variants of established languages such as Chinese or those, like Caribbean Creole, Cornish or Gaelic spoken by a small number of people (36). In the context of that degree of ethnic and linguistic diversity, good luck with, for instance, making the delivery of a borough council's services 'representative'. It may sound like a reasonable diversity aspiration, democratically sound and responsive to the community, but it is arithmetically impossible. How can 'being representative' be a practical, rather than a merely rhetorical, objective? A council could respond to that level of diversity through three interlinked approaches:

- fostering alertness to the diversity of the residents it serves by increasing the diversity of its employees;
- enabling employees to share their own differences with each other across the organization and increasing the collective understanding of diversity;
- supporting employees to have the confidence to adapt the design and delivery of those services to meet the different needs of people in the borough.

Firstly, a significant mix of difference in the council's people will alert its teams and departments to the range of differences among the borough's residents – its different shaped families, types of religion, cultures, lifestyles, working lives and so on. Councils need not be representative so much as culturally sensitive in the broadest sense of that phrase. They need to understand that there is enormous breadth in the way people live and be sufficiently self-conscious about the reality of those differences. The recognition and valuing of diversity among its employees will greatly enhance the council's ability to do this and respond to the lived experience of their residents.

Secondly, employees need to share that learning and the insights from their own differences across the organization, so that all their colleagues gain the benefit and, in whatever they do, are then more able to challenge the assumptions the organization is making about the services and products it provides.

Thirdly, people need to be supported by their managers to have the confidence to flex the services and products to match the different ways their residents and customers perceive, access and use them.

This three-pronged approach of using the diversity of your people is a way of raising awareness of the diversity of your customers. Learning from each other's insights about difference and being confident to adjust and adapt products and services is a framework that works equally well for companies in the commercial sector where they have a direct relationship with customers, or are operating nationally or globally across different cultures or in relation to different ways of doing business.

In a report published in 2018, *Diversity: The New Prescription for the NHS*, I argued that diversity plays an indispensable role in the provision of effective health services (37). In part I was drawing on work by the leading researchers in the field of diversity and health, Professors Michael West and Jeremy Dawson (38). They looked at the effect of hospitals trying, as much as is actually possible, to represent the populations they serve in the people they employ. What they discovered has a rather uncomfortable starting point. There is much research, they reported, that 'suggests that people unconsciously favour members of their own social groups'. That means we have learned to be nicer to people who are like us. But however hard that is to own up to, it can have a positive outcome when employees are deliberately drawn from a range of groups of people who are not like each other. Michael explains it thus:

> What we found was that much of the explanation resided in patients' reports of civility. What appears to be the case is that when the diversity and mix of frontline staff matches that of the surrounding population, the staff behave more civilly in total to the people that they interact with because they cover the range of 'people like me'. What that does is create a culture of civility. And that civility does not stop at the boundaries of staff–patient interactions. What it is likely to do is to spread across other relationships as well.

Michael and his team's work uncovered that each group's unspoken (and often unrecognized) unease or hostility to those who are not like them can nonetheless be turned to the advantage of the NHS by recognizing that when treating 'our own' with civility, we role model civility to our colleagues. Diversity in employees can thus create an overall increase in civility.

The police face a similar challenge with the pressure 'to be representative'. They are at the service of increasingly diverse communities. They have, in some cases, learned how to adapt policing to this rather well. Many years ago, I personally experienced the hostility and lack of ease that they projected in relation to gay people. In 1995 I was nearly arrested for what I later described as 'Being in Possession of a Gay Sexual Orientation'. It was the night before Gay Pride in London. I was eating outside in Soho when the police decided to clear the pavement. 'Disabled access', they said. As they overreached their mission and tried to move us from our tables, I realized that my bag had been stolen. I tried to report this to one of the officers and he literally said, 'Move on sonny', despite the fact that I was 38 and trying to report a crime. I persisted and he threatened to throw me in the back of a police van for being 'obstructive'.

I discovered subsequently that these were police drafted in from Essex for the event and they hadn't yet quite got the hang of how to oversee Pride. How did this change? I saw that happen with the police in Brighton, where I live, 15 years later. Looking at the data the police realized that, in a city with a long-established and sizeable gay and lesbian population, crimes against them, ranging from the petty to the violent, were going unreported. Even if they were reported they weren't being dealt with sensitively and with respect. So they weren't getting the evidence to convict. More than that, even if they got the defendants to court, lesbians and gays were just too frightened to go into the witness box. To tackle this they set out to build trust with gay people across town. Gradually they created better relationships. The situation improved markedly. Trust was built so that crimes were reported, witnesses did go to court and criminals were convicted and punished.

What is interesting about this is that neither of the officers involved in this exercise was lesbian or gay. They had simply identified a policing problem. Crimes against a section of the local community were being committed and going unreported and unpunished. Diversity may have been a lens through which the issue was first spotted, but the work that the officers did turned it into a policing priority not a diversity scheme. But was there any need for those who took this initiative to be 'representative' for there to be recognition of a policing problem? They just had to be good police officers and the Brighton police as an organization had to be open enough to become aware of the issue and then be prepared to act and adapt.

From the many sessions I have done over the years with the police, it emerges unmistakably that trust is key to the police obtaining evidence and earning and maintaining the necessary respect for their authority in order to protect the public. Thus there are definite policing reasons to recruit and promote officers of all kinds and from all groups in a community. A diverse population needs to see a diverse police force. But the diversity in the police also needs to be articulated on the basis of a clear argument that it does indeed build trust and help them to unearth evidence of crime that would otherwise not be forthcoming. That it builds respect with the public whom they serve. The presence of Black and Brown police officers may well contribute to creating this greater trust. There is also evidence that, on its own, it doesn't.

Professor Jennifer Eberhardt in her recent book *Biased* described her work with Oakland Police in California evaluating their behaviour when stopping drivers (39). She found that 'when officers were speaking to black drivers, they were rated as less respectful, less polite, less friendly, less formal and less impartial than when they spoke to white drivers'. She and her team then combed through nearly 500,000 transcripts of car stops, tallying the words that signified respect and scoring them. This confirmed their initial conclusions. However, something unexpected also emerged. 'Black officers were just as likely as white officers to exhibit less respect to black drivers. The drivers' race trumped the officers' race'. The lack of respect correlated to the race of the driver, not the race of the officer.

This points towards the problem lying in the overall culture of the police, not just its representative composition. Police officers, whatever their ethnicity, are being institutionalized into particular attitudes towards certain members of the public. This suggests that race is not the only lens through which to look at the reform of the police, that a lack of representation is not the sole cause of their failures to treat Black people and people from ethnic minorities equally with other members of the community. There appears to be a more extensive issue in their organizational culture. If the police are to describe accurately their reasons for diversity in local forces, they have to be clear about the policing dividend, how it will build trust, how it will help to create positive cultural change and how it will reduce crime and increase the protection of the public, not just repeat the surface logic of representation.

The smart business thing to do

'What gets measured gets managed' is one of the most frequent incantations in business. It's usually attributed to the great US management theorist,

Peter Drucker. Except he didn't say it. More than that, he didn't really think it. He wrote in *Management: Tasks, responsibilities, practices*, 'Work implies not only that somebody is supposed to do the job, but also accountability, a deadline and, finally, the measurement of results – that is, feedback from results on the work and on the planning process itself' (40). Measurement is only significant insofar as it is a form of accountability and an opportunity to learn. Targets are about responsibility and reflection, not just numbers. The more interesting question about targets is why they were or weren't achieved, not whether. As Drucker elaborated in 1990, they are one part of a complex set of relationships that make things happen in organizations. He told one of his clients: 'Your first role… is the personal one… It is the relationship with people, the development of mutual confidence, the identi-fication of people, the creation of a community. This is something only you can do. It cannot be measured or easily defined. But it is not only a key func-tion. It is one only you can perform' (41).

The measurement mantra has been criticized on and off for over 60 years. In 1956 VF Ridgway from Cornell University's School of Management published research, the intention of which was admirably clear from its title: *Dysfunctional Consequences of Performance Measurements*. It was summed up by one business columnist a decade or so ago as: 'What gets measured gets managed – even when it's pointless to measure and manage it, and even if it harms the purpose of the organization to do so' (42).

Nonetheless targets, and diversity targets in particular, are very popular in business. There is also no doubt that when used carefully they can draw attention to the problem and they can stimulate action and accountability. When it launched in the UK, the 30% Club established a set of targets for women in FTSE companies. It was set up in 2010 with the aim of achieving a minimum of 30 per cent female representation on FTSE 100 boards by 2015 and on FTSE 350 boards by 2020. The first was reached in 2018, and the percentage currently stands at 36.1 per cent. The second was reached by the following year and is currently 34.2 per cent. By 2023 they aim to reach at least 30 per cent representation of women on all FTSE 350 execu-tive committees. In 2020 their latest data shows that women only occupy 21.3 per cent of those places (43).

These kinds of targets are most useful as headlines to create change and overcome what Professor Iris Bohnet, the Academic Dean of Harvard Kennedy School and author of *What Works: Gender equality by design* and a doyenne of research into diversity, calls 'the intention–action gap' (44). However, what numbers you settle on obviously need careful consideration.

If it were going to be 'representative', for instance, the 30% Club would need to be called (according to the World Bank's current global population figure for women) the 49.584% Club (45). But the reason for '30%' derives from two different impulses. The first is achievability. When Helena Morrisey, the founder, started trying to raise interest in the campaign in 2010 she says companies were initially dismissive. 'A typical response ran: "This is a women's issue. What's it got to do with me?"' The breakthrough came when she managed to convince male chairs to recruit other male chairs to the cause because, she argued, 'it's not a women's issue, it's an economic issue. Look at the bottom line' (46). To some extent, although this is never said out loud by any of the founders, but has been quietly said to me, 30 per cent was a figure that 'wouldn't frighten the horses', to recall the famous quote at the turn of the century by actor Mrs Patrick Campbell. It was good tactics because 30 per cent was thought to be achievable and that it would suffer less resistance from those who were not keen to support any change or any target.

The other source of the ubiquity of 30 per cent comes from separate work done in 1977 and 1988 by Professor Rosabeth Moss Kanter and Professor Drude Dahlerup on the effects of increasing women in business and in politics (47). Their work established and led to wide acceptance of what became known as critical mass theory. Rosabeth observed from her research that 'the relative numbers of socially and culturally different people in a group' were 'critical in shaping interaction dynamics in group life'. More recently, exemplifying how widely accepted the ideas around critical mass have become, *Time Magazine*'s Washington correspondent, Jay Newton Small, summarized it as:

> When women reached 20 per cent in the Senate, they went after the Pentagon to reform the military's sexual-assault protocol. When they reached 25 per cent of Hollywood producers, they took down Harvey Weinstein and his casting-couch culture. And when they reached a third of the White House press corps, Fox's Roger Ailes, NPR's Michael Oreskes and other serial harassers in the media began to get called out. Somewhere in that zone, when women comprise 20 per cent to 30 per cent of an institution, things begin to change (48).

However, there is no linear relationship between just the numbers of people in minority-status groups in an executive committee, board or a team and positive outcomes for the organization. There is awareness that flows strongly from the mere presence of difference, as we'll come to see in Chapter 5. But as Iris points out, it's not just the percentage of difference on the board or exec that matters but 'how the board members are chosen, how the boards are organized and what the rules of engagement and decision making are'. Moreover women, people from Black and Asian backgrounds, lesbians and gays do not all think and act the same as each other. When they are in small numbers, they may feel, and are often seen, as token representatives. As a result, they may well judge that they need to stick together. However, the more difference there is in a team, the greater the critical mass of people from minority-status groups, the more inclusively managed and led it is, the more those people can and will express their personal view and the more alliances and disagreements can happen productively outside identity groups and across the whole team. Crucially the target is not enough on its own unless, for instance, the women are not only different because they're not men but also because they can express what they think with ease. Furthermore the men and women need to be different from each other in terms of background, experience and the ways they frame the world and their approach to the business, as well as just the difference in sex. It's not just who or how many you are, but how you behave and how you frame decisions. The difference in personal experience matters.

It is significant that the 30% Club, despite its narrowly focused title, identifies three wider 'strategic pillars' in describing what it wants to achieve: influencing those with power to drive change; activating chairs and CEOs as members; enabling future women leaders. Pulling all those levers has shown that what has operated most effectively for them is generating a level of social pressure in business to advance talented women. They created a new norm. If businesses didn't hit the 30 per cent, they were asked to 'comply or explain'. With the support of significant business figures and of government they, in effect, deployed embarrassment. The standard became compliance. Failure to reach the target was socially penalized. 'Named and shamed – the two FTSE 350 firms that have no women on the board... and the 39 with one "token" female director' shouted the headline on This Is Money website in November 2019 when the Hampton-Alexander Review that 'champions more women on FTSE Boards and in leadership' announced its annual figures (49).

The UK government, by announcing voluntary targets and using that review to monitor them, became what one of the doyens of behaviour change, Cass Sustein, called 'norm entrepreneurs' (50). By setting a form of social incentive for boards, rather than regulation, they had enhanced the atmosphere for change. Other governments have preferred to use mandatory tools. There has been wide discussion over the years about the effect of quotas, much of it focusing on the decision by the Norwegian Parliament in 2008 to legislate for a 40 per cent compulsory quota of women on the boards of publicly limited liability companies. The results in the short term did not appear to support any conclusion that quotas were positive. As Scott E Page says, 'the evidence from the Norwegian case reveals a negative effect of gender diversity. The Boards that most increased their gender diversity performed less well after the law was implemented'. However, as he also wisely pointed out, 'these findings should not be surprising, except to those people who believe that diversity bonuses occur by magic' (51).

Scott's research into the context reveals that there are a number of reasons why it didn't work well in the short term. Norway's main industries are in sectors that are heavily male dominated. They have a scarcely populated female pipeline of talent. Therefore a relatively few number of women ended up on a large number of boards. They had less experience. There were other activities in the sectors, like acquisitions, which affected the companies' immediate profitability, not to mention the 2008 crash. Also, given the complexity of inducting and acclimatizing a significant number of new people onto boards in a relatively short space of time, it is hardly surprising that 'more women' didn't produce a miraculous financial uplift. However, in the long term, women at an earlier stage of their career now have the definite prospect of training and pitching for board roles in the future. The pipeline of female directors is growing. Quotas can break the cycle of lack of opportunity, as can targets. As we will see later, targets are at their most effective when aspirational and backed by a clear articulation of their purpose as a talent strategy to develop the business.

In April 2017 Boston Consulting published a paper called *The Mix That Matters: Innovation through diversity* (52). They studied 171 German, Swiss and Austrian companies to investigate the relationship between the diversity of companies' management teams and the revenues they got from innovative products and services. The findings were dramatic. It showed that 'companies with the greatest gender diversity (8 out of every 20 managers were female) generated about 34 per cent of their revenues from innovative products and services in the most recent three-year period'. The evidence also suggested that 'having a high percentage of female managers is positively correlated with disruptive innovation, in which a new product, service, or business model fully replaces the version that existed before [such as what Netflix has done to DVD rental stores and what Amazon is doing to retail]'.

So, if we just recruit more women, will we automatically get more innovation? Well, no. The findings of the study were very specific and on one point quite emphatic. The authors were clear that 'one thing that *doesn't* seem to have an effect on innovation is the *overall percentage* of women in a company's workforce'.

For the diversity rationale to be effective the target and the outcome have to be explicit and specific. The head of an English department at one of the UK's largest universities asked for our help in diversifying the academics through the recruitment of some new lecturers. Starting as ever with the *what it's for?* question, we asked why the department needed greater diversity. It was going gangbusters: high application numbers, great student degree attainment, loads of research income, excellent academics, good position in the league tables. What was the problem? It's very simply stated, the head replied, 'There is great literature across the world being written in English by people who are not English. I want to reflect that contemporary canon of literature in our academics.' What the department needed was cultural (and geographic) diversity. It would look like ethnic diversity, but it was much more specific than that. They wanted to recruit academics with cultural and regional insight into literature in English. They really wanted Chimamanda Adichie or Binyavanga Wainaina or Arundhati Roy to join the department.

So, taking all the preceding into account, where does that leave us? How can businesses and organizations frame an effective top-line approach to diversity? The evidence and our experience suggests that the rationales for diversity that are effective are ones that lay out the reasons for it quite specifically, don't set abstract targets and understand precisely how diversity will further the business or organization's goals.

Three examples.

When we embarked on creating Diversity by Design, I was introduced to an inspiring South African. By the time I met Chris Brink he was VC of Newcastle University. He is a mathematician, specifically a logician, and he taught and researched maths, philosophy, logic and computer science in South Africa and Australia before coming to the UK in 2007. Five years earlier he had been appointed as the rector and vice chancellor of Stellenbosch University. Stellenbosch is the birthplace of apartheid. DF Malan, the first apartheid prime minister, was a Stellenbosch resident. Hendrik Verwoerd, the true architect of apartheid ideology, was a professor of sociology at Stellenbosch University before entering politics. His successor, John Vorster, was a student leader at Stellenbosch, and eventually chancellor of the university – as was Vorster's successor, PW Botha.

Just eight years after the end of apartheid and the first free elections in South Africa, Chris took over as VC. He was the first 'outsider', non-Stellenbosch alumnus or academic, to do so. As he told me, he immediately did two key things:

> The first, within weeks, was to state in front of a university-wide assembly that 'Stellenbosch needs more diversity.' The second, once the usual arguments of the 'Yes, but...' variety were being trotted out, was to give an *educational* rationale for why more diversity would be good for the university. The claim I made was that quality needs diversity.

What is especially fascinating about the situation he found himself in was that the post-apartheid ANC government wanted more diversity too. However, Chris had spent significant times when he was at the University of Cape Town (UCT) in the 1980s fighting what the government wanted. Liberal universities resisted apartheid interference in higher education by defining academic freedom as 'the right of each university to decide for itself: who shall teach, who shall be taught, what shall be taught, and how it shall be taught'.

Chris was now placed in a somewhat ironic situation. He was faced with 'a different category of risk, namely of being ordered by the state to do something I *did* want to do'. He realized that if he stuck to those principles of academic freedom and Stellenbosch continued to 'decide for itself who shall teach, who shall be taught, what shall be taught, and how it shall be taught', it would continue largely to recruit from the plentiful supply of what he calls 'mostly young white Afrikaners from what, as in the UK, were called "good schools"'. The university wouldn't transform. To achieve that he would instead have to develop a rationale that had its roots, drive and motivation not in the politics of the post-apartheid ANC government but in the new educational mission of the university.

At the heart of it, he explained, was this idea. It's worth quoting at length:

> Diversity has an inherent educational value. That is why we need more of it. The university is an educational institution. Our business is about knowledge. That means that we all have to learn, all the time. Students learn through their lectures, their assignments, their tutorials. Staff learn through their research, through their interaction with the community and through their teaching. One way or another, we all have to learn and keep on learning. And we will learn more from those people, those ideas and those phenomena that we do not know, than from those we know only too well.

We need around us people who represent the rich spectrum of South African life and we need the diversity of ideas that are new to us. We need to pursue this diversity of people and ideas to increase the quality of our core business, which is to learn. Only in this way, I believe, can we really meet our responsibility to our students. We need, and we wish, to prepare our students to become active and confident participants in a multicultural and globalized society. Whatever the advantages may be of a mono-cultural institution, they do not include the opportunity to meet and engage with many different viewpoints and to learn about many different environments. One reason why our engagement with diversity of colour is so urgent for us in South Africa is that engagement between Black and White people is such a powerful training ground for engagement with different ideas (53).

This approach, widely admired, achieved significant results in diversifying the university.

The second example is interesting not so much for its rather startling objective, but for how the company in question decided on it. In 2016 BHP Billiton, the largest mining business in the world, set 'an ambitious and aspirational goal to achieve gender balance globally by 2025'. And it was indeed particularly 'ambitious and aspirational', as it would mean, according to *Fortune Magazine*, employing another 21,000 women by the middle of the next decade (54). In December 2017 in a speech to the UK campaign group, Powerful Women (full disclosure – I sit on their Board), their Group Treasurer, Vandita Pant, admitted, 'That is no mean feat... [it] is a huge leap for BHP as a year back women represented less than 17 per cent of our workforce.'

How did they decide on this goal? Mining, along with other engineering and traditionally heavy industries, is facing a dual challenge. Firstly, the workforce in the sector is older. Only recently the salary survey in *The Engineer* showed that the average age among engineers is 47.6, two years older than the 2018 average (55). In the next decade, mining, along with others in the sector, is going to see a drop in numbers on a very steep gradient as a result of retirement.

Secondly, the industry is requiring a wholly new and different range of skills. As Athalie Williams, BHP's chief people officer, says:

The increased use of technology and automation at mine sites (will) boost the diversity of hiring, as it will allow BHP to recruit from sectors outside mining... For us it's given the space to have conversations and to understand how our organization works in a way that we wouldn't have done if we hadn't set the target (56).

At the first I-triple E (the Institute of Electrical and Electronics Engineers) Vision and Challenges Summit in San Francisco in May 2017, the distinguished former Dean of the School of Engineering at Stanford, Professor James Plummer, echoed this, advocating:

> broadening engineering education to include more liberal arts exposure and more life skills, with the aim of preparing future engineers for unpredictable careers. Engineers will need communication skills, the ability to work in teams, global knowledge, and an entrepreneurial outlook as much as they will need technical depth for the future (57).

Oil, gas and mining – the resources industries – went from having pictures in their glossy publications of men in hard hats on oil rigs, to photos of men and women in hard hats on oil rigs. How much will that change continue into the future? As Athalie says, 'The resources industry hasn't traditionally been attractive to women. How do we rebrand and make people see that future roles in mining are not a White man in a hard hat with a dirty face but a place of technological innovation?' (58).

Starting from those two points, BHP ran its data to find out the effect on the business of employing more women. They looked at teams in 'their most inclusive sites' and discovered that they performed 'at least 15 per cent better than company average – on safety, production, cost efficiency and employee engagement and... there was a reduction in injury frequency of up to 68 per cent and up to 15 per cent greater accuracy in production forecasting', according to Vandita. The reason for this, their research told them, was that 'in our most inclusive sites, people are more engaged, share ideas and collaborate to make things better. They respect and value diverse views and experiences.'

Their goal, even though 'aspirational', flowed from two key business imperatives for the changing future of the company: the numbers of employees and the skills they will need into the next decades, and the data showed that they could enhance performance through greater diversity.

The third example comes from one of the very few people of colour to be CEO of a Fortune 500 company, Ajay Banga of Mastercard, who has just retired from the position after 10 years. In 2019 in a 'Talks at Goldman Sachs' interview, he spoke of how financial inclusion has become a significant part of their strategy (59).

His starting point was the 2 billion people in the world who are excluded from banking. Mastercard no longer issues cards. It now describes itself as a 'technology company in the global payments business' and it processes billions of transactions around the world annually. These 2 billion people are not just in the emerging markets. There are an estimated 25 to 40 million people who are 'underbanked or unbanked' in the United States and 70 million or so in Europe. He described reaching these people as core business. It's not philanthropy. They are mainly lower-income people, but by engaging them now, they can become a significant group of future customers. That connects them to Mastercard's core business for the years to come.

Their exclusion from banking has a substantial effect on their lives. He told of how when he came to the United States in his thirties he couldn't hire a car or get a phone because he didn't have a credit history. Reaching these people draws them into the circle of Mastercard's business, which is providing the means to make those kinds of transactions even when you don't have that kind of credit history.

Mastercard, he says, has now reached 380 million of those 2 billion – 19 per cent. They are individuals with low and middle incomes and small and micro entrepreneurs. 'I make a small loss on them, but changing the way they interact with the money they get, the money they spend, their pensions etc, that changes the way cash operates in an economy. And that's extremely beneficial to our company. We can do well and do good at the same time.'

Consequently Mastercard is able with some confidence to state its diversity commitment in terms of a key business objective. Even if they express it in a rather impenetrable way:

> The complexity of the current economic climate demands creative and innovative business approaches and presents the opportunity for growth in developing markets by addressing unexpected or counter-intuitive consumer needs. Shifting demographics, increasing purchasing power of non-traditional segments and a trend towards customization present a compelling case for viewing Mastercard's business efforts through a diverse lens (60).

In other words: 'There are large numbers of potential new customers, many of whom are currently on low incomes and excluded. They won't yield immediate returns. But in a cashless world they will be our customers of the future. They are vital to extending the pipeline of our business.'

These three examples are not comprehensive or perfect. But they give us powerful clues as how to make a statement about a company's diversity that is effective in delivering results and can take all your people with you.

You can harness the Power of Difference to develop a specific rationale for diversity in your company by exploring:

- what the business/team is trying to achieve. What are the goals? What kind of diversity, and why that kind of diversity, will help you to meet those goals?

- how you can make diversity an approach to acquiring and promoting the talent you need to achieve those goals.

- how you can have a talent strategy driven by diversity not a separate diversity strategy.

- how you can be receptive and adaptable to the differences in your customers rather than 'representative'.

- how your people can see that diversity is the 'right thing' when it furthers core business objectives.

- what are the right targets to set so that they enable you to value what different groups can bring, and open up the space for reflection and learning.

- how you can avoid generalizations so your diversity statements are about specific business goals rather than personal passions.

02

Inclusion is not just about being nice to people

Jo Berry's father was Sir Anthony Berry MP, a Government Deputy Chief Whip. He was killed by a bomb that exploded at 2.54 am in The Grand Hotel in Brighton on the last night of the Conservative Party conference in 1984.

The bomb had been planted by Patrick Magee, who had joined the Provisional IRA barely into his twenties in 1972. It contained nine kilogrammes of gelignite and used a timer from a video recorder. He placed it behind a panel in the bathroom of room 629 and programmed it to detonate 24 days later.

The IRA issued a statement in which they claimed responsibility in chilling tones:

> Mrs Thatcher will now realize that Britain cannot occupy our country and torture our prisoners and shoot our people in their own streets and get away with it. Today we were unlucky, but remember we only have to be lucky once. You will have to be lucky always. Give Ireland peace and there will be no more war (1).

From the conference stage she responded equally defiantly by calling the bombing:

> an attempt to cripple Her Majesty's democratically elected Government... That is the scale of the outrage in which we have all shared, and the fact that we are gathered here now – shocked, but composed and determined – is a sign not only that this attack has failed, but that all attempts to destroy democracy by terrorism will fail (2).

The Northern Ireland conflict seemed at the time extreme, vicious and intractable.

I met Jo and Patrick through my involvement with the Forgiveness Project, which 'shares stories of forgiveness in order to build hope, empathy and understanding'. Twenty years later, on the anniversary of the bomb and of her father's murder, I invited Jo and Patrick to share the extraordinary private conversations that had led them to work together, for the first time in public in front of an audience in a church in Brighton.

Jo had decided soon after her father's death that 'somehow I would come to understand those that had killed my father and that I would find a way of bringing something positive out of what had happened'. So during 1985 and 1986 she travelled frequently to West Belfast 'to find real human beings involved in the conflict and to hear their stories'. To begin with she had a lot of anger. 'There was anger against God, anger against whatever made this happen. Just anger. Rage about how something like this could come about, you know. Why can't we have peace?' That started to change when she found that 'people in Northern Ireland were really happy to hear what I was saying. And what I was saying was "let's find a solution, let's look beyond the labels". And I said... I wanted to learn, to understand.'

She also was very public, later on, in saying that she would be happy to meet Patrick. 'People would ask me "Why do you want to meet him?" And really it was just to hear his story... about why he planted the bomb. What had happened, before, after and to be in dialogue.'

Patrick had been arrested, convicted and given eight life sentences with a recommendation that he serve a minimum of 35 years. In the end he served 14 because he was released as part of the Good Friday Agreement in 1999.

In 2000 the opportunity did finally arise for Jo to meet Patrick in Dublin. It was arranged by a friend, Ann Gallagher:

> I arrived at her house and she said, 'Jo will you cook, I've got to make phone calls?' So, I'm cooking in her kitchen and then the doorbell rings and it was Patrick. I remember thinking I just really wanted to reassure him that it was going to be OK to meet me. And I thought maybe he will be more scared than me. I don't know whether Patrick remembers this but I shook your hand and said, 'I'm really pleased you've come'. Do you remember what you said?

Patrick replied, 'Something to the effect of "thank you for inviting me". I certainly was scared, I'll tell you that'.

What is fascinating about their conversations, which I have chaired twice more since 2004, is that Patrick doesn't apologize, which was deeply unsettling at first. Yet, on reflection, something far more profound happens in their interaction than an apology.

Patrick said to the audience in 2004:

I wouldn't like anybody here to go away thinking that there's somehow been
a major transformation in my view of what I've done in the sense that I would
renounce the use of violence... I do think there's lessons for all people who take
up arms in that it should only be as a last resort when every other action has
been tried and tested... I have to continually and will continue to ask myself:
'were there other actions available to me as an individual and available to the
movement I was a part of?' Where I am at present, I can't see any. I'll debate the
point. I'll argue the point. But I can't see any. The reality we faced then refuted
that notion, any notion, that there was another way of doing it.

For Jo hearing Patrick justify what he did in this political and military way
is the hardest part of their relationship. Her response recalls the stark reality
of it for her and her renunciation of violence:

the bomb didn't work for me. It changed my life forever and I'm still dealing
with that legacy. I can still see that there are things happening in my life,
difficulties which were as a result of choices that I made after the bomb because
I was so traumatized... There were many other people in Brighton whose lives
were also changed. So for all of us it didn't work. To me violence can never work.
Everyone loses out. Those that are violent and those that have the violence done
to them. But what do I do with those feelings, that's where the choice is? Do I
harness those feelings and transform them and bring them into a different kind
of future? And the answer is, yes I do.

Patrick argued that day in Brighton that in certain circumstances violence
was justifiable and Jo argued that it never was. That imbalance between
their world views and the tension it creates ebbs and flows in emotional
prominence in their lives. Jo's hurt on the one hand and Patrick's self-justification on the other, generated by their different positions as perpetrator and
victim, is a material dynamic in their exchange and will never disappear. But
Patrick also described the transformational impact Jo has had on him since
they first met:

I've never come across anyone so open and with such dignity... I had this
political hat on my head, the need to explain... but then I have to confront
every single time I've met you, and perhaps more so now because where we are
and the day that it is and that I'm sitting with someone whose father I killed.

I'm here in Brighton 20 years after your father's death and I will not shirk my responsibility for that. It was an Irish Republican Army operation but whatever the legitimacy and the political arguments behind it, the fact is I was part of it and I killed your father. And every time since, that's been at the forefront of my mind. I'm sure that's what I suddenly had to confront… There's no hiding behind politics or rehearsed arguments. The line might be sincere but it's inappropriate. At the moment we met we were communicating as two human beings.

Jo echoes this transformative effect of their engagement with one another:

For me meeting you today, 20 years after you planted the bomb that killed my father, is part of something that I've yearned for and searched for and worked very hard for, for years and years. To reach this point where I can sit with you and listen and understand, it means so much to me. I feel us being together does bring something positive out of what happened… and gives a lot of signs for the future. And it seems every time we meet, you're more open and vulnerable and on a day like this I really do appreciate that. I don't think we're finished meeting. And however hard it is and uncomfortable and however much sometimes I want to shut the door and be more 'normal' I won't because I think the gains are greater than I can imagine for both of us.

In a conversation that lasted 90 minutes or so, the transcript reveals that the word 'hear' was said just over 30 times. Every three minutes either Jo or Patrick said it. Hearing lies at the heart of their ability to have a meaningful conversation. Not to reach agreement. You can't agree about a murder. But the result of their preparedness to hear each other, to include each other, has led to their commitment to working together for a peaceful future for Northern Ireland and elsewhere. They now collaborate, albeit sporadically, through her organization Building Bridges for Peace, which 'promotes peace and conflict resolution throughout the world' (3).

If you think of the many challenges of creating an environment in your own workplace that could reliably be called 'inclusive', they may rather fade in the face of Jo and Patrick's. The two of them have managed to craft, out of the most extreme of circumstances, an environment that is able to be inclusive of a murderer and his victim's child. Their personal interests on the face of it could not be more divergent. Yet through preparedness to do so they discovered each other as humans and found values they could agree on and pursue through their joint work.

A model for inclusion: difference not similarity

Their experience offers a useful paradigm for inclusion. Most importantly it focuses those involved in diversity on the fundamental truth that inclusion is about difference not about similarity. It is about conflict or potential conflict rather than agreement. It faces you up to the challenge of negotiating between competing interests rather than living a fantasy where everybody just gets what they want and says what they choose, without needing to adjust for its impact on others. It's about productive disagreement rather than winning the argument. The only agreement it requires is the desire to achieve a common interest rather than a sectional one. Inclusion is about hearing leading to collaboration.

One of the most celebrated definitions of diversity and inclusion was coined by Vernā Myers, now VP Inclusion Strategy at Netflix, when she said, 'Diversity is being invited to the party. Inclusion is being asked to dance' (4). If the party is your company, then joining in the dancing is how you can influence the work. But the invitation to dance can't just come from or to certain parts of the business or certain groups in the company. The invitation has to be made by everyone and to everyone and then you all have to agree on what dance you are dancing. Inclusion is not a chaos of individuality or biasing one sectional interest over another or giving into the blaring volume of the most dominant voices. It is structured participation for all your employees to achieve joint outcomes. It only works through a consensus about what you are trying to achieve together. And an agreement to communicate – speak, hear, learn and discuss – in order to achieve it.

Giving space and expression to all voices is the way that inclusion is usually characterized. A recent article in the *Harvard Business Review* (5), for instance, argued that while diversity is vital, 'without inclusion… the crucial connections that attract diverse talent, encourage their participation, foster innovation, and lead to business growth won't happen'. It goes on to identify four levers that drive inclusion, two of which are 'inclusive leaders' and 'authenticity'. It emphasizes under the first that inclusive leaders should ensure that they are 'making it safe to propose novel ideas', 'empowering team members to make decisions' and, primarily, 'ensuring that team members speak up and are heard'. In relation to authenticity it points out that 'It's not surprising that everyone expends energy by repressing parts of their persona in the workplace in some way.' One of the aims of inclusivity is to understand this and mitigate it. This is the kind of observation that gives rise to the pervasive cliché that people must be able 'to bring their whole selves to work'.

On the face of it, and this article is absolutely typical in the diversity canon, this approach is perfectly sensible. It must be right that not only should companies recruit and promote a diversity of talent but they should also be under an obligation to ensure that those people feel included when they get there and their voices are heard and valued. So far so simple.

Yet it is also axiomatic in movements for social change – and pursuing diversity is in part a logical extension of those movements into the work-place – that all voices are not equal. You can draw that conclusion from history. The Rights of Man were literally that and for centuries women did not have the vote. Despite holding 'these truths to be self-evident, that all men are created equal, that they are endowed by their Creator with certain unalienable rights', the United States had hundreds of thousands of slaves, human beings owned as property by others (6). Gay sex has been decriminalized in a number of countries in only the last 50 years and remains illegal still in over 70 (7). Discrimination against people with disabilities at work has only relatively recently been banned in many jurisdictions and rights at work are still not guaranteed to people in the gig economy in the UK, let alone to workers on poverty wages in the developing world.

It would be naïve to assume that those power imbalances within society weren't reflected in organizations. As a generalization men as a group have more power than women; White people more than Black people; straight people more than gay people; middle-class people more than people from working class backgrounds and so on. The data on who succeeds more than others in companies bears this out. So, when we talk of 'inclusion' whose voice is to be 'included'? Whose should be heard? Should it only be the voices of the less powerful? Do we need to get into an 'oppression Olympics' to work out what the pecking order is? Should everyone bring their 'whole selves to work' or should some people, specifically the more powerful, leave some of their 'authentic self' at home? This needs to be unpicked.

First a bit of history

The notions of equality and rights, as they have been broadly understood in Western societies, were inherited from the Enlightenment. This intellectual movement began to articulate, through the idea of the power of rational thought and argument, the political ideals of universal freedom and equality. Through just over a century of revolutions, from the English in 1688 through the American, the French, until it descended into the Reign of Terror, and the successful uprising of liberated slaves in Haiti led by Toussaint Louverture, the framework that underpins much of our understanding and practice of human rights emerged. Notwithstanding the towering and continuing inspiration of these ideals of rights and freedoms there lurked within their expression a damaging contradiction. When Enlightenment intellectuals turned their attention to the social standing of women or of non-White people, pretty much to a man, their reason deserted them in favour of prejudice. Their ideals aspired to universality, but their writings talk just about White men. They contradicted their own ideals. The same Enlightenment thinking that is the deep background to people's work on diversity today also sparked the need for the focused campaigns by women and people of colour for their equality.

While women had to fight a long struggle to gain universal suffrage, property rights and to escape being chattels of men within marriage, over three centuries theories of racial superiority continued to be used in justification of the enforced, unpaid labour of slavery, the subjugation of countries in the pursuit of empires, the industrialized genocide of the Holocaust and the horrors of apartheid. After the Second World War and the Holocaust, however, the tide began to turn. Anti-racism started to take the moral high ground in most democracies. The world, through the United Nations Universal Declaration of Human Rights, attempted to tip the scales of rights and freedoms in the direction of a true universalism.

But still, over the decades that followed, the fine words and good intentions in those democracies didn't deliver for minority-status groups. The Enlightenment had airbrushed them and the post-war era barely begrudged them any real taste of equality. What little progress there was, was painfully slow and small. As Kenan Malik, the columnist, has observed in relation to the civil rights movement in America, 'the struggle for black rights… (was) squeezed between an intensely racist society on the one hand, and an often-indifferent left on the other'. The consequence of being stymied by either hostility or disinterest inevitably further fanned the sparks of identity-based struggles and resulted, Kenan continues, in:

> many black activists in the 1960s ceding from integrated civil rights organizations and setting up separate groups, giving rise to the Black Power and Black Panther movements. And that Black radicalism provided a template for many other groups, from women to Native Americans, from Muslims to gays, to look upon social change through the lens of their own cultures, goals and ideals (8).

The term 'identity politics' was coined in 1977 by a Black lesbian organization called the American Combahee River Collective, which argued that the most radical politics came from people placing their own experiences at the centre of their struggles. But, as Kenan observes, they crucially insisted 'that such struggles were necessarily interwoven with broader campaigns for change. Identity politics of that time provided a means of challenging oppression as a specific part of a wider project of social transformation'. However, a wedge was beginning to be driven between identity politics and that wider project.

The first crack opened up when the trades unions and the Left turned out not to be quite the natural allies that women and Black activists had hoped. The TUC in the UK remained ambivalent to women's organizations. Unions largely regarded women's demands for equality as a distraction from their core constituency of working men. Where there were women at work, the unions often argued for a strict application of the marriage bar and not only refused to campaign for equal pay but instead tried to maintain the pay differentials in favour of men (9).

Similarly, despite Black workers joining unions in large numbers in the fifties and sixties in the UK, they were not unambiguously welcomed. Notoriously in Bristol in 1963 Black communities boycotted the bus service because of the refusal of the Bristol Omnibus Company to employ Black or Asian crews. Far from getting behind the boycott, the local Transport and General Workers Union supported the bus company. The campaign lasted for four months until the company finally backed down and overturned their colour bar (10). In 1968, the dockers joined the London Smithfield Meat Market porters' strike and marched in support of the MP Enoch Powell who had become the mouthpiece of anti-immigrant hostility in his incendiary 'Rivers of Blood' speech (11).

Ambivalence on the left was met by hostility on the right. With the advent of the Reagan and Thatcher era, the dominant politics became deeply uninterested in any kind of collective rights. Reagan had voted against the Civil Rights Act of 1964 and the Voting Rights Act of 1965 (12) and his Presidency turned away from the legacy of his predecessors JFK and LBJ. Margaret Thatcher distanced herself from the radical social reforms of the 1960s Labour governments. In an interview in *Women's Own* in 1987, she famously said, 'You know, there's no such thing as society. There are individual men and women and there are families' (13). Later that year at the Conservative Party Conference she marked a further turn towards traditional conservative ideas, when she said in her leader's speech, 'Children who need to be taught to respect traditional moral values are being taught that they have an inalienable right to be gay' (14).

Not only did separate identity groups spring up in response to that political coldness and antagonism, but the idea of 'identity' itself took on a wholly new meaning in the second half of the 20th century. It was now being used to describe the idea that you had 'an identity' and you needed to find it in order to fulfil yourself. This defined a new concept and expressed a modern social phenomenon. Its coinage is widely credited to the developmental psychologist and psychoanalyst, Erik Erikson, who, in *Childhood and Society* published in 1950, analysed the development of personality as going through eight clear stages. The fifth of them, which covers adolescence from 12 years old to 18, he called 'Identity vs. Role Confusion'. 'In the social jungle of human existence', he wrote, 'there is no feeling of being alive without a sense of identity' (15). In 2018 Dr Marie Moran, from University College Dublin, trawled popular books and magazines, corporate and business literature, and political statements and manifestos published before the middle of the 20th century and made the startling discovery that there was 'no discussion at all of "identity" in any of the ways that are so familiar to us today, and which, in our ordinary and political discussions, we would now find it hard to do without' (16).

Thus, in the two decades from the sixties to the eighties, personal identity became a modern obsession and individual empowerment was more often than not emphasized over collective change. Identity largely took over from politics. Who first said 'the personal is political' has been credited to famous feminist after famous feminist, although each of them in turn has disavowed authorship. But whoever did say it first, it's now been turned on its head. The washing of politics through therapy made social progress a question of personal fulfilment. The political became almost entirely personal.

Finally, the third quarter of the 20th century saw an explosion of consumerism and individualism, reaching something of a peak with the ideas of the neoliberal economists that the origins of freedom lay in market choice, choosing what we want apparently without constraint. As Milton Friedman, one of both Reagan's and Thatcher's foremost economic advisors, said in 1980, 'A free society releases the energies and abilities of people to pursue their own objectives' (17). This made individual choice the conduit for your identity. The market was where you found yourself and how you became individual. The idea is curiously contradictory, however, because in that marketplace manufacturers make the same clothes, sports gear, shoes, make-up, kitchen designs, in fact anything you can think of, available to everyone, as long as they can afford it. But people still feel that buying these mass consumer goods is a sign of their individual style and identity or at least that of their tribe. Millions of people get the same Calvin Klein underwear, celebrity branded perfume, signed Nike trainers and so on, and yet continue to feel that each says a lot about 'who they are'. As the house journal of the Prindle Institute for Ethics puts it, 'The way you dress, the way you decorate your home, and the range of your hobbies express a nascent identity, allow you to take it for a test drive, and provide pathways for changing it in a kind of ongoing identity feedback loop' (18).

The point of this whirlwind historical tour was just to illustrate how the minefield of current identity politics, which shapes much of the landscape of diversity and inclusion today, was birthed by the Enlightenment, whose universalism nonetheless was flawed by the omission of women and Black people, who were then, with other minority status groups, cold shouldered by traditional politics and so started to go it alone. Those struggles then became filtered through the ubiquity of personal self-improvement and were finally driven to self-centredness by the individualism of the market. Shaped by the Enlightenment, failed by traditional politics, inveigled by therapy and captured by the market of individual choice, the politics of identity we are experiencing today found a style and character. This style and character, however, has been exacerbated by the divisive megaphone of social media since the early 2000s, and become more individualistic, increasingly subjective, too self-centred and in most cases delinked from the bigger picture of fundamental social, or in the focus of this book, organizational change. Solidarity between groups and the building of alliances, inspired by the pursuit of the common aim of finding a way to live and interact amicably together, has been compromised by dominant trends in identity politics that segregate people into smaller and smaller groups, emphasizing their own sectional interests over shared possibilities and reinforcing feelings of belonging by stressing differences as unbridgeable rather than a route to benefits that are mutual.

If that's the history, what does it mean for the present?

So what impact does this have on your organization? How do managers run their team or departments in an 'inclusive' way? Whose voices are to be included? What weight is to be given to subjective experiences? Can inclusivity ever exclude people? If so, on what grounds and who decides those grounds? How do you take account of the variety of voices in any one group?

To start with it's important to beware of people setting themselves up as gatekeepers of the group voice. Their own experience, important as it is to hear it, does not make theirs the only valid view or perspective from their group. At the very core of inclusion must be the recognition of the diversity of voices across all your people and the diversity within the different groups. It may be obvious to say it, but it seems to need restating all the time. Do not make assumptions. Not all people of colour see their relationship to race in the same way nor share the same values. Not all lesbians and gays have the same political outlook. Not all people who are encompassed by the spectrum that arcs from those who have surgically transitioned to those who choose to identify socially as gender non-conforming articulate their place in the world in the same way. Yet there seems to have emerged an orthodoxy in diversity plans, strategies and actions that regularly and without hesitation lumps people together under catch-all acronyms like BAME and LGBT, assumes they each have just a single voice, and allows that one voice to represent the entire group's viewpoint.

For instance, observe the reaction to Kanye West's support for Donald Trump. Many commentators and snipers on social media couldn't compute his outspoken defence of the President, his wearing a 'Make America Great Again' hat when he met with Trump in the Oval Office in October 2018, or his comments about 400 years of slavery being 'a choice'. Many could only see all that as some kind of betrayal of the fact he's Black. But there are other alternatives. As a billionaire he might just be in favour of a President who gives tax cuts to the rich. Despite being an artist of extraordinary flare and talent, he may also be just politically naïve or downright unintelligent. Or maybe he's simply a Black man with agency who's made up his own mind about his own politics. It's as mistaken to question his political choices on the basis of his race as it was for Joe Biden to say to the radio presenter Charlamagne tha God, 'I'll tell you, if you have a problem figuring out whether you're for me or for Trump, then you ain't Black' (19).

Someone once told me, during the campaign on the age of consent – when we were trying (and succeeding) to build the widest consensus around equalizing it at 16 so that young gay people were treated identically to their straight friends under the law – that I was the kind of gay man 'that heterosexuals liked'. It took me a few seconds to realize that this was meant as an insult. To which I only managed to reply, 'What, all of them?' In the same vein, Pete Buttigieg – 'Mayor Pete' – now the US Secretary of Transportation in Joe Biden's Cabinet, a gay man in his late thirties, a Christian, a Veteran, a Rhodes Scholar and recently married to his first serious boyfriend, was roundly condemned by some q***r activists for being insufficiently gay. 'The gay equivalent of Uncle Tom' (20) one of them put it, who was 'playing the nice, well-behaved gay man who's choosing convention over revolution' (21). Which accusations conveniently seem to forget that swathes of gay men want precisely that kind of white picket fence world of a nuclear family and monogamy. Many of them don't spend their time being sexually non-monogamous at drag nights in leather bars, but rather going to church and helping at the local community carnival. And lots of them probably do both! But Mayor Pete is exactly what lots of gay people are or want to be. And what lots of others reject being. The point is that one is not more authentically gay than the other. Kayne West is no less Black for supporting Donald Trump and became no more Black when he disavowed that support in July 2020, albeit apparently to run for president himself.

The variety of these voices within minority status groups, however, doesn't mean to say that there isn't a shared experience that flows from a form of common identity. There is. Both positive and negative. The former can be exhilarating as any newly out-of-the-closet lesbian or gay will tell you at their first Pride parade or after the first full-on gay kiss they had in a club surrounded by other gay people, who at that moment are definitely their tribe.

Similarly, skin colour is 'a superficial route to an understanding of human variation', as the genetic scientist Adam Rutherford puts it. 'There are many more points of genetic difference between Africans, than between Africans and anyone else in the world – two San people from different tribes in southern Africa will be more different from each other in their genes than a Briton, a Sri Lankan and a Māori' he points out (22). This scientific reality doesn't mean that we can or should deny the social and cultural significance of race in expressions of shared identity. There have been many, many writers and artists and speakers who have gloried in the richness of a common Black experience. Particularly Americans.

As Langston Hughes, the poet of the Harlem Renaissance, wrote in 1926, 'They'll see how beautiful I am/And be ashamed /I, too, am America' (23), so Muhammad Ali wrote in his autobiography 'I am America. I am the part you won't recognize. But get used to me. Black, confident, cocky; my name, not yours; my religion, not yours; my goals, my own; get used to me' (24). The actress Viola Davis said in an interview in *Essence* magazine in 2011 'As black women, we're always given these seemingly devastating experiences – experiences that could absolutely break us. But what the caterpillar calls the end of the world, the master calls the butterfly. What we do as black women is take the worst situations and create from that point' (25).

The Nobel Laureate Toni Morrison echoed that on the publication of her 1987 novel *Beloved* when she said, 'I really think the range of emotions and perceptions I have had access to as a black person and as a female person are greater than those of people who are neither... So it seems to me that my world did not shrink because I was a black female writer. It just got bigger' (26). That celebration, as we will see in Chapter 3, is not just a life-giving burst of energy that catalyses the power within and enables people to put it to use in the world, but it also is an act of, if not defiance in a world that does not value you for who you are, part of rebalancing the playing field.

There is of course the other side of that joyful and celebratory coin, which also binds together those who belong to minority-status groups. They have a shared experience of disadvantage and discrimination, which can range from simple rudeness or individual acts of harassment, to the denial of opportunity and ambition at work, to violence, injury and even murder. At the moment they experience that discrimination because of their actual or perceived membership of that group, the group has salience. Its members share an understanding of the world. It means something profound to the reality of being a woman to be subjected to sexual harassment or be disallowed the true reward for your abilities at work in favour of a man; to be Black and denied a job or persistently disrespected in everyday life or treated as less than equal by the police; to be gay and have to hide it or to be mercilessly bullied at school or at work if you don't; to be gender transitioned or non-conforming and be threatened in the street or rejected by your family and colleagues because of it; to be physically disabled but thought to have no intellectual or bodily skill. These moments, these life experiences, are real, damaging and are visited on people in minority-status groups with pervasive regularity.

It is important that managers show they understand that discrimination is a shared experience in these cases and that the voices of people who have suffered it, or are fearful about suffering it, need to be listened to. However, while this acknowledgement of the collective experience of a group – positive and negative – is crucial to tackling discrimination, it would be wrong to allow that understanding to lead to a failure to recognize, and so to deny, the variety of individual different voices within that group. For instance, the founding of #BlackLivesMatter in 2013 and the turbo charge it has given to discussions and campaigning against racism, has resulted in a striking and vibrant range of people of colour disagreeing with each other about the significance of race in their understanding of the world and in campaigns for justice and equal rights. BLM itself expresses its mission as: 'to eradicate white supremacy and build local power to intervene in violence inflicted on Black communities by the state and vigilantes' (27).

One of the great contemporary Black American writers, Ta-Nehisi Coates, has powerfully put the notion of White supremacy and the common interests of Black people at the centre of his writings. In 2014 in *The Atlantic* he wrote:

> Black nationalists have always perceived something unmentionable about America that integrationists dare not acknowledge – that white supremacy is not merely the work of hot-headed demagogues, or a matter of false consciousness, but a force so fundamental to America that it is difficult to imagine the country without it (28).

Ibram X Kendi, the author of *How to Be an Anti-Racist*, wrote:

> There is no such thing as a nonracist or race-neutral policy. Every policy in every institution in every community in every nation is producing or sustaining either racial inequity or equity between racial groups. Racist policies have been described by other terms: 'institutional racism', 'structural racism' and 'systemic racism', for instance. But those are vaguer terms than 'racist policy'. When I use them I find myself having to immediately explain what they mean. 'Racist policy' is more tangible and exacting, and more likely to be immediately understood by people, including its victims, who may not have the benefit of extensive fluency in racial terms. 'Racist policy' says exactly what the problem is and where the problem is. 'Institutional racism' and 'structural racism' and 'systemic racism' are redundant. Racism itself is institutional, structural, and systemic (29).

But the voices who put race front and centre of the struggle for equality and in all policies by government and organizations, while currently highly influential, are not the only ones. As Batya Ungar-Sargon, the Opinion Editor of *The Forward*, put it in a piece in July 2020, 'Since George Floyd's horrifying murder, an anti-racist discourse that insists on the primacy of race is swiftly becoming the norm in newsrooms and corporate boardrooms across America.' She goes on to identify a group of Black intellectuals who:

> having experienced being Black in America... scramble the racial lines of today's debate... What unites them into an emerging and increasingly influential

intelligentsia is their rejection of the racial essentialism they view as ascendant in our current moment – the idea that one must prioritize race over everything else to combat racism (30).

One of them, Chloe Valdary, the former *Wall Street Journal* writer and founder of the start-up Theory of Enchantment, puts it bluntly: 'Racial essentialism is very reductive and actually oppressive. Ironically, it reduces us as individuals to our immutable characteristics, which is precisely what we were supposed to be fighting against' (31).

Another very eminent Black voice, the historian Professor Adolph Reed Jr, a long-time critic of Barack Obama and of many Black Democrat politicians, has challenged from a radical left-wing perspective. He is concerned more with class and the structure of the economic system and their twin effects on people of colour. 'Race politics is not an alternative to class politics; it is a class politics, the politics of the left-wing of neoliberalism.' His trenchant and critical view is that there are self-appointed voices whose main interest is the 'protection of the boundaries of racial authenticity as the exclusive property of the guild of Racial Spokespersonship' (32).

In Britain the Equiano Project, founded in 2020 to focus on debates around race, culture and politics, and named in honour of Olaudah Equiano who in the 18th century was the first political activist in Britain's African community, states that it explicitly rejects 'the conflict-driven approach of addressing "race-relations" and we challenge the notion that racism alone is the cause of all racial disparities'. They continue, 'We oppose racism, reject racial essentialism, challenge identity politics and critique the notion of race itself' (33).

John McWhorter, professor of linguistics at Columbia University and self-confessed 'cranky liberal Democrat', in his recent book, *The Elect: Neoracists posing as antiracists and their threat to a progressive America*, calls 'America's Third Wave Antiracists', 'medievals with lattes'. Acknowledging that he knows 'quite well that white readers will be more likely to hear out views like this when written by a black person, I consider it nothing less than my duty as a black person to write it'. 'The medieval Catholic', he says:

> passionately defended prosecuting Jews and Muslims with what we now see was bigoted incoherence, rooted in the notion that those with other beliefs and origins were lesser humans... right here and now we are faced with people who harbor the exact same brand of mission, just against different persons.

In 1500, it was about not being Christian. In 2020, it's about not being sufficiently antiracist... Third Wave Antiracism... exploits modern Americans' fear of being thought racist, using this to promulgate an obsessive, self-involved, totalitarian and unnecessary kind of cultural reprogramming... Its adherents preach with such contemptuous indignation, and are now situated in the most prestigious and influential institutions in the land – on their good days they can seem awfully 'correct'. However, there is nothing correct about the essence of American thought and culture being transplanted into the soil of a religious faith (34).

You don't have to take one side or the other in this scintillating argument to recognize that there is an argument. There is no single Black voice. None of these thinkers and activists is arguing that the understanding of racism should not be one of the central perspectives in tackling discrimination against Black and Brown people in society. But their differing opinions dramatize the reality that if organizations allow a single view to set up as the gatekeeper of minority experience, they will drown out other equally legitimate voices. It is a peculiar feature of modern identity politics that the struggle for diversity is too often matched by a demand for a rigid conformity. There is a dangerous interpretation of inclusion threatening to take hold that boils down to, *to be inclusive you need to speak like this, think like this, behave like this. And if you don't... we'll exclude you.*

Striving to create an inclusive environment cannot mean closing down difference. It must require us instead to find ways to host difference constructively. Furthermore, if only certain voices are given credibility, people in the same group who dissent from those views will justifiably feel excluded. Shutting out dissenting voices can have the serious consequence of corroding, and ultimately undermining, the trust of your people in the integrity of your organization's processes and leadership.

Three days after protests erupted in response to the killing of George Floyd in 2020, a data analyst called David Shor at a progressive consulting firm Civis Analytics in Washington DC, posted a research paper by Professor Omar Wasow, a Black academic at Princeton. David Shor's job was to think about how Democrats can win elections (35). The academic paper was looking at an issue that Omar had been studying for 10 years. His question was whether the reaction to violent or peaceful protests, and how they were reported in the media in the 1960s, affected the way people voted. Omar concluded that 'in the absence of white antipathy to black uprisings, the "law and order" coalition would not have carried the day... In this counterfactual scenario, the United States would have elected Hubert Humphrey, lead author of the Civil Rights Act of 1964, rather than Richard Nixon'.

Despite the long and distinguished history of this debate, most vibrantly between the followers of Martin Luther King and those of Malcolm X, about the relative effectiveness of peaceful or violent protest to achieve change, Twitter piled on. 'Minimizing black grief and rage to bad campaign tactics for the Democrats is BS', went one. When David Shor replied that 'it was about violence driving news coverage that makes people vote for Republicans. The author does a great job explaining his research', his tweeting critic replied, 'You need to stop using your "intellect" as a vehicle for anti-blackness'. This person then tweeted to David Shor's boss: 'Come get your boy' (36). The boss did exactly that. David Shor lost his job.

Where this matters in relation to inclusion is that Civis appeared to have legitimized only one right response to George Floyd's death. There was no room for other voices since, the Tweeter had argued, merely to suggest that there was a debate to be had between different kinds of tactics to achieve change was, in itself, 'anti-Black'. David Shor was not in his tweets critical of #BlackLivesMatter. His impulse was entirely liberal. He was merely giving space to an argument that has ever been part of the Civil Rights movement.

While maintaining that 'Civis was founded on the principles of free speech', its CEO, in firing David Shor, rather undermined that claim. An employee told one journalist that the only reason for the firing 'that was communicated that I heard, were the client and staff reactions to the tweet'. This employee asked to be quoted anonymously, 'for fear of professional repercussions' (37). The Tweeter, and those employees and clients who had joined in, had not only defined Shor's 'guilt' – that he was 'anti-Black' – but had done so at the same time as unilaterally redefining the 'crime' – what constituted being 'anti-Black'. According to them even to air dissent, even though in this case by airing the research of a black academic, was to exhibit racism. By responding as they did, Civis effectively denied the debate between a diversity of Black voices.

This is one way that companies can significantly undermine trust. If the response to a Twitter storm is a PR move to save immediate face and reputation, rather than to enable a course of action that can embrace disagreement and diversity, your people will unsurprisingly feel anxious about expressing their views. This is not to say that actual racism towards colleagues, or discrimination against women or gay people, is to be given airtime freely within your organization. But it is to suggest that denying the legitimate expression of different respectful views about vital social issues undermines trust rather than builds it. In order to make inclusivity real, companies have to create the space for those genuine differences of view to be expressed and explored in order to be able to co-exist. Not as agreement, but as a way forward. Regulating discussion by defining opposing views to your own as bigoted and illegitimate does not create inclusion. Personally coming down on one side of an argument shouldn't mean that you don't think there is a discussion to be had. You wouldn't frame debating and testing the best way to implement a project or the right way forward for a particular part of the business in those terms. If you suppressed disagreement and alternative views on those important strategic issues by attacking the person who brought them to the table rather than discussing their view, you'd reinforce the iron grip of groupthink. So why would you want to do that about diversity, just because it's personal, can be emotionally charged and so can be such difficult territory?

Echo chambers

In his book *Rebel Ideas*, Matthew Syed explored the difference between 'information bubbles' and 'echo chambers' (38). The former is where 'people on the inside see only their side of the argument and *nothing else*'. The best example of a bubble is a cult. Denying members access to any information from the outside is crucial to keeping it intact. But it simultaneously makes members very vulnerable to outside ideas that, if they are encountered, open a crack in the carapace of the organization and empower members to leave.

Echo chambers, on the other hand, are significantly different from information bubbles. Through the way they operate, the presence of opposing views actually strengthens the existing opinions of those shouting inside them. It transpires that the more people in an echo chamber hear those opposite opinions, the less it changes their mind. Instead, it further reinforces their original position. Matthew Syed quotes two studies, one by Seth Flaxman from Oxford and the Pew Institute (39) and the other led by Christopher Bail of Duke University (40). Both reached this similar conclusion. When exposure to opposing views does take place, 'people become more polarized... It was as if exposure to different views confirmed their prior convictions.' These echo chambers are increasingly the way social media work and how they polarize views on the big social issues.

This way of operating emerged particularly on talk radio in the United States and the UK with the rise of the so-called 'shock jocks' in the late eighties. They developed the tone and style of attack in relation to social and political issues that we now see everywhere in the cultural and political battles of our time. It has spread from radio, stridently onto partisan TV, to Facebook and Twitter, the latter brilliantly described by the US comic, Michael Che, as 'like everyone you hate having your phone number'.

Matthew describes the key element to this kind of rhetoric as not seeking 'to persuade [their] audience to cut themselves off from alternative voices… Instead [they seek] to delegitimize alternative voices… [They] attack the integrity of those who offer different views and defame their motives… [Their] insistence is not [just] that opponents are wrong, but that they are malicious.'

That is the powerful, yet corrosive, formula of current social and political debate that has flowed directly from the identity politics of the left and the right. Disagreements should be about views, visions and values. But now they are about 'identities'. Who you are matters more than what you say in this daily diet of polarized politics and it is having disastrous consequences not just in society at large but within organizations and businesses. The diversity of voices, the possibility of dialogue, is being shut down by describing anyone who disagrees with the group gatekeepers as '-ist' or '-phobic'. The mechanism is not to talk about the issues but to delegitimize the other person. Not to argue with their views but to dismiss them outright.

What's inclusion for?

In this current atmosphere it's worth going back to rather basic questions: What is the point of inclusion? What are we trying to achieve by spending hours writing, speaking, agitating and arguing for it and for its importance to organizations? To start with let's determine what it's not. It's not about excluding people or their views or their experiences. It's not about cancelling them because you disagree with them. Rather, in companies the point of inclusion is to engage employees by – recalling the *Harvard Business Review* article quoted at the start of the chapter – attracting diverse talent and, having done so, encouraging their participation that in turn fosters innovation and leads to business growth. Put very simply, the point of inclusion is to make it possible for all employees to get along well together and thus be able to collaborate for success. It may sound soppy or a bit basic, but 'getting along together' is a highly aspirational and laudable goal. It is also fraught with difficulties and challenges. One client of ours recently wrote to me after an inclusive leadership session I had led in their NHS Trust and said, 'Beforehand some people may have been thinking that inclusion is the nice and pink and fluffy stuff. Actually, it seems to be as though it is anything but. I started to think during the session that on the contrary it's where all the muck and bullets are!'

She is quite right. Ultimately getting along with each other is the underpinning of any enterprise that is social, and businesses are, at their core, social. They may have hierarchy and structure, but for them to work successfully over the longer term, they cannot be autocracies run by imposition from the top. Successful organizational cultures are negotiated between the people who create and live in them. Businesses agree principles and then those who inhabit them have to engage in the serious effort of making them work practically, which is where the muck and bullets come in, because it's not as easy as it sounds.

As we saw earlier the framework for diversity and inclusion is descended from the notion of Rights developed in the Enlightenment, which for all its faults and omissions, remains pretty robust. However, as powerful as the idea of Universal Rights is, each individual Right cannot be absolute. Because often they clash. And when that happens, who gets to judge the primacy of one over the other?

When the United Nations General Assembly proclaimed the Universal Declaration on Human Rights in Paris on 10 December 1948, the fourth paragraph of the preamble sets out one of its primary aims: 'Whereas it is essential to promote the development of friendly relations between nations' (41). In other words, one of its core purposes was to enable peoples to 'get along'. The first and second articles laid down the fundamental principles that 'All human beings are born free and equal in dignity and rights. They are endowed with reason and conscience and should act towards one another in a spirit of brotherhood' and 'Everyone is entitled to all the rights and freedoms set forth in this Declaration, without distinction of any kind, such as race, colour, sex, language, religion, political or other opinion, national or social origin, property, birth or other status'.

Article Eighteen declared: 'Everyone has the right to freedom of thought, conscience and religion'; Article Nineteen: 'Everyone has the right to freedom of opinion and expression'; and the first part of Article Twenty-six: 'Everyone has the right to education'.

On 9 October 2012, a masked Taliban gunman boarded a school bus in the Swat Valley in Pakistan and asked, 'Who is Malala?' He then shot her on the left side of her head. With extraordinary medical care in the UK, the support of her family and a seemingly bottomless supply of grace and resilience, Malala not only survived but has thrived as one of the globe's greatest advocates for the education of girls. In December 2014, aged 17, she became the youngest person to receive the Nobel Peace Prize (42).

The Taliban, the Sunni Islamic fundamentalist political and military organization, was founded in 1994 in Kandahar in South Afghanistan. They believe in the imposition of an extreme form of Sharia Law stemming from a niche interpretation of Islamic jurisprudence. This includes, alongside all sorts of regulations about men and beards, forbidding music, technology, photography, men and women competing in sports such as football and chess, women working and, crucially in Malala's case, girls attending school or university (43).

The question may be a long way from your world of work, but, if you asked the Taliban if they were pursuing their right to freedom of religion and if you asked Malala whether she was pursuing her right to education, they would both say yes. But clearly those rights clash.

The Taliban vs Malala is an extreme case, but it serves to illustrate the point. Rights do conflict when for instance the pursuit of an extreme, in this case religious, ideology is brandished as an absolute. Rights in the outside world can be irreconcilable but in organizations these conflicts have to be resolved, not with one side 'winning' but with both sides finding accommodation.

Rather more locally, and emotionally closer to home perhaps, an example of precisely that burst into the media in 2019. Between February and October at Anderton Park school in Sparkhill in Birmingham, a group of Muslim parents protested against a programme being taught in the school called 'No Outsiders'. It was developed in 2014 by the deputy head, Andrew Moffat, and its vision is: 'Inclusive education, promoting community cohesion to prepare young people and adults for life as global citizens', under the strapline: 'All Different, All Welcome'. It involves educating kids about the reality of a world that includes people of different faiths or sexual orientation and families where for instance there were two parents of the same sex. As Andrew says, it is designed 'to teach kids that we're all different and that's fantastic'. The teaching is done with story books like the one with a story from the New York Zoo – which happens to be true – about Tango who 'was the very first penguin in the school to have two daddies'. In another there is boy who wants to dress as a mermaid. All very innocuous sounding to the average liberal parent (44).

But a group of the Muslim parents certainly didn't see it that way. The placards outside the school proclaimed: 'Say No to undermining parental rights and authority'; 'My child, my voice'; 'Say No to sexualization of children'. Amir Ahmed, one of the leaders of the campaign, told Sky News, 'This is converting children with a heterosexual background towards believing that homosexuality is fine. That's socially divisive because it's changing the moral position of family values' (45). He added in a BBC interview, 'Morally we do not accept homosexuality as a valid sexual relationship to have'. When asked if that wasn't 'homophobic', he replied, 'That's like saying if you don't believe in Islam you're Islamophobic. We don't believe in homosexuality but that does not make us homophobic. We respect individuals as human beings' (46).

The clash was fraught for both sides. The parents were very angry and Andrew was scared for his family and husband. Eventually they found a way forward. The programme was paused briefly in order to meet with and listen to the parents. Andrew made adaptations without in the school's view compromising any of the messages. He described one such example in the *Huffington Post*:

> So what does that mean to celebrate LGBT? That word 'celebrate' is an interesting word to talk about in a primary school. Do we need to use that word? What does it mean? So I thought: 'OK, we'll drop the word.' I'll celebrate being gay. I'm happy being gay, but I'm not going to ask you to celebrate me being gay in the same way you can celebrate being Muslim. I don't have to. I can accept it and I can embrace it but I don't have to celebrate it. That helped (47).

However, the situation was not resolved without eight months of protests and finally a Court injunction against the protesters with some lingering damage to community relations and some continuing and serious reservations about some of the thinking and ideology that underpins the programme.

One of the more intriguing aspects of the clash sprung out of the messages on the placards. How much were the parents' feelings just about a hostility to homosexuality driven by religion and how much were they about a deep sense of loss of parental authority? Investigating this I spoke confidentially to someone who had engaged informally to see how they could help. By their own admission they were unsuccessful. But they shared an insight into one underlying dynamic that was never openly acknowledged, which was that those parents' protest was influenced as much by a conservative view on relationships as by their perception that a predominantly White, middle-class group of people were seeking to impose their values onto a group of working-class Muslims.

Creating inclusion requires sensitivity both to the multilayered aspects of those kinds of clashes of views and also that negotiations between the needs of different groups at work necessitate a steady build-up of trust and of tolerance. While there may be two or more 'sides', the point of inclusion, while recognizing the differences, is not to widen the divide. Revelling in the purity of one's position plays no useful part in this process. Rather, tolerance and negotiation are key because what trumps the divides between people in organizations is the need to be able to work together. The process of inclusion is the journey through difference towards collaboration.

Inclusion must embrace disagreement

Current identity politics, amplified by the echo chambers, has compromised that journey by casting disagreement as opposition or, worse, hatred. People endlessly assert a right or demand that others behave towards them in a particular way. But what obligation does the other person have to accede to such a demand? Asserting something neither makes it happen nor makes it right. Organizations can establish principles, dictate policy and lay down rules. But for all that to create a working culture, to generate an environment of true inclusion where all their people willingly and enthusiastically live it out in their day-to-day working lives, the needs of different groups have to be couched in a desire to be able to get along with each other to achieve common goals. And to do that they have to negotiate, in the most humane sense of that word. Inclusion comes not from brandishing competing demands at each other but from realizing our reciprocal duties towards each other. Successful working cultures are willingly embraced not wilfully enforced.

Consider a seemingly uncontroversial step towards inclusion, which is the current fashion that people put their 'preferred pronouns' at the bottom of their email signature or Twitter profile. A number of businesses have embraced this idea with the best of motives. In June 2020 the BBC wrote to all its 22,000 employees encouraging them to do this because it 'lets colleagues know your pronouns and shows that you respect other people's too. It's really simple.' The email said that it was a 'small, proactive step that we can all take to help create a more inclusive workplace… and a culture where everyone feels comfortable introducing themselves with pronouns' (48). The only problem with it is that it doesn't make everyone feel comfortable.

The main reason for this is that the idea of 'preferred pronouns' flows directly not from a desire to be 'nice' to transpeople, as it's so often characterized, but from a theoretical and campaigning perspective that everyone has an 'innate gender' and therefore there is a need to state your pronouns as separate from your physical sex. This is not widely accepted. In fact, it is highly controversial. Many, probably most, men and women believe that who they are in this respect is a question of their sex, not of an 'innate' gender. They also argue that what is given in evidence of this 'innateness' are reinforcements of harmful stereotypes, which they reject. So, however much you might wish there weren't, there is a considerable disagreement about this apparently innocuous proposal. On the one side, there are people who see this as a 'small, proactive step' to be inclusive. The other side experiences it as being put under pressure to conform to something with which they profoundly disagree, to submit to a form of coerced language.

That disagreement matters when businesses set up a new norm that everyone is then expected to follow. People who disagree with the underlying idea experience that as a form of social intimidation because it has consequences if they don't participate. If it is expected that you put a pronoun into your signature, that leaves women who do not want to with a dilemma. What if they don't accept the idea of an 'innate gender'? Either they include pronouns, in effect aligning themselves with a position with which they profoundly disagree, or else they reveal their views in the workplace and suffer the possible penalty.

As one women put it to me, reflecting a widely held view:

> I've heard many people tell me they don't mind doing this as a courtesy. That's a personal choice and I respect the reasons why some people make it. But I've also heard many activists declaring that anyone who won't comply is obnoxious, mean, hostile and unpleasant. 'Misgendering' is hate speech, they say. People who won't do it are transphobic.

Clearly they aren't, however, they just don't agree that there is an innate 'gender identity'. They are gender critical rather than gender ideologists.

Quite apart from these ideological issues there can also be external practical consequences for women who work in sectors where they are discriminated against and seriously underrepresented. If they declare their female pronouns, they particularly fear exclusion as a result of bias. The Royal Society of Chemists, in a 2019 talent report, analysed gender bias in publishing in the chemical sciences (49). Often it was very 'subtle' or even 'inadvertent', but women were invited to review less often, their work was more harshly received and their initial submissions more frequently rejected. These 'small biases' led to a 'significant cumulative effect'. In that context you may prefer as a women to hide your sex rather than advertise it, as many do, using just their initials.

These kinds of issues around race or homosexuality and religion or gender ideology and feminism are some of the trickiest questions involved in how to create inclusion. Like all aspects of diversity, they are deeply personal and rightly give rise to powerfully felt passions, stemming from the intensity of social inequality. Consequently they can feel overwhelming to deal with at work. But when an organization does take them on and supports managers to hold the ring on these difficult discussions, it gains the prize of enabling the voices of all of its employees to be properly heard, which in turn makes it possible for them constructively to combine to create joint solutions.

That is the essence of inclusion. It must embrace reasonable disagreement. Bernie Mayer, the Professor of Conflict Resolution at The Werner Institute and a facilitator at the Industrial Relations Centre at Queen's University, Ontario, argues that:

> the mistake so many managers make (and conflict professionals too) is to identify their goal in conflict as prevention, containment, or resolution. Those all have their place, but the more important challenge is to create the space for conflict to occur in a constructive way, for people to raise difficult and contentious issues, and for leaders to be exposed to often uncomfortable disagreements. Otherwise, problems fester, important views are squelched, and effective communication is inhibited (50).

An inclusive framework has to pair equality with diversity. That doesn't mean allowing every difference of view. So-called race 'science' insists that Black people are inferior to White people. That is not compatible with equality. But holding to the science of biological sex being binary does not exclude transwomen. It simply makes the point that transwomen are transwomen and women are women and that while being diverse from each other they both deserve equality. There is a difference in a business saying that it will not tolerate harassment, bias or prejudice towards a colleague and requiring that employees adopt a belief system with which they disagree.

One of the most moving moments I ever experienced personally in this discussion was at an event where I was on a platform with the long-time trans activist Jacqui Gavin. Formerly in the RAF and then a civil servant, she was the first ever chair of the Transgender Network in the Department of Work and Pensions and then Chair of 'a:gender', the cross-government support network for transgender and intersex civil servants. In front of an audience at one of the big four consultancies, we each gave our own contribution, Jacqui including in hers that she had been called Scott before she transitioned many years before.

Finding that we were intrigued by some of the things that each other had said, we started to talk between the two of us in front of everybody, exploring where we agreed and where we had differences. Then we threw it open to the floor. One of the HR team confessed that she was really thrown by 'all these issues about "misgendering" and "deadnaming" and pronouns'. Jacqui replied reassuringly, 'The first thing is to calm down. It's fine. Just take your time about it and ask.' Then she added, causing a wave of admiration and warmth through the room, 'I wouldn't be here if it wasn't for Scott's bravery. He is part of me. I carry him with me everywhere I go.'

Afterwards person after person came up to us to tell us that they had never seen that conversation between a gay man and a transwoman engaged with such ease. But above all they showed their unbounded respect for Jacqui's honesty and openness. She had given them a way into the issue. Her story, from childhood and Scott to adulthood and Jacqui, is full of complication, courage and happiness. Hers a real insight into a life lived. The way she tells it, with authenticity and truth, opens up a difficult subject, rather than closing it down.

Being yourself at work matters, so no one should have to 'cover'

Authenticity has become a buzz word in diversity. But it's often interpreted, almost by default, as a licence to do and say whatever you want. Managers and colleagues justify their behaviour by saying, 'that's just who I am. I am bringing my whole self to work.' But this puts the emphasis on the wrong word. 'Bring your whole *self* to work', they say with the accent on 'self'. But the word to underline is *work*. When you are at work, you inevitably, and with good reason, surrender a degree of individual expression – 'authenticity' – in the name of appropriate behaviour – agreed rules and boundaries. How do you balance the two?

In his 2013 report *Uncovering Talent*, Kenji Yoshino, who is the Chief Justice Earl Warren Professor of Constitutional Law at New York University, asks, after quoting the usual litany of diversity deficits in large companies, 'Why have inclusion programs stalled on these fronts?' (51). In response to his own question he suggests:

> one intuitive answer is that these initiatives have not lived up to the core
> ideal of inclusion. The ideal of inclusion has long been to allow individuals
> to bring their authentic selves to work. However, most inclusion efforts have
> not explicitly and rigorously addressed the pressure to conform that prevents
> individuals from realizing that ideal.

The report, and his longer book on the subject, uses the concept of 'covering' to investigate this. It's a highly valuable tool to understanding where that right balance lies between personal expression and company behaviour. As he explains:

> 'covering' differs from the more familiar term 'passing'... When an individual
> passes, she is ensuring that others around her do not know she possesses a
> particular identity. When an individual covers, she has disclosed that identity
> but seeks to mute its significance. Covering is a much more universal dynamic –
> while only some groups have the capacity to pass, all groups have the capacity
> to cover.

He lists four axes along which people cover: Appearance, Affiliation, Advocacy and Association and gives examples. Respectively: a Black woman might straighten her hair to de-emphasize her race; a woman might avoid talking about being a mother because she does not want her colleagues to think she is less committed to her work; a veteran might refrain from challenging a joke about the military, lest they be seen as overly strident; a gay person might refrain from bringing their same-sex partner to a work function so as not to be seen as 'too gay'. Also, any number of employees of all descriptions might simply be not speaking up. They may not be bringing their whole voice to work about what matters in the company or in their team.

What is most useful about this concept is that it can embrace the experience of the whole workforce. In the extensive research Kenji did across 10 different industries, he found that 61 per cent of all respondents reported covering along at least one axis at work. Eighty-three per cent of LGBorT individuals, 79 per cent of Blacks, 67 per cent of women of colour, 66 per cent of women and 63 per cent of Hispanics cover:

Covering occurred with greater frequency within groups that have been historically underrepresented. At the same time 45 percent of straight White men – who have not been the focus of most inclusion efforts – reported covering. This finding seems particularly promising, given that a model of 'inclusion' should, almost by definition, be one in which all individuals can see themselves.

We worked with one company in which a very senior executive had his assistant put into his diary an 'unmoveable client meeting', on 22 December. In the session we did with the Executive Team he, with some degree of anxiety in such a competitive work environment, admitted that this was actually his six-year old's nativity play. What he should have done was to book a day's leave like women typically do. But he covered to such an extent that, strictly speaking, he committed a disciplinary offence. He lied. Admitting that he was wrong, and explaining why he covered, led to a very useful discussion that gave insight into two issues. Firstly, he and his senior colleagues understood more about the pressures to cover that other types of people were feeling in the organization. Secondly, they explored how they could make sure that men could take time off to spend with their children and not suffer any disadvantage in relation to promotion or performance reviews.

Covering is not a question of being excluded, but rather it's about the terms on which people feel that their inclusion rests. Investigating and understanding how different groups of your employees experience the need to cover provides great insight into the culture of your team or the whole organization. The realization that everyone covers to a greater or lesser extent can unify your people in working out what are the unspoken rules that are pushing each of them back into their particular closet. Inclusion means not just reinforcing the bonds and common interests within groups by, for example, setting up staff networks. It also strengthens ties across groups – and the diversity of voices in all the different groups – that can bring them together in a common cause. Understanding and investigating where employees are covering helps managers and organizations to see where people are holding back, not expressing themselves, hiding their views, feeling pressured into discomfort or experiencing anxiety or outright hostility. In other words, it can tell you where their voices are not being fully included. Tackling this will significantly increase engagement by your employees and will be a unifying process. It will show you whether and where there is a gap between the actual experience of your people and the expressed values of your organization.

It is those company values that can provide the framework for making inclusion a reality. They can, if effective, both inspire constructive disagreement between a diversity of views and describe its boundaries. In the last decades all organizations have adopted values that aspire to define their character and ethos. It's obligatory. But, with the best will in the world, how often do they really guide the day-to-day way the business works? They are too often too bland to matter or too banal to inspire adherence.

A few years back, someone showed me the values of one large US company, as an example. They were concise, powerfully worded and principled: 'Communication. Respect. Integrity. Excellence.' Unfortunately they were the values of Enron, which you may recall, through accounting loopholes, misleading the board, creating temporary companies and a whole bunch of other murky off-the-books accounting practices, managed to hide billions of dollars in debt from failed deals and projects that led to it filing for bankruptcy in 2001 and to convictions for bank fraud, securities fraud, wire fraud, money laundering, conspiracy and insider trading, among other crimes, for 16 of its former employees. So much for their Values. So much for 'Respect' and 'Integrity'.

Value statements like that can either be trite slogans that have no effect on behaviour at all or just state the obvious. According to the Aspen Institute survey of corporate behaviour, '90% of value statements reference ethical behaviour or use the word "integrity", 88% mention commitment to customers, and 76% cite "teamwork and trust"' (52). But what is the point of specifying any of those as values as if they are exceptional or define anything distinctive about a company? I often apply a 'reverse meaning' test to these kinds of statements to see if they describe anything at all distinguishing. If you apply that to many value statements you can see how they don't really help to define anything useful at all. Submitting the Aspen results to the test, who would want to work for a company whose values were: 'dishonesty and deceit', 'a disregard for customers' and 'people working solo in the face of a redolent atmosphere of distrust'. Now those could have been the Enron values.

In a paper for the international Business School, INSEAD, their Professor of Organizational Behaviour, Charles Galunic, researched the effect of values on companies by looking at Fortune 100 firms (53). What he found was that a successful *process* of determining values is what helps to clarify what is core to the business. As he says 'a wrestling match with your culture can be a valuable exercise and is the real value behind espousing corporate values'. What was clear was that 'companies who show more dynamism around their values – those that change them over time – outperform firms who kept theirs stable'. He went on to argue that this is because 'these firms are... more actively engaged in a conversation about who they are, what their culture is and in which direction they are taking their business, precisely because they are wrestling with their organizational culture, rigorously defining and articulating it'.

It's not so much the values that make a change in performance or the company stand out from its sector peers, it's the process of working them out. Businesses are very complex social groupings and so there will be a wide range of values that your people would consider important. As Charles points out, this means that:

> not all of these values are in perfect harmony ('Stability' versus 'Innovation'), and so listing a bare minimum may reflect a lack of adequate attention to the trade-offs inherent in any corporate culture. Grappling with the full set of core corporate values probably reflects a greater willingness to work through the trade-offs.

Powerful values, stated at the highest level, can describe the core elements of what makes a company culture both innovative and also inclusive of the widest range of voices within the organization. Those values would include 'embracing healthy conflicts of ideas', 'valuing and engaging in constructive disagreement' or 'listening hard and being able to challenge assumptions'. Not just saying it, but meaning it too. As a colleague once said to me as I tried unsuccessfully to persuade him that he just didn't get what I was saying, 'I *am* listening. I *am* understanding. And I *am* disagreeing with you.'

Margaret Heffernan, a considerable expert on the art and practice of collaboration, gave a great example of the value of productive conflict in a TED talk she gave in 2012 (54). She told the story of the scientist, Alice Stewart, who discovered the devastating effects of X-rays during pregnancy in causing cancer in children. She worked with a statistician named George Kneale. Margaret describes George as pretty much everything that Alice wasn't:

> Alice was very outgoing and sociable, and George was a recluse. Alice was very warm, very empathetic with her patients. George frankly preferred numbers to people. But he said this fantastic thing about their working relationship. He said, 'My job is to prove Dr Stewart wrong.' He actively sought disconfirmation. Different ways of looking at her models, at her statistics, different ways of crunching the data in order to disprove her. He saw his job as creating conflict around her theories.

Alice and George, says Margaret, 'were very good at conflict. They saw it as thinking.'

To come full circle, Jo Berry and Patrick Magee have found that the essential conflict between them has, through a process of hearing and valuing difference, created a place for them to be able to talk together, work together and to make a difference in the world together. Conflict, their diametrically opposed situations in Jo's father's murder, was the starting point. How they dealt with it is what delivered the extraordinary outcome. They are the antithesis of an echo chamber. They recognize each other's specific pain – Jo's grief, Patrick's fight for a united Ireland. They have crossed extremely tricky waters – every bit as personal and challenging and fraught with anger and fear, as the issues of religion and homosexuality, feminism and gender ideology or differences over #BlackLivesMatter. Through their efforts to hear and try to understand each other they have found a way to include each other so they can collaborate. If they can do it, in the face of all those challenges, can their experience inspire organizations, and their managers and leaders, and you, to do so too?

You can harness the Power of Difference to create real inclusion so all employees' voices are heard by exploring:

- how employees experience inequality, bias and disadvantage as a group. How that influences their experience at work.

- how your business / team can encourage and support the diversity of individual voices and recognize that people who appear to have the same identity do not speak with one voice.

- how managers can be confident to support productive disagreement and recognize that dissent is central to innovation and making good decisions.

- how everybody – not just some people – can be supported to bring their 'whole selves into *work*', not just some people.

- how you can discover who in the organization is covering. Kenji suggests a four-point plan:

  o reflect – on who is covering in your organization, where and why?

  o diagnose – find out where and how it is happening. Talk to your people and ask them to respond in their own words.

- o analyse – the relationship with the company values and whether the company is really living up to them.

- o initiate – leaders to 'uncover' themselves (share your stories).

- how you can ensure that discussions about what the organization stands for are not static.

- how to develop effective values that reflect complexity and make the value of disagreement central to how your team or organization works.

03

Diversity is not a minority sport

Great things happen at Berkeley. It is one of the 10 campuses of the University of California. Ranked seventh in the 2021 Times Higher Education World University league table, Berkeley has lots to boast about over its 150 years.

In the 1960s you'd have found well-dressed male students in ribbon ties, tweed jackets and even suits. The young women wore check patterned, knee-length skirts or floral dresses, both with cardigans. Revisiting the photos of the time is slightly surprising as these smartly dressed, conformist looking students were the leaders of the first radical student protests of the 1960s in the United States. Berkeley was famous not so much for free love as for giving birth to the Free Speech Movement. Joan Baez came and sang to the protesters and, as a result of the campaign that lasted all through the autumn of 1964, the students won the right, for the first time, to engage in political activity on campus.

One of the protest leaders made a speech celebrated ever since as iconic in student activism. In front of 4,000 people on the steps of Sproul Hall at the centre of the campus, renamed after him in 1997 as the Mario Savio steps, he proclaimed:

> There's a time when the operation of the machine becomes so odious – makes you so sick at heart – that you can't take part. You can't even passively take part. And you've got to put your bodies upon the gears and upon the wheels, upon the levers, upon all the apparatus, and you've got to make it stop (1).

Surprisingly not noted in the list of achievements on Berkeley's website is something possibly more significant than those protests and that speech. It happened two years earlier. Ed Roberts enrolled into the political science course for a BA and went on to earn an MA and then, although he never finished it, signed up for a PhD. Why was this extraordinary? Because aged

14, Ed had caught polio. He was paralysed from the neck down except for two fingers on one hand and several toes. He slept in an iron lung and outside of it he breathed using a technique called 'frog breathing' when you force air into the lungs using facial and neck muscles.

In 1952 when he got ill, doctors told his family that in all likelihood he'd spend the rest of his life as 'a vegetable'. Later he is reported to have said, 'If I'm a vegetable, I'm going to be an artichoke, prickly on the outside, with a big heart in the middle' (2). With that big heart and that prickly insistence on not accepting the world as it is, but campaigning to make it as it could be, Ed Roberts will be remembered as one of first and leading people to create the disability rights movement. He has been called the 'Father of Independent Living' (3).

With the staunch encouragement of his mother, Zona, and despite the attitude of some of the university employees – one of them was reported to have said, 'We've tried cripples before and it didn't work' (4) – he was admitted, accommodated with his 800-pound iron lung and given full access to academic and social support. Zona remembers that he, and still only a very few fellow disabled students, 'named themselves the Rolling Quads and began to do the activism on campus... like the curb cuts. They didn't happen until Ed and the Quads went there' (5).

Curb cuts, or dropped kerbs as they are also called, are those little inclines at the edge of pavements that slope down to the road. What would any of us with a suitcase on wheels, a baby buggy, a shopping trolley, sack trucks or even a wheelbarrow do without them? When Ed and the Rolling Quads campaigned for access like that on campus there was barely a handful of students in wheelchairs. Even now Berkeley's Disabled Students' Programme, which will include people who are not in wheelchairs, serves just 3,500 students (6) out of the 42,000 (7) enrolled at the university campus – a mere 8 per cent. Yet every day, hundreds of thousands of students and university employees of all abilities use those curb cuts without thinking and without acknowledging a man who slept in an iron lung and whose sheer persistence and reputed charm changed an aspect of outdoor space for all of us, for ever.

The dropped kerb is the perfect metaphor for trying to understand minorities and diversity. It is where the needs of even a really quite small minority, and the insights that flow from them, can change the world for everybody. In this case, the catalyst to change the design of practically every pavement across the globe, to the advantage of the entire world, was a tiny group led by a man The Smithsonian, who proudly has his wheelchair as an exhibit, describes as 'a model – a joyful, positive model – of independence' (8). As Ed

Roberts once said, 'Our number one issue is still old attitudes towards us, and those old attitudes see us as helpless and unable... [but] disability can make you very strong and very able' (9).

That is the paradox that lies at the heart of this chapter. Minorities have specific needs and suffer specific disadvantage and frequently violence, deprivation and assault. If you ignore those needs and issues in how you understand those people's lives you will ignore an underlying reality. Yet at the same time if you only ever see people as 'minorities' – and throughout I will include women as a 'minority-status' group as they experience many of the same disadvantages – you are in danger of seeing them only in terms of that disadvantage. You will miss the strength that their life experience brings to them, to society and to organizations. Ed Roberts, through his insistence to be taken seriously as a student, did not so much 'put his body upon the gears... upon the levers, upon all the apparatus, and... make it stop' than he threw his weight behind the apparatus and, through his life experience and his actions, sped up the cogs, pulled the levers and took part. His example shows that if we miss the very ability that came out of Ed Roberts' 'dis-ability', we don't see the way he asked the world to change how it sees potential.

Differently different

Dame Stephanie 'Steve' Shirley's life has been devoted to the triple focuses of her ground-breaking business career in technology, her marriage and caring for her autistic son Giles until his too early death aged 37. In the Gresham lecture she gave in 2011 she remarked:

> Several City organizations committed to diversity, employ people on the autism spectrum, often starting as interns... Managers have commented that learning to understand the communication difficulties of those with ASD (autistic spectrum disorder) has helped them to communicate with their whole team more effectively (10).

The same is being discovered in Team Domenica, which is based in Brighton, and is run by someone rightly admired for her bloody-minded persistence when she comes across an issue that requires tackling. She is Rosa Monckton. Her daughter, the eponymous Domenica, who was Princess Diana's last godchild, was born with Down Syndrome. When she was nearing the end of her official schooling at 16, Rosa realized there would be nothing to support her into any level of independence. So she started a project to do just that for her and for the many other young people in that situation. The Team vision is 'for people with learning disabilities to be valued in the workplace, to reach their full potential and feel included as members of society'. Now, after just four years, they support over 70 candidates (as they call the young people) and have achieved a 75 per cent success rate getting them into work, compared with a 6 per cent rate nationally (11).

In a similar way to Steve Shirley's City organizations, the managers who take the Team Domenica candidates into that work have commented that, whatever the stresses and pressures of managing those young people with often very acute difficulties with life and social interaction, the benefit that flows from it is that they have come to see them as just differently different from the rest of their team. Not as 'other' but on a spectrum of difference.

Sometime around the point that BC turned into AD, Seneca, the philosopher and dramatist, said, 'There is a noble manner of being poor, and who does not know it will never be rich.' What he meant was there was a richness and morality beyond money. He didn't mean there was some nobility that flowed simply from the fact of being poor.

Minorities do not have virtue as a result of being minorities. What gives you direction as an individual from one of those groups is who you've decided to become through that experience, how you collaborate with others inside and outside the group, and make wider alliances to end the discrimination against you. But because of the way societies have decided to mistreat them, members of minorities often have to claim that they are, in and of themselves, 'Good', 'Great', 'Proud', 'Powerful' or 'Beautiful'. Minorities often feel that they have to try to level the playing field by overstating the value of their players. If they don't, the rest of society isn't going to. If they don't rescue dignity and self-worth from the litany of discrimination and ill treatment that is the sometimes intermittent, but all too frequently the regular, story of their lives, no one else will.

You can see why people feel like that. Given what the world projects onto them, it is often a strenuous uphill struggle for those who belong to minorities to reach the position where they believe in their own self-worth. One particular take on this journey was analysed in *The Velvet Rage: Overcoming the pain of growing up gay in a straight man's world* by the US therapist Alan Downs, published in 2005. He was quite explicit that, while he could only tell the gay man's story, other people who had grown up with personal characteristics that also set them outside the norm – the Black person growing up in a society shot through with racism, the Jew growing up in the shadow of insecurity that all might be taken away from them again as it was by the Holocaust, the woman whose ambitions were stereo-typically limited by her parents or teachers – could also have a similar experience.

Alan's contention is that spending one's formative years being signalled to by your enveloping environment in endless, constant and subtle ways that you are not the norm, is damaging. That lack of reinforcement of who you are takes a deep emotional toll. As he says, 'Velvet rage is the deep and abid-ing anger that results from growing up in an environment when I learn that who I am as a gay person is unacceptable, perhaps even unlovable'. And he goes on, 'This anger pushes me at times to overcompensate and try to earn love and acceptance by being more, better, beautiful, more sexy – in short, to become something I believe will make me more acceptable and loved'.

He grew up in an evangelical environment, which he says meant 'that clearly, because I was Pentecostal, I was going straight to hell for being gay. Hence my own experience with shame. I often say the God of my childhood had anger-management problems'. But his point is even more reinforced by the experiences of those gay men and lesbians who grew up in very support-ive environments with parents who gave them all the love they should to their child. Yet they still have to overcome the barrier of coming out which, in my experience and that of many gays and lesbians I have spoken to, is as much psychological as it is to do with the external context. Despite all the love and support, they cannot avoid and so are damaged by all the societal signals that chip away at their self-esteem. So they still need to go on a jour-ney of self-discovery in order to end up in a place of contentment with themselves. As Alan is careful to make clear, 'the problem is not being gay. The problem is the invalidation we went through as children' (12).

Why norms too often aren't norms at all

As he says, this is not just a gay story, nor is it just a psychological one. Not being the norm in whatever way has serious consequences, when the setting of that norm has not involved you nor taken your experience into account. Caroline Criado Perez launched a memorable and successful campaign in 2017 to get Jane Austen onto British bank notes – the only women apart from the Queen to be so. In her highly persuasive book *Invisible Women*, she makes the case that the framework for approaching, seeing and solving so many issues in societies is underpinned by a pervasive and damaging exclusion of female experience and realities. Instead it is based on men's lives and male experience (13). The data collected, the issues prioritized, the framing of problems are all slanted in one direction. Towards men. Why this is so detrimental is that because, from just 50 per cent of the world's experience, a norm is created. It is claimed as universal, when in fact it is partial. This does harm not just to women but to those around them, their families, their health, their political engagement and, above all, to all of us through the way that their marginalization deprives towns, organizations and societies of so much insight.

As she says, right at the start of the book, 'Seeing men as the human default is fundamental to the structure of human society.' She quotes Aristotle to show just how long this has been the case. In the 4th century he wrote in his treatise *On the Generation of Animals*, 'The first departure from type is indeed that the offspring should become female instead of male.' In our own times, as she points out among many, many examples, Apple mirrored this when they produced their 'comprehensive' health tracker. It could track everything related to health. Except one element. Periods. Which made it rather less than 'comprehensive'. When Siri was launched it could, according to Caroline, find 'prostitutes' and 'Viagra suppliers' but not 'abortion providers'. It understood 'heart attack', but if you were a women who had been raped and told Siri, she replied – despite her artificially generated female sex – 'I don't know what you mean by "I was raped"'. The brilliance of the technology turned out to be deeply flawed on the distaff side, mainly because the data sets that were used to underpin its algorithms were overwhelmingly informed by the male experience.

Examples of this kind of bias overpopulate the debit side of the ledger of the life experience of people who belong to minority-status groups. For six years the global consultancy McKinsey has been publishing its *Women in the Workplace* study (14). In 2020 they concluded from research in the United States that:

> women continued to lose ground at the first step up to manager. For every
> 100 men promoted to manager, only 85 women were promoted – and this gap
> was even larger for some women: only 58 Black women and 71 Latinas were
> promoted. As a result, women remained significantly outnumbered in entry-level
> management at the beginning of 2020 – they held just 38 percent of manager-
> level positions, while men held 62 percent.

The percentage of women in senior management has remained practically the same over the years of the study rising just 1 per cent to 33 per cent. And at that most rarefied level of a company, where the carpets are thicker and everyone's description begins with a 'C', the Executive, the numbers may have risen slightly faster from 17 per cent but still they have only reached a lamentably small 21 per cent. Broken down by ethnicity, that top echelon in 2020 is 19 per cent White women, 66 per cent White men; 3 per cent women of colour and 12 per cent men of colour.

Progress is small and this hasn't changed significantly since the Chartered Institute of Management in the UK reported a few years ago that 'Male managers are 40% more likely than female managers to be promoted into higher roles… [and] while women comprise 73% of the workforce in entry and junior level roles, female representation drops to 42% at the level of senior management' (15). Not only is promotion less likely for women but they are often tested against much different standards. Allyson Zimmermann, of the global non-profit Catalyst that for over 40 years has been working 'to build workplaces that work for women', quotes their research that showed that 'women are promoted based on performance, while men are promoted based on potential. Women are being held to a higher standard' (16). The cartoonist Bob Thaves memorably captured that higher bar for women when he drew a 1982 cartoon strip with two men looking at a poster of Fred Astaire and one of them saying: 'Sure he was great, but don't forget that Ginger Rogers did everything he did, backwards… and in high heels' (17).

In 2019 Ipsos Mori surveyed a representative sample of people across 28 countries to try to understand these different ways in which men and women were judged as suitable for promotion (18). The results for the UK were that: 26 per cent of those people thought intelligence is one of the most important factors helping women get ahead, compared with 17 per cent who said the same for men; 37 per cent said working hard is key for women's success, compared with 29 per cent for men; 29 per cent said having connections is important in men succeeding, almost twice as many as the 15 per cent who said the same for women, and one in 10 (11 per cent) of Britons said a woman's looks are a key factor in helping them get ahead, while just 4 per cent said the same for men. In short if you're a women and work long hours, spend time networking and you're what is thought to be attractive, you could get the chance to be promoted, but you'll still earn less than the men. In fact 7.4 per cent less, which is the 2020 UK-wide gender pay gap according to the Office of National Statistics (19).

In 2019 the Royal Bank of Scotland's former global human resources director, Anuranjita Kumar, had over 600 hours of conversations and meetings with over 500 male and female Black and minority ethnic professionals, including 125 from the UK (20). She concluded that candidates from Black and Asian backgrounds stood 'only an 8 per cent chance of promotion to chief executive, chief financial officer and other senior director roles'. They were 'however capable... found to be consistently overlooked because their cultures and religious beliefs are seen to be at odds with most company's "private members' club mentality"'. Just 4 per cent of the applicants she interviewed were successful, and all reported that 'they felt obliged to adopt western mannerisms and to tone down their natural accents during the interview'.

These differential norms are not only excluding, they are potentially physically injuring or fatal. One of the most disarmingly eloquent statistical transgressions uncovered by Caroline Criado Perez is that in a car crash 'women are 47 per cent more likely to be seriously injured than a man and 71 per cent more likely to be moderately injured'. And most alarmingly '17 per cent more likely to die'. And why is this so? For the simple reason that the design of crash-test dummies is based on the male body, despite the fact that men and women are anatomically different in a number of very significant ways. On average, women are shorter, their legs need to be closer to reach the pedals and they need to sit up straight to see clearly over the dashboard. Let alone the differing shape of their hips and pelvis. All of which makes the effect of an impact profoundly different on male and female bodies. So, women are suffering injury and death in cars for the simple reason that they are not men.

Facial recognition software has been around since the 1960s but advanced rapidly around 2012 as the development of cameras, technology, data sets and computers all gathered pace and power. However, by 2016 an MIT researcher, Joy Buolamwini, who went on to found the Algorithmic Justice League as a result, made a hugely influential discovery. She first experienced this bias when she was an undergraduate. Facial recognition programmes she experienced would work fine on her White friends but didn't recognize her face at all. What her MIT research showed was that if the person in the photo was a White man, the software was right 99 per cent of the time. But the darker the skin, the more errors arose, to the extent that their sex was misidentified in up to nearly 35 per cent of images of darker skinned women (21). In a number of studies it has emerged that the reasons for this are that the original data sets widely used to create the algorithms for facial recognition were estimated to be more than 75 per cent male and more than 80 per cent White (22). Another data bias was discovered by researchers at the Georgetown Law School, also in 2016, when they calculated that, while

117 million Americans were in facial recognition networks used by the police, African Americans were most likely to be singled out because mug-shot databases had been used in which they were disproportionately represented due to the high level of arrests of Black men (23).

This is the regular experience of minorities. However, it is important to be clear that highlighting this research is not, at this point, to comment on the niceness or lack of it in individual men, White people or anybody else you work with. Their individual behaviour may range from being perfectly decent to being careless or unaware about its impact or to being downright unpleasant and prejudiced. But what the research points towards is that discrimination against minorities in organizations, while being experienced in personal interactions, is amplified by becoming embedded in the processes, among them: the narrow range of data bases; the blindness to their bias; the failure rigorously to make decisions on hiring and promotion based on evidence rather than uninterrogated assumptions about groups of people; and ultimately a failure to redesign recruitment, promotion and appraisal to enable managers to make much better decisions and judgements about their people's talent and skill. Individual prejudice and preference certainly play a part in all of this, but the central issue is the way in which biases are absorbed by systems in organizations and then reproduced by their practices and procedures that managers frequently fail to question rigorously in the light of the unfairness and imbalance of their outcomes.

Over 50 years ago the Black activist Stokely Carmichael talked about the 'pervasive operation of anti-black attitudes and practices... which permeate society on both the individual and institutional level'. The 1999 Macpherson Inquiry into the murder of the Black British teenager Stephen Lawrence didn't coin the phrase 'institutional racism', but it did engage with Stokely Carmichael's idea and bring it into illuminating common usage in the UK, specifically in relation to the Police (24). The report acknowledged the controversy and debate around the concept when it said, 'Taking all that we have heard and read into account we grapple with the problem.' But they settled on a definition, which is still helpful today to describe behaviours and decisions that are driven by obliviousness, carelessness or actively held negative stereotypes and are then reinforced by the culture and environment of organizations. Institutional racism the report said is:

> the collective failure of an organization to provide an appropriate and
> professional service to people because of their colour, culture or ethnic origin.
> It can be seen or detected in processes, attitudes and behaviour which amount

to discrimination through unwitting prejudice, ignorance, thoughtlessness and racial stereotyping which disadvantage ethnic minority people.

This formulation identifies a range of motors of prejudice that are boosted by the failure of the institution itself in which they then flourish. This is not just true of racism. Unchecked bias in processes affects all minority-status groups. However, it is people that have racist, sexist or homophobic beliefs, not organizations. Those human behaviours collectively build cultures that make the issues organizational. If the humans change the organization will do too.

Isabel Wilkerson, the author of *Caste: The origins of our discontents*, focuses on three caste systems that have stood out in history: 'The lingering, millenniums-long caste system of India. The tragically accelerated, chilling and officially vanquished caste system of Nazi Germany. And the shape-shifting, unspoken, race-based caste pyramid in the United States.' She defines caste as 'structure. Caste is ranking. Caste is the boundaries that reinforce the fixed assignments based upon what people look like... Casteism is the investment in keeping the hierarchy as it is in order to maintain your own ranking.' In defining it this way she gives us a very useful framework to understand the way in which such structures operate. There is a continuing script in which the actors play their assigned roles and say the lines they have been given by centuries of the artificial ranking of human value. As she says, 'Caste is insidious and therefore powerful because it is not hatred; it is not necessarily personal. It is the worn grooves of comforting routines and unthinking expectations, patterns of a social order that have been in place for so long that it looks like the natural order of things' (25).

Diversity's contradictory problem with minorities

These norms, and the ways minorities are judged against them, are every-where in our lives and, particularly at work, they create a problem for pro-gress on diversity. Those of you trying to find meaningful and accurate ways of achieving a change in the diversity numbers, and so open up more oppor-tunities for the breadth of talent and experience that actually exists in soci-ety, have to juggle two contradictory ideas. On the one hand, you have to acknowledge the reality for people outside the norms – the minorities. You have to collect the kind of data above that is so depressingly negative. Then you have to make it understood and acted upon in your companies and organizations. As a result, in order to create what the management books used to call 'a burning platform' to engender some urgency, you can end up simply reinforcing in the minds of, particularly the senior management whom you are trying to influence, the minority status of those employees. In order to collect and analyse data and make the case you have to single out their experience as 'other'. Simultaneously though, you also want to change the norm so that it really does embrace the breadth and diversity of human experience and can be based on, and grow from, the combination of difference. This new norm needs to embrace the value of what everyone can bring through who they are, through their different backgrounds and life experiences. The new norm needs to serve the needs and aspirations of the whole rather than just a part of any talent pool. As Robert Putnam, the US political scientist, in his ground-breaking essay *E Pluribus Unum*, put it, 'The central challenge for modern, diversifying societies is to create a new, broader sense of "we"' (26). That is also true for organizations.

The way many companies go about widening diversity, however, is to accept the norm and in effect 'rent a minority'. This was parodied by the columnist Arwa Mahdawi when she started a site called precisely that (27). Her website rentaminority.com is, according to its front page:

> designed for those oh-shit moments where you've realized your award show, corporate brochure, conference panel is entirely composed of White men. For, like, the fifth year in a row. Suddenly you're being called out on Twitter and you need to look not-racist and not-misogynist fast. Actually doing something meaningful to disrupt institutional inequality would be way too much work; so why not just Rent-A-Minority instead?

And, as she said in her TED talk (28), companies have actually been in touch!

When organizations approach diversity like this, I often say to them – and I know it is a bit of a sound bite, but people do jot it down – achieving true diversity is not 'spicing up the stew. It's changing the recipe.'

So a new approach to diversity needs to transcend the obvious flaw in a majority/minority paradigm that emphasizes a default way of seeing people along the Aristotelian line: men/not men, White/not White, straight/not straight and so on. Also this default isn't created by numbers but by power and influence. You don't have to be in a minority to be treated as minority status. Black and Asian people, for instance, are not in the minority. Not globally. Kwame Kwei-Armah is the Artistic Director of the Young Vic theatre in London and a leading force in rebalancing the commissioning and producing of Black and Asian work in UK theatre. On one New Year's Day he tweeted, 'It's 2020 n I'm resolved 2 talk it as I see it. Pls stop calling me BAME. I'm not an ethnic minority. I'm part of the global majority' (29).

Yet in diversity-speak, people continue to use 'BAME' – Black, Asian and minority ethnic. Even if the British context can't fully acknowledge Kwame's global perspective, what is damaging is that the acronym just lumps together a whole group of people who come from vastly different cultures, geographies and ethnicities. They are all people with a personal and family heritage that matters to them individually. Would you ever say in conversation, 'She's BAME. He's LGBT' rather than 'He's Nigerian', 'She's from India', 'He's gay'? The acronyms are a form of herding that lacks salience to people's lives except when they can verifiably describe a group experience, positive or negative. How much does the daughter of a wealthy Indian heritage businessman who lives in one of the smart squares in Kensington in London have in common with someone from an ethnically similar background who was burnt out of their home in Grenfell Tower just down the road, except when they are both the victim of racism? When the T was added to LGB it seems to have been based on an assumption that sexual orientation and gender identity embraced the same experiences of life. But do they? Someone once asked me if I was LGBT? I said, 'Well you can't be all of them.'

In a recent Civil Service blog called, 'Please, don't call me BAME or BME!' the writer, who works in the Government's Race Disparity Unit, echoed this: 'Personally, I have never referred to my ethnicity using BAME or BME, and I don't like it when they are used to describe me. Like many ethnic minorities, I proudly refer to my specific ethnic identity – my background is Indian' (30). She suggested convincingly that the phrase of common usage in the UK should be 'ethnic minorities'. 'Ethnicity is not a colour palette. It is a technical term used in the Census, as well as an important part of an individual's identity.' She added, 'Most people rightly recognize that using a lower-case 'i' for Indian or 'b' for Bangladeshi is wrong, so why wouldn't we use 'W' for White and 'B' for Black ethnic groups?' Later commenting, 'if policy makers, programme providers and those tasked with communicating this work use acronyms and terms that people do not understand, their efforts will have a limited impact'.

In September 2020 a group in the UK came together under the umbrella of #BAMEOver. In their rules of engagement they say, 'We reject BAME. The term unhelpfully blends ethnicity, geography, nationality – and in doing so erases our identity and reduces us to an "other".' At the conference they convened, one of the speakers, Ozzie Clarke-Binns, put it bluntly:

> When we look at a word like BAME to me it seeks to solve a problem that doesn't actually exist. In essence it is the need to characterize everyone in opposition to whiteness. We are human beings, we should define ourselves in the affirmative of who we are and how we like to define ourselves, not as the negative or as lacking something in relation to whiteness (31).

The #BAMEOver Terms of Reference begins with the unambiguous statement:

> We do not want to be grouped into a meaningless, collective term, or reduced to acronyms. We are African diaspora people. We are South, East, and South East Asian diaspora people. We are Middle East and North African people. We are ethnically diverse. We are people who experience racism (32).

That expresses forcefully those moments when group experience and identity is indeed the dominant force in people's lives. When you are discriminated against, whatever the multi-layered experience you may have of your own identity in life, you know you are part of that group. This is a literal or metaphorical 'fist-in-the-face' moment. When you are hit or verbally abused or clearly discriminated against because of who you are, you know why. Belonging to the group has meaning through that, albeit negative, experience. The philosopher and Jewish author, Hannah Arendt, wrote, 'One truth that is unfamiliar to the Jewish people... is that you can only defend yourself as the person you are attacked as. A person attacked as a Jew cannot defend himself as an Englishman or a Frenchman. The world would only conclude that he is simply not defending himself at all' (33).

However, outside those circumstances if you make the assumption – not least by routinely just using one of the acronyms – that the group experience is somehow homogeneous, then you will fail to reflect the variation between individuals. You risk blurring the individual life chances and limiting the contributions to the world, or at a more granular level, to your company, of the very people you are trying to support. In a landmark lecture in 2008, Baroness Jane Campbell, the disability campaigner, made a strong case that we must be alert 'to the diversity of the characteristics and experiences of disabled people, and to the causes of the barriers which prevent equality'. She warned of the danger of the 'overly narrow representation of disabled people… which denies the complexity of people's lives, the multiplicity of their identifications, and the cross-pulls of their various affiliations. The rich diversity of disabled people has too often been reduced to the wheelchair symbol' (34).

The emphasis on identity and understanding group disadvantage has got society a long way in creating visibility and respect for groups of people who have previously experienced wholesale prejudice. Where there has been progress it has considerably transformed the ways that they are seen by the rest of humanity. It has created change. That change in turn has enabled the flowering of a great diversity in the individual experiences and ambitions of the people in those minority groups. The obligation now is properly to acknowledge that very diversity and actively take it into account.

All of this emphasizes the paradox that I alluded to above. These appalling examples of disadvantage and discrimination are real and impact on the lives of people in those groups every day at home and at work. But, despite the necessity of doing so, the more you talk about the reality for minorities, the more the diversity solutions that companies produce focus on that status and reinforce their 'otherness'.

The flaw in flexibility

It has become very common in companies to enable flexibility for women in order to accommodate their need to work and also fulfil their family responsibilities. The dominant narrative is that what holds women back is an imbalance between family life and work life. The almost universal response to this is that companies need to take steps to relieve that pressure for women. Many companies are clear that they have managed to improve the number of senior appointments of women by making flexibility at work not an optional but a standard part of their offer to those women.

Recently, however, the larger narrative has been challenged by two scholars of sex inequality at work, Professors Robin J Ely and Irene Padavic (35). Their discoveries chime with many senior women with whom we at Diversity by Design have shared their work. One of those described her experience in the Boardroom as typical of the several public companies of which she has been a director: 'Many organizations hide behind the work/family narrative. When there is Board discussion on gender diversity one of the members inevitably pipes up that some women are bound to make the choice to work differently in order to accommodate family obligations. "It's in the genes".'

What Robin and Irene found when they were working with what they diplomatically just call a 'global consulting firm', was that the more time they spent with people at the firm:

> the more we found that their explanations didn't correspond with the data. Women weren't held back because of trouble balancing the competing demands of work and family – men, too, suffered from the balance problem and nevertheless advanced. Women were held back because, unlike men, they were encouraged to take accommodations, such as going part-time and shifting to internally facing roles, which derailed their careers.

Men and women were experiencing similar levels of distress over the pull between family and work, but they were being encouraged by what the company was offering to deal with it in directly opposite ways. Even if it was unspoken, women were being expected, and expecting, to take the flexibility. But the men, while feeling the same upset at missing their children and guilt about how they weren't spending enough time with their families, expected to carry on at work. Instead of resolving the tension, they submerged their distress, burying it by working too many hours and by hiding their feelings.

On wider investigation, the Professors established that the problem was that the work/family narrative was being used as an excuse for what was actually the fundamental issue that really held all women back, which was 'the crushing culture of overwork at the firm. The unnecessarily long hours were detrimental to everyone… but they disproportionately penalized women because, unlike men, many of them take accommodations, which exact a steep career price'.

What happens with the provision of flexibility in the context of that kind of culture is that women take the accommodations, or – and this is very significant – it is unquestioningly assumed that they will want to do so at some stage in the future because they will want to have a family, even if they haven't got children right now. Conversely it is assumed that the men won't take them. And then, by and large, they don't.

It is this blanket assumption about women's family obligations – whether or not they have children – that is damaging their careers. The men of course champion the women to be able to work flexibly because they want to appear supportive. However, according to the research, what this support actually demonstrated was that they were projecting their own feelings of conflict about work and family onto women and then benefiting from the good feeling that came from being able to show that they understood what women were going through.

The upshot is that what is precisely designed to support women's advancement in fact reinforces the narrative that holds them back. Reading this research it struck me that this was yet another moment when, attaching a specific issue only to a minority-status group, far from being liberating in terms of their career, could in fact be limiting. The consulting firm Accenture, in a recent piece of work *When She Rises, We All Rise*, identified 'men being encouraged to take parental leave' as 1 of 14 key factors that are most likely to affect change and influence advancement for women (36). When you think about it, it seems obvious that, if companies want men and women to rise to the full extent of their abilities equally, then making parental leave available and actively encouraged to both sexes is a powerful symbol that there will be no penalty for enthusiastically balancing work and family. It goes against the old norm and indicates a new one if men's active participation in taking leave to look after their children is highlighted, rather than just women's. It may seem basic but one way to get real change in the advancement of women is for companies to shape their family policies equally around men and women. Yet largely they don't. The way flexibility is typically focused on and taken up by women currently holds them back and provides no solution to men. In the end no-one benefits. Men don't get to spend more time with their children and women don't get promoted. The only thing that comes out of it really well is the age-old narrative that women are solely the homemakers and men are properly the hunters.

Still the work/family tension narrative in relation to women has a powerful grip. While the Covid-19 lockdown had such a profound effect by obligating many people to work very differently at home and predominantly online, the sharing of the burdens of family and work might have been expected to shift to a more equitable balance between men and women. But a University of Sussex study in the summer of 2020 showed that this was a false hope (37). They asked 2,000 mothers who have a male partner about how the lockdown had affected them and their child and discovered that while:

> many dads have stepped up and undertaken more childcare over this period…
> our findings show that women are still overwhelmingly taking on the role of
> primary carer, and with schools closed, primary educator… the prolonged
> school closures and home working are likely to be having a disproportionate
> impact on women's participation in the workplace.

The researchers found that, even with both parents at home together, 67 per cent of mothers who worked were still the default parent. In a situation where the most flexibility was available to both parents, the women's experience was still determined by the dominant narrative that it is they who experience the work/family tension and adapt accordingly.

It is significant too that Robin and Irene's research showed that the work/family narrative swept up women without children as enthusiastically into its embrace as it did those with kids. Childless women were also less promoted. Women with children were said to need the flexibility because of family, but then all women were seen through that lens. The minority/majority frame for diversity tends to do that. It reinforces the stereotype, which is odd, especially when these stereotypes are being applied by those who are advocates of diversity. It is prejudice that lacks the intelligence to tell people apart. It is bigotry that is sufficiently obtuse not to be able to see people as singular human beings rather than just as a cluster. Those who oppose prejudice and bigotry and support diversity are supposed to be the clever ones and not do that. But companies and diversity professionals fall all too frequently into the trap of lumping people together into acronym labelled boxes. This has arisen partly because solving the diversity *deficits* and creating the diversity *dividends* are typically collapsed into one. But as we explored in Chapter 1, while they overlap, they need separate approaches and focus. If you approach diversity as a 'minority issue' you will fall into all the traps described above, which is also relatively easy to do, not least because that's the way the law is framed.

More traps set up by the labels

The Equality Act 2010 was a very considerable advance in the human rights story in the UK. It was designed specifically to give legal force to the defence from discrimination on the basis of: (i) age, (ii) disability, (iii) gender reassignment, (iv) marriage and civil partnership, (v) pregnancy and maternity, (vi) race, (vii) religion or belief, (viii) sex and (ix) sexual orientation.

It was devised on the basis of recognized diversity deficits. It works pretty well when applied as a legal remedy against prejudice and unfair treatment. But it is only one half of the necessary approach to the challenge of creating real diversity in an organization or society at large. It is based on a perfectly reasonable assumption that prejudice and bigotry will come at one of a group as it comes at all of its members. The law is expressed as a protection against that discrimination.

Organizations must deal with those inequities but not by perpetuating only group identities among employees. People who discriminate don't care about who you really are. Your individuality. They don't care about your actual background, life, religion, politics or views. Whether you're mixed race or bisexual or have mental health challenges that they can't see. No nuance for them. It's the one time those in a minority group do experience the world in exactly the same way. For all the enormous diversity within minority groups, the irony is that possibly the few times those who belong to them have an experience that they share precisely, is in a moment created by the ignorance of intolerance. Companies really should not reproduce that.

In the experience of discrimination, people in minority-status groups do undeniably have something in common, but in their individual lives that may well not be the case. Organizations have to be cautious in the extreme in how they approach diversity so as not to make inaccurate assumptions about people in minority groups. A few examples from our work:

- Some years ago, working in a university we came across a young lesbian from one of the Latin America countries who was linked up by a well-meaning student counsellor with a member of the faculty who came from the same country. Unfortunately, he was a staunch Catholic and was very hostile to homosexuality.

- In many of the NHS environments in which we have carried out diversity projects there have been great disagreements between women, between gays and even between trans staff over the issue of self ID for trans people. Yet the trusts continue to make the faulty assumption that all 'LGBT' people have the same views on this issue.

- In one university, 'BAME students' were deliberately dormed in the same residences. However, considerable tensions then erupted between some Black and Asian students who were gay and others who were observant, rather traditional Muslims.

There is a danger in ignoring these divisions within minority groups if we are to tackle diversity successfully. The Equality Act and policies that seek to outlaw unfair treatment in companies are perfectly justifiable as a minority-based approach. It is quite reasonable to see employees as part of a group when the discrimination is directed at them precisely because they're part of a group. However, when it comes to creating real diversity in organizations you have to make a clear distinction between deficits and dividends. A minority-based approach leaves companies stranded dealing with only the former. What organizations need to value is not just who people are but what they can bring through that experience.

One of the go-to tools in the diversity professional's toolbox is the staff network or employee resource group. But, too often they are more evidence of a flawed tick-box approach to diversity unless they are consciously focused outwards to the company rather than inwards towards themselves. If not, there is a real risk that they will play precisely into the majority/minority paradigm of diversity, rather than transcending it. If focused on the minority rather than the company, they can set up a false sense of commonality within the group and not acknowledge its own diversity nor the very valuable role they can play in the wider company's success.

One of the ways to avoid this hazard is to set up these networks explicitly as a way of bringing another, different set of voices into the enrichment of the strategy and goals of the whole company. Usefully staff networks can have three objectives:

- bringing different voices to contribute to company strategy from new angles, to frame the company goals in a new light, to add texture and insight from distinctive points of view;
- support each other personally in the achievement of their ambition in the company because they have a good chance of understanding what each other may need to succeed;
- host events in the company on issues of real strategic importance to the business or sector *that are not about them*. This puts them into the mainstream of key issues and debates in the company and gives them the opportunity to show people from the minority-status group as experts in industry issues.

A dramatic example of this in practice can be seen in the work we did with the lesbian and gay staff network in a large global drug company, that 'discovers, develops and commercializes innovative medicines in areas of unmet need' (38). What emerged very strongly from the discussions was the extent to which there was a clear match between people's personal stories and life experiences and the core goals of the company. Two of its main markets are diagnosis, treatment and cure of those people affected by HIV/AIDS and Hepatitis C. Focusing on both of these issues requires an informed and sensitive understanding of, and response to, the health needs of, particularly, gay men.

As a result, it was clear that there was a personal involvement in the company's inspiration to 'address unmet medical needs for patients living with life-threatening diseases around the world' (39). That meant that there were individual experiences in that group of people that could make a considerable contribution to the development of ways of working, for instance, in locations where the environment for homosexuals was legally and/or socially hostile. Between them they could add significant insight to the development of a corporate narrative of how to work successfully in such environments. They would be able to explore the ethical and personal dilemmas those situations exposed. One specific challenge, for instance, was how to develop relationships that had integrity with customers who were homophobic, in order to achieve the desirable objective of reaching the patients who needed their medical products. In addition the network had the seniority and spread of different skills and capabilities to be able to plan carefully how best to influence the company in a positive way to add to the achievement of its overall goals. It wasn't just the fact that the members of the group were lesbian or gay, but the power of their network lay in bringing their highly informed contribution together with their experiences of life as gay people to the realization of the company's mission.

Minorities shed light on the bigger questions

Making real the contribution of a minority to the mainstream underpinned the original style and approach of Stonewall, the lesbian and gay equality lobby. From its inception it was an organization that was able to forge broad alliances, often with those who disagreed with its view, around bigger principles and that way build popular support.

So when campaigning on fostering and adoption, doubts were raised by opponents about whether lesbians and gays 'should be parents'. That question can only be answered with prejudice, because being lesbian or gay or being heterosexual does not predict your ability as a mother or father. The statistics of abuse and neglect testify that there is nothing inevitable about heterosexuals parenting well. To think that is to confuse the biological ability to have children with the parental capability to look after them. Equally among lesbians and gays there will be vast differences in the quality of their parenting.

But if you strip out the intolerance that lies within that question, you find much more interesting ones. What does anyone need in order to be a good parent? What makes a good parent? How can we, as a society support that? So those of us in Stonewall never argued that in effect 'gay was good' and so all gays were going to be great parents. That would have implied some virtue in and of itself in being gay. What the campaign wanted was not the right to be parents, but the opportunity to contribute to one of the great responsibilities of society, which is to bring up the next generation well. By projecting the question onto that bigger canvas it turned the objections based on prejudice and stereotyping towards the question for all of us, of what was best for children and how lesbians and gays could contribute as members of society to that. That way we were able to build much broader support by raising our sights from the experience of lesbians and gays as a minority, to a question of much wider significance for all parents. Transcending prejudice, the issue then became how can we support parents to be their very best?

Staff networks really make an impact in companies when they embrace that kind of bigger principle. One that is wider than their own self-interest. Diversity by Design was a few years back engaged by one of the banks. The first project was to work with the four staff networks focused on: family and flexible working; gays and lesbians; women and men's equality; and race and ethnicity. Our job was to help them find a common agenda on which to collaborate in the company. To start with we struggled. We went round and round for quite a while. Until a young gay guy, who hadn't been in the bank very long, overcame his shyness in one session and opened up about the language he'd noticed around the office. What he'd overheard hadn't in the main been aggressive but was just casually disagreeable, enough to be unsettling to him as a new person in his job.

His remarks fired up a conversation that started to weave a pattern. What emerged was not about language that was specifically hostile to minorities, but an insight into the culture in the bank and the lack of respect with which everybody seemed to treat everybody else. There was an absence of curiosity between people. Assumptions were made about everybody. Crucially, this was affecting the way people across the bank were communicating and working together. It was affecting banking. By finding the bigger conversation, the minority networks had been able to articulate an insight into the mainstream company culture. The starting point was a minority perspective, but the impact was the same for the whole bank as the wheelchair-inspired drop kerb was for all parents with buggies. The four networks were able to go to the leadership and engage the entire business in a conversation about a cultural issue that was affecting the performance of the bank. They had essentially moved from tackling a diversity deficit to finding a diversity dividend.

Members of minorities at work need to be protected from the discrimination that is too regularly visited on them. They also need to be supported as individuals to follow their own aspirations to the level of their ambition. They are not 'other'. Every employee is 'differently different'. To get the real dividend from diversity it is important to move away from a majority/minority model and create a culture where it's not who you are that matters, but what you bring *through* who you are. This challenges one of the most powerful set of assumptions that underlie so many of the decisions that businesses make about their people. What do you value in them? What constitutes merit?

How 'merit' is by and large not actually merit

What Ed Roberts brought to our lives was the inspiring demand to be seen for what he could do, what he could bring to the world, for what his disability had taught him about his abilities. His campaign to overcome a physical restriction on his and other wheelchair users' mobility on a campus freed the rest of us. His abundant capability to live independently and encourage others to do so and be seen to do so lay in what the world saw as a significant lack. His merit lay in what he had learned from his experience. He showed just how much the idea of what someone is capable of, and what their skills and ambitions could be, is all too often judged against the narrowest idea of merit.

How many times have you heard a manager justify the appointment of someone who is very much in their own image on the grounds that they were 'the best person for the job'? Were they 'the best' or was the manager merely using themselves as the benchmark for assessing their skill and suitability? Sir John Parker's report into the ethnic diversity of UK boards in 2016, calculated that over half of the FTSE 100 companies do not have any directors of colour at all (40). In 2019 the recruitment agency Green Park, who every year publish their *Leadership 10,000* review of the 'gender and ethnocultural diversity of FTSE 100 Leadership', identified that among the top three roles (Chair, CEO and CFO) people of colour numbered only 3 per cent, with no improvement since 2014 (41). Can this really be because White people all have more merit as Board members and senior management than Black people? It may be more likely that those appointing were simply valuing people from their own experience and backgrounds over those whose were different. What they really prize in colleagues is similarity.

That's in large part because most people who have got to senior positions in organizations think they have got there entirely through their own efforts, 'forgetting the social scaffolding within which their success took place' as the Nobel Prize Winner, Angus Deaton, put it recently (42). If it was your group that set the rules then when you win the game you need to believe that you did it through your own brilliance. Once you frame it like that, you don't only justify your own position as being fair and right and reached solely through your own talent, but all that needs to happen is that the minorities get better at whatever role or job they are doing, and at how to play the game, and that way they'll catch up. As Sheryl Sandberg said in the title of her book, all women need to do is *Lean In* (43). Women just need to fix themselves and their careers will take off. When actually what needs to happen is not for women or people from Black and Asian backgrounds and the rest to 'lean in', but for organizations to reach out and change the basis on which they make judgements about their people. Life experience is what creates the difference that we all can bring.

The kind of self-justification that leads to homogeneity is what Scott E Page calls 'the meritocratic fallacy' (44) and Caroline Criado Perez 'the myth of meritocracy' (45). This claims everyone is competing from an equal starting point and that success is simply a question of personal merit. But what is merit? The men at the top are not all universally brilliant, neither do they all deserve to be there. But that hasn't occurred to many of them. It hasn't crossed their minds that a large part of the reason they got there might be because they are men and the networks and advantages that has given them, rather than because they are super talented. As I often say, one of the most telling performance indicators for success in diversity in the future might be when companies start to appoint large numbers of truly mediocre women to the very top jobs.

Chris Brink, when faced with the challenge of transforming Stellenbosch University, talked extensively about the idea of 'merit in context'. As is the case in the UK, university acceptance in South Africa is largely based on exam results. And what is extrapolated from that is that people with better exam results have a higher intellectual ability. And, furthermore, the better the scores, the more meritorious the person. But is that really true? This kind of faulty assumption is applied regularly in reverse, for instance, to working-class young people, young people from lower socio-economic backgrounds. As Chris says:

To say that school-leavers whose parents could buy their way into 'good schools' are of higher merit than school-leavers who struggled in adverse circumstances, on the sole evidence of their respective school-leaving results, seems a peculiarly narrow definition of the word 'merit' (46).

Yet there is a casual acceptance that school leavers who get lower grades are less able. But firstly, you have to ask, less able for what? What skills are you looking for and what skills do high exam grades demonstrate that you have? How good a predictor are they anyway of future job performance? And secondly, how much do those grades depend on the circumstances in which they were achieved? This attitude to merit pervades not just school exam results but also the almost unchallenged reliance by companies, other organizations and universities employing academics, on technical skills and graduate qualifications or length of experience as the signifiers of future high performance, rather than life experience or the difference that someone can bring to a team.

Chris understood this quite profoundly and realized that he needed a dramatic way of demonstrating the value of widening the flow of talent into the student body as part of the transformation of the university. So he devised an institution-wide prize called 'The Vice-chancellor's Award for Succeeding Against the Odds'. It was a large cash sum to students – usually three or four per year across the university – who had succeeded in rising above difficult circumstances.

The money was much higher than existing awards and it attracted deliberately a great deal of public attention. It was presented at the year's official academic opening, in front of an audience of thousands in the great sports hall, with the same pomp and ceremony as the award of honorary doctorates. Chris explained his thinking in his speech at the first ceremony:

In line with our vision statement, Stellenbosch University strives to be an academic institution of excellence, with a national profile and an international reputation. Quality must be our benchmark. If so, we have to ask a simple but profound question: how do you judge quality relative to context? Some of us take for granted an environment, which for others is only a dream. If so, is it not the case that our performance, no matter how well merited on the basis of our own efforts, also owes something to the environment within which we live and work?

Consider two hypothetical cases. One is a student whose parents are well-educated professional people, reasonably affluent, and who comes to us from one of the so-called 'good schools', where she enjoyed every possible facility for sharpening the mind. The other is a student whose parents have had little formal education and who live in poverty, who comes to us from a historically disadvantaged school in a gang-infested area. If the former student comes to Stellenbosch with a school-leaving mark of 90 per cent, and the latter comes with a school-leaving mark of 70 per cent, is it possible for us to say that the former is a better student than the latter? And if we do, would that be right?

As he explained later when he came to the UK as a Vice-Chancellor:

> The claim I made was that performance is relative to context. In a different country and under different circumstances, I am reminded of these words whenever I hear school-leaving results being equated with merit. The students who won the Vice-chancellor's Award for Succeeding Against the Odds all had life stories to tell which made it impossible to regard them as anything other than meritorious. Most of them barely scraped into university, yet all of them performed well – some outstandingly well – towards the end of their studies, and in later life. All that the award really did was to give them a chance, by removing financial worries and showing appreciation for the route they have travelled. And a chance was all they needed (47).

For companies to make progress on their diversity, they need to examine their idea of merit. They need to allow themselves to think more widely about what they value in people. This will give them the opportunity to realize that life experience can make an equal if not greater contribution to a person's ability to do their job as any academic or technical qualification. Managers and those hiring and promoting would be invited by that changed idea of merit to understand both the valuable experience employees might have gathered from succeeding through any disadvantage they have experienced, and also, beyond that, to value that person's individuality and the particular and personal nature of their talents and ability to succeed. People in minorities belong to their group – and will share key aspects of that group experience – but they are also individuals with differing abilities and ambitions. It is a mistake to see those in each group as simply the same. This, by the way is also true of those in the majority. They will also have life experiences that may well deviate in a profoundly personal way from the dominant narrative of the majority groups they belong to. What matters is that the company values in every individual what they can bring through who they are, what their experience has taught them as much as their school or college or last employer.

It is complex for companies and hiring managers to do this because in this new framework for diversity they are being asked to see the person and the context, the minority and the individual, to value the technical as well as the life experience. To add to that, people are wary of identifying difference. Even embarrassed by doing it. Often they think the right thing to do in order not to discriminate and to treat people from minorities fairly is to pretend that everyone is the same. In the course of our work, for instance, people (almost always white people) say: 'I just don't see race'. And I always say to them, 'if you don't see race you really are missing something. But if you only see race, you're really missing something too'. As the educator Anthony Peterson has pointed out there is a curious paradox about race. 'We tell our children that race is real and that race doesn't matter. When in fact the opposite is true. Race is not real. But race does matter' (48). It matters in discrimination. But also it matters in what your people bring through their culture, geographical heritage, language, customs, the shape of their families, ways of living, eating, cooking, sharing. This is true not just of race but of the experience of all your people. Organizations should be curious enough to create processes of hiring and promotion, building their strategies, developing their innovation to value the myriad influences and insights that flow from the lives of minorities and majorities so they can transcend the norms and create the new company 'we'.

You can harness the Power of Difference to ensure that the perspectives from minorities enhance the effectiveness of the whole organization by exploring:

- Ed Roberts' story and remembering that 'old attitudes see us as helpless and unable... [but] disability can make you very strong and very able'. What are the fresh insights minority voices bring?
- how minority voices are heard in the business;
- the many voices within minority groups in the business;
- how to avoid stereotyping minorities in the business;
- how to question assumptions and avoid achieving the opposite result of what you intended with a policy (see women and the work/family narrative above);
- the most effective way to establish minority networks by focusing on three outward facing questions:

- o How can they bring new voice, insights, perspectives to the formulation and execution of the whole company strategy and how does meeting their (minority) needs enhance the achievement of the aims of the entire company?
- o How can they support and advise each other to advance their talent to the benefit of the whole company? What do they specifically need?
- o How can they host discussions, seminars, Zooms that are not about them but rather about the key issues facing the company, the industry and the sector and then feature voices from their particular group as experts on them?
- how you can see everyone in your team as differently different, rather than just seeing minorities as 'other';
- how minorities can help you reframe the traditional idea of merit by valuing life experience;
- how you can challenge assumptions about the norms in your organizations.

04

Unconscious bias is an excuse

On 18 February 1895 at 4.30 in the afternoon, as the Hall Porter of the Albemarle Club in London recalled, the Marquess of Queensbury delivered a letter containing his now famously misspelt accusation: 'To Oscar Wilde, posing Somdomite'. Thus began the persecution of Wilde by his lover's father that brought about his downfall and made him one of the most famous homosexuals of all time.

Oscar sued for libel. Queensbury countered by accusing him of soliciting more than 12 young men 'to commit sodomy'. On 3 April, the first day of the trial, Oscar arrived at court, accompanied by liveried servants, in a stylish four-wheeled Brougham carriage pulled by two horses.

In the dock he was dismissively magnificent and witty. Replying to questions from his counsel Oscar recounted an attempted blackmail by a man who had come into possession of a letter to his lover, Alfred Lord Douglas. Oscar told the man that he 'would gladly have paid... a very large sum of money for the letter as I consider it to be a work of art'. The blackmailer, alluding to its obvious homoerotic content, had replied that another rather more 'curious construction' could be put on it. Oscar quipped, 'Art is rarely intelligible to the criminal classes.' When the blackmailer said that he'd been offered £60 by someone else for it – several thousand pounds today – Oscar had advised him to take it, 'as he himself had never received so large a sum for any prose work of that length'. As the laughter subsided, the judge said he would clear the court if there was any more noise (1).

On the wall of a cubicle in the loos of the library at Sussex University, where I did a law degree, someone had written in felt pen, 'My mother made me a homosexual.' Underneath someone else had added, 'If I send her the wool, will she make me one too?'

Oscar's behaviour at the trial and the lavatory wall joke are not unconnected. The significance of the graffiti lies not just in its wit but in the words 'a' and 'one'. It shows that, in people's minds, there is such a type of person as 'A Homosexual'. You could be 'one'. In her ground-breaking article 'The Homosexual Role', published in 1968, the sociologist Mary McIntosh showed how the transformation was made from describing someone being engaged in 'homosexual acts' to them being 'a homosexual person' (2). From acts into a complete actor. By the late 19th century in Britain the homosexual was becoming established as a description that characterized certain individuals and not others. The invention of The Homosexual is relatively modern. Oscar Wilde crystallized the template.

One of the reasons humans are able to learn and adapt so quickly is because we are excellent at making generalizations about the world based on very limited experience and using them to navigate it. Inevitably that creates stereotypes. They develop over time from observations of actual language and behaviour. But then, deprived of the context that would explain or understand their origin, they are distorted and exaggerated to create a misleading picture of a whole group. Through repetition, this becomes embedded as a way of seeing those people. On the positive side stereotypes are dead handy. But on the other hand, they are just deadly.

In Oscar's gay prototype, while his defiant wit may have been cover for shame and wounds inflicted by a wholly unsympathetic society, it also sparkled luminously. Many gay men have since sought a place in the world by attempting (sadly too often unsuccessfully) to emulate him. Camp and deflective humour is often the weapon of choice by gay men. When generalized though, all gay men then become, in the eyes of non-homosexuals, witty, glamorous and 'such fun', which I can assure you from personal experience is not always the case.

In a world where, if you're Black, you are judged by 'the colour of your skin' and not 'the content of your character', you may well be attracted to excel in sport, where achievement can be measured with accuracy without reference to race. Bias may create barriers to your entry, but sporting success is unarguable when calculated in goals or seconds. Similarly in the music industry. Your success in downloads and earnings is unchallengeable. But then the erroneous attribution of those abilities to your race entrenches a stereotype of all Black people excelling in (and loving) sport, rap and hip hop.

While stereotypes can be positive, in the main they fuel judgement and persecution. It is not a coincidence that the creation of The Homosexual in the late 19th century coincided with the enactment of the gross indecency laws. Now they were identifiable, homosexuals could be and, to shore up the family in a time of increased sexual division of labour, society needed them to be, identified and punished as outsiders. In apartheid South Africa, racial stereotypes were weaponized to enable systems of laws designed to separate and victimize groups of people, deny them freedom and, in Nazi Germany, to justify mass murder.

Stereotypes gather partial truths and forge them into bias and discrimination. They belittle those to whom they are applied in order to shore up the power of dominant moralities. They sustain differences in status and regard in society by reducing groups of people to a single set of characteristics that, once moulded into prejudice, justifies the expulsion of the people in that group to the other side of a boundary. Stereotypes not only organize the world, they also police it. Humans judge and categorize each other by these biases. In general, bias rounds humans up and disadvantages and limits us. In the most extreme cases, it kills us.

What happened when we legislated against bias?

In the 20th century the damage done by discrimination began to be widely acknowledged. The formal response was built on the Bills of Rights from the revolutionary era and the Enlightenment. Sickened by the genocidal catastrophe that had resulted from the very worst kind of stereotyping – that Jews were at the heart of an international conspiracy to control the world and yet also, contradicting that view, an inferior race – the world came to an agreement in The Universal Declaration of Human Rights that established rights in relation to freedom of association, thought, opinion, religion, conscience, life, health and a standard of living, and the prohibition of slavery and torture. It was a starting point for what has become, in many countries, a well-articulated legal framework that condemns prejudice in action and provides remedies to the injured. Governments have established that bigotry and discrimination against groups of people are not acceptable and have enacted legislation to make this official.

In the UK, 1968 brought the Race Relations Act, 1970 The Equal Pay Act, The Sex Discrimination Act in 1975, the Disability Discrimination Act in 1995 and the Employment Equality (Sexual Orientation) Regulations in 2003. The European Convention on Human Rights was incorporated into domestic British law as the Human Rights Act 1998. Despite pledges to review the HRA by the British Conservative Party, this legislation currently guarantees a range of rights and legally bans prejudice. Yet, predictably, it didn't just disappear.

In the UK the first case under the Race Relations Act was brought, only months after the Act was passed, by Mahesh Upadhyaya who had come from Aden in 1961 (3). Once he was earning decent money, he tried to buy a house for his family in Huddersfield. In an interview to mark the 50th anniversary of the Act, he said that after they had looked round one they liked, 'I rang the developers, George Haigh & Sons, later that day. The person on the phone said, "Are you the coloured family who had a look around earlier?" I said that we were. The person on the phone said, "Our policy is not to sell to coloured people because that will jeopardize the sales of our other properties".' 'No Irish, No Blacks, No Dogs' then, as the signs famously said on B&Bs in Notting Hill in London in the 1960s. The Court ruled that by saying what they did Haigh & Sons behaved unlawfully (although the case was dismissed on a technicality).

In the years since these Acts the situation has not entirely improved. Survey after survey of employees in companies has demonstrated that the experience of harassment and discrimination is still ubiquitous. Equal pay remains an issue, as does the gender pay gap. Many lesbian and gay people are still bullied. Black and Brown people tell stories of their experiences every day of racism, carelessness in language, outright aggression or of their apparent invisibility. Jews continue to experience anti-Semitism with alarming frequency. The rate of unemployment among people with disabilities is significantly higher, evidence of the inability of employers to see beyond the physical to potential. Opportunities for particular groups of people are still being denied. Things might have improved. But even if prejudice isn't any longer an all-day event, it is still an everyday event. How could this be so?

How could bias and discrimination have been outlawed and yet still be so prevalent, particularly as social attitudes surveys show a consistent move towards more liberal and open-minded views? When the British Social Attitudes Survey was first published in 1983, just under 60 per cent of White people said they would mind if a close relative married someone Black or Asian (4). But in June 2020 Ipsos Mori reported that 89 per cent of people in the UK say they would be happy for their child to marry someone from another ethnic group, 14 percentage points higher than in 2009 (5). Today an overwhelming majority of people, 93 per cent, disagree with the statement that 'to be truly British you have to be White', an 11 per cent improvement on 2006. Noticeably the proportion who agree with the statement has fallen from 10 per cent to 3 per cent in the last 14 years. The number of Britons who say they have a mixed-ethnic background almost doubled between the Census of 2001 and the following one in 2011, to about 1.2m, slightly more than 2 per cent of the overall population (6). Between 1989 and 2019 the proportion of the population that thought that gay relationships were wrong fell from 40 per cent to 13 per cent (7). And so on.

While social attitudes improve, bias and discrimination nonetheless stubbornly remain. People are increasingly comfortable it would appear with their daughter marrying a Black guy. But he's often still less likely to get a job he applies for or a promotion. Parents are rightly as delighted by their son's gay civil partnership as they are by their daughter's marriage to a man, yet the *Harvard Business Review* reported in 2018 that in Australia, the United States and the UK 68 per cent, 46 per cent and 35 per cent respectively of gay men and lesbians are reluctant to come out at work (8). We know from a persistent result in the NHS's Workforce Race Equality Standard that people from Black and Asian backgrounds are almost one and a half times as likely to be put through formal disciplinaries than their White colleagues (9).

These biases make themselves apparent at work in many both subtle and unsubtle ways. There is a now very widely used experiment originally designed by Kathleen McGinn at Harvard Business School in 2000, which has become known colloquially as 'Heidi and Howard' (10). Howard is a successful and very well-connected Silicon Valley tech entrepreneur, counting Steve Jobs and Bill Gates in his network. In the case study he describes how he reached these lofty heights. Students are given the narrative and asked to evaluate his performance. Rather unsurprisingly they think he's highly competent and effective. They also like him and want to work for him. However, he's fake. He doesn't exist. The case study actually describes the career of Heidi Rosen, a serial tech entrepreneur, one-time Vice President of World-Wide Developer Relations for Apple, who describes herself on her own website as 'a venture capitalist, corporate director, Stanford lecturer, recovering entrepreneur and Mom'.

When the students find out that they were reading about a woman rather than a man, their attitudes change in a highly significant way. They still found her competent and effective. But they didn't like her and they didn't want to work with her. What is celebrated as self-confidence, enterprise and success in a man is perceived as arrogance and pushiness in a woman. Example after example has demonstrated that women are forced into this trade-off between competence and likeability, which flows directly from the stereotype that attempts to define women. In breaking out of it they suffer consequences.

Many businesses and organizations have grappled for some time with the continuing presence of bias and why it was happening. They were scratching their corporate heads about how social attitudes seemed to be improving, but bias continued to pervade the outcomes of recruitment, promotion and the experiences of their employees. They were searching for solutions. Senior managers had always thought that decisions in business were guided by wisdom and experience that drove conscious judgements and decisive actions. That way organizations ended up with the 'best person for the job' and the right way forward for the company. As time went on many of those same bosses made public commitments not just to outlawing discrimination but positively to pursuing diversity. Then they discovered that, despite their good intentions, the diversity figures changed at a glacial pace, if at all. Certain groups of people continued not to advance and get opportunities as much as other ones did.

How business thought unconscious bias training was the cavalry

In the 1990s the concept of 'unconscious bias' rode to their rescue. In 1995 Anthony Greenwald a social psychologist at Washington University, and a psychologist from Yale called Mahzarin Banaji, published the first paper which 'describes an indirect, unconscious, or implicit mode of operation for attitudes and stereotypes' (11). More than that, by 1998, they reckoned they could measure these hidden biases. A team led by Greenwald developed the Implicit-Association Test, the IAT, computerized it and made it available to anyone to use in order to discover their unintentional preferences (12).

It turns out that while explicit expressions of bias have been outlawed by legislation and increasing social disapproval, according to implicit bias theory, we have merely pushed our racism, sexism and homophobia into the recesses of our minds. Our prejudices are hidden in a place where we do not act on them until they are triggered, whereupon they leap out and affect our judgement. We are not aware of these biases. They have been buried in our unconscious. So the IAT will tell you something about yourself that you didn't know.

When you take the test it first alerts you to the four categories it will use. For instance, with the race test it will show you Good, Bad, Black People, White People. It lists eight words associated with each of 'good' and 'bad' and displays six neutral pictures each of 'Black people' and 'White people'. You are then asked to press the E key or the I key as swiftly as possible when you see any of the categories on their own and then in combination with the words. This shows how fast you put the different words and pictures into positive or negative groups either on their own or together. The test measures the speed of your reaction in pressing the key. Crucially it is that speed that gives you the verdict on your implicit bias.

While it has become hugely popular, there has been a slew of criticism, academic and political, of the IAT. Much of it justified. A number of the critiques have questioned what exactly is meant by 'unconscious', some whether bias is in fact implicit and a number of others have questioned whether the results tell us anything about how we actually behave.

People from ethnic minority backgrounds and women certainly are at the receiving end of behaviour by White people and by men that they experience as racist or sexist. But there can be a range of reasons for the behaviour, as we saw in the Macpherson Report definition of institutional racism in the previous chapter. It might be that those White people and those men are being actively prejudiced, where the bias is quite conscious. But it could also be that in many of those cases they are behaving and speaking, making judgements and taking decisions the negative impacts of which they are just not aware. Or that they were just being careless or insensitive in their use of language. Is it the biases of which people are unconscious or of the impact that they are having? Saying that doesn't diminish the effect of these every-day harms, or excuse them, but understanding how they are generated should help organizations to go about tackling them. Many businesses continue to think that the IAT and an understanding of the 'unconscious' nature of bias does that. But how much are they trying to fix the people rather than trying to transform the processes of recruitment, appraisal and promotion, designing out the bias to create better outcomes?

The idea of 'unconscious' bias also implies that you can't control it. But does the fact that you are unable to control aspects of your behaviour necessarily mean that you are unconscious of it? There is a whole raft of damaging behaviours that result from an inability to restrain our impulses: drug addiction, obesity, sexual risk taking and problem gambling, for instance. People struggling with these issues are often only too conscious of them and the effect they are having on their lives, but that knowledge doesn't mean they can manage them.

How the test generates its results has also been radically criticized. Not only does the IAT just measure the speed of your reactions (and how reliable a guide is that to your behaviour?) but also the judgement that the participant receives about their apparent bias is based on a cut-off point. But is there any evidence that people above and below that point really differ fundamentally in their preferences or more importantly in their behaviour?

The US journalist Jesse Singal rounded up the views of a group of critics in 2017 for an article in the *New York* magazine (13). They ranged from 'the question of what the IAT is really measuring [as in, can a reaction-time difference measured in milliseconds really be considered, on its face, evidence of real-world-relevant bias?] to the algorithms used to generate scores to, perhaps most importantly [given that the IAT has become a mainstay of a wide variety of diversity training and educational programmes], whether the test really does predict real-world behaviour'.

The authors of the test have increasingly responded to these criticisms by saying, rather unconvincingly, that their view is that contrary to the claims of its original fanfare, the results of an IAT are not definitive about someone's behaviour but just a prompt to get people thinking about implicit bias and how it may affect their judgement. They warn that people should not overinterpret their results. More recently they have been even less definite in claiming that an individual's result in an IAT necessarily predicts their actions.

What is so disturbing about the effect of the IAT is not that it may help us to focus on the prevalence of racism or sexism or homophobia. That can only be a good thing. The problem is that it limits the response. In a 2020 documentary on Channel 4, a group of 11- and 12-year-old children in a well racially mixed school were part of an experiment that involved them all being put through an IAT (14). They were then told the results. These asserted that 70 per cent of them had a preference for White people. The commentary intoned, 'The majority of the class showed an unconscious bias towards White people. Eighteen out of twenty-four showed a significant preference for White people, two showed a Black preference and only four had neutral or no bias.' One girl described her skin colour as 'mixed' and said, 'My dad and mum usually say it's olive.' She then added, 'even though I *look* different to White people or Black people I don't really think of it as a way of me *being* different'. She said on hearing the result, 'We usually think of White people with better connotations. We don't necessarily think that Black people have bad connotations, we just find it easier to have good connotations with White people.' Being racially mixed it may not be surprising that she understood her experience of the world in Black and White, even while she attributed 'better connotations' to White people. But what she said scarcely illustrates that her attitudes were 'unconscious'. It's not entirely clear why she needed to be put through the IAT to discover something she was easily able to articulate anyway, nor to have it presented to her as scientific-sounding feedback.

The most common reactions among the kids were different expressions of guilt. One girl, when she realized at the end of the test that the results have been 'collected and sent', said, 'I thought they would come for me.' 'Who are "they"'? said the teacher. 'The Police', she replied, 'knocking on my door'. A young Black guy said, shocked and sounding as if his self-esteem had taken a bit of blow, 'I didn't know this about myself.' Another said, 'I was thinking we can beat this', but then added, crest fallen, 'obviously not... and that was a bit disappointing'. And one boy, with the kind of vibrant red hair that in many circumstances can lead to being bullied, said, 'They say not to feel bad about it, but you still feel bad about it because you've done something wrong.' None of this was a recipe for future action. Taking the IAT merely provoked a wave of self-reproach. All based on a test that the inventors are now saying is really an awareness raising tool rather than a scientific predictor of behaviour.

We need to do the work, not beat ourselves up

The IAT's impact as a tool of change is flawed in two important ways. Firstly, it rests on a premise that, while people may behave in ways that are racist or sexist, because the biases that drive that are 'unconscious' they are not able to control this behaviour. This is profoundly pessimistic as it undermines the possibility of any transformation. Rather than being helpless puppets of their impulses, as the IAT implies, people need to do the work to gain awareness of and understand their biases and then to challenge them. Bias is not a fixed state of being. It's a culturally and socially created set of views and actions that can be transformed, individually or collectively.

Secondly, the IAT fosters the idea that White people's reaction to #BlackLivesMatter or of men to #MeToo should be to examine their own imperfections, rather than join with people of colour to act against racism, or with women to challenge the prevalence of sexism and violence. In this way the IAT just distracts attention from tackling the real problems, which are the causes of discrimination and the need to expunge it from organizations and society. Instead, it implies that the way forward is personal self-improvement. Rather than a collective effort, what we apparently need is group therapy. Instead of focusing mass action on goals that will end bias against Black people, women and homosexuals, what we require is a global movement of personal remorse and self-flagellation.

In conversations about race this has reached something of a peak with the concept of 'White privilege'. Imported from the United States, its use has been much debated in the UK. Against a wholly welcome surge of urgency about the need to wrestle racism to the ground in organizations and society, something strange has occurred. We seem to be talking more about White people now than Black people. The focus has shifted from talking about racism to talking about 'privilege'. There are two problems with this. I know that by those who subscribe to this analysis of White 'privilege' and White 'fragility' – that has made so much money and profile for its premier advocate, a White woman called Robin Di Angelo – I will be accused of just being defensive. I also realize that, as a White person, I am caught in something of a Catch 22, because any criticism of this framework ends up with one being accused by its adherents of merely being evidence of my 'fragility'. However, my criticisms stand.

Firstly, the concept of privilege falls very differently on US ears than it does on British ones. To Brits it has echoes of public schools, of Etonians in top hats, of champagne, of horseracing at Royal Ascot. In essence, of class, wealth and life beyond the curtain that divides Business Class from Economy. So when we talk to those who are poor and White, unemployed and White, parents with children on free school meals and White, the idea that they have 'privilege' has little or no resonance with them.

For example, the Office of National Statistics measures the average 'Attainment 8' score for children in school (15). These are their results in eight GCSE-level qualifications including English and maths. It also disaggregates them for the ONS ethnic categories and also for those children who are poor enough to be on benefits and thus eligible for free school meals. In the 2018 to 2019 school year in England the average score for all pupils was 46.7 out of 90. Chinese children scored an average of 64.3, Asian, Mixed Race, White and Black children scored respectively 51.2, 47.6, 46.2 and 44.9.

However, if we compare children from poor families, those on free school meals, with those overall scores we can see that there is a poverty penalty for each group, which varies considerably. For Chinese children the penalty is 10 per cent, for Black children 12.3 per cent, for Asian children 14.5 per cent and for Mixed Race children 22.7 per cent. Their White school friends, however, are living with a penalty for being poor, which is over double that of their Black school friends, of 30.7 per cent.

This is not to deny racism. It is rather to argue that the concept of 'privilege' brings only the narrowest sliver of insight to exploring the complexity of relationships between White people and Black people, or women and men, when they are both disadvantaged. When it comes to race, people of colour experience the constant gaze of society that sees them as different, as not belonging, their image and abilities frequently distorted through the lens of bias and stereotypes. White people do not suffer that for being White. Women similarly experience the constant drip, drip of everyday sexism from men. But when you and your children don't have enough to eat, or you have no job, your ethnicity or your sex is overwhelmed by the impact of your poverty. If you are poor and White, or poor and male telling you that you are 'privileged' is more likely to drive you away from embracing diversity than towards it.

Secondly, more than that, the notion of 'privilege' attached to any one group of people – in this case White people – is so static that it defies the possibility of change. It's as if White people, in a way that is reminiscent of Calvinist predetermination, were born with original sin. A condition that never alters. Racism stops being the problem and is replaced by the issue of White people who are incapable of escaping their inheritance. Defeating racial inequality is seen in terms of the problem of being White rather than the power and potential of being Black. It condemns any idea of solidarity between Black and White to the bin, in favour of unending division. It disrespects the progress made by activists against racism over the last decades and the optimism through struggle that was Martin Luther King's Dream. In no way does it urge me to take responsibility for listening, trying to understand and acting against the bias that I have acquired and the effect that the things I say and do may have on the lives of Black people I know, work with, pass in the shops or even am married to. And in relation to the last, if I take against the concept personally it's because it says the relationship between me and my husband, a man in his own words 'proud of being an African and a Nigerian', can in this analysis only be seen through the microscope of race, only as a partnership between me, the inevitable vessel of racism, and him, the victim of my 'privilege'. Neither of us believes that.

In a conversation recently with a Consultant who works in an NHS Trust that is a client of ours, she and I talked over the problem we both had with this concept of 'privilege'. So, two consultants, one in diversity and one in medicine; one White, gay and male, the other British Nigerian, straight and female. We badgered at the word, raking through what lay behind it and what it was trying to express. In her view what was important about it was how it reached to encompass the constant nature of the experience of being Black, and in a minority, and of racism. But its drawback was that in her experience in the hospital where she worked, she had considerable privilege, over and beyond many of her colleagues, simply because she was a consultant. The hierarchy of the NHS gave her power that it did not give to others. It wasn't the underlying idea that worried her, despite some anxiety at the inflexibility that was at its core. It was the word itself and what it means to most people. So she was coming round instead to the idea of 'hindrance'. The experience of being Black in the UK meant that even now in 2020 her 10-year-old daughter's friend was told in the playground to 'go back to where you came from'. The unremitting nature of those kinds of experiences, from childhood onwards, creates a hindrance in Black lives that each person of colour has to overcome. That idea of a consistent hindrance that needs to be surmounted seems to express the pervasiveness of racism, or for that matter the similar experience women have in the face of constant sexism, in a way that translates it into something that could be meaningful for the widest audience. It also focuses our attention properly on the effects of bias, which if we are going to challenge it effectively, is better defined in terms of actions rather than as a state of mind.

However, seeing it as the latter continues to exert its grip on diversity work. By 2018 the original article that described the IAT had been cited 4,000 times. It is claimed that the test has now been taken by more than 14 million participants (16). It has leapt out of the lab and into extensive use by both public service and business. What seems to make it so popular is its instantaneous verdict. In just 10 minutes it enables you to uncover all the bias in your psyche. Around it has grown up an industry of 'Unconscious Bias' training that has an enduring life in companies and bedevils work on diversity.

Professor Iris Bohnet estimates that in the United States alone in 2019, $8bn was spent on diversity training that almost invariably has unconscious bias shot through it as a guiding principle (17). However, she quotes from one of the most comprehensive reviews of almost 1,000 studies of training exercises on diversity, made by Professors Elizabeth Levy Paluck from Princeton and Donald Green from Yale, which concluded that there was a 'dearth of evidence' as to whether they work (18).

Nonetheless, it's the standard corporate response to diversity crises. In 2015 the then CEO of Starbucks, Howard Schultz, encouraged their baristas to write #racetogether on coffee cups and 'talk to their customers about racial tension' (19). This was mercilessly lampooned on comedy and talk shows. And pretty swiftly halted. Barely three years later two 23-year-old Black entrepreneurs, Donte Robinson and Rashon Nelson, were waiting to meet a potential business partner at the Starbucks in Rittenhouse Square in Philadelphia (20). Rashon asked to use the loo when they arrived but was told it was for paying customers only. They sat and waited. A barista asked them whether they wanted to order anything. They said no they were just there for a quick meeting. The next thing they knew the police showed up, having been telephoned by the manager, and, according to Rashon, told them, 'Get out, you have to leave. You're not buying anything, so you shouldn't be here' (21). They, reasonably, explained they were there for a business meeting. The man they had arranged to see had now arrived, but they were arrested and handcuffed and taken to the police station. Another customer fortunately filmed the whole incident and it was watched over 10 million times online.

Just over 10 days after the incident, no charges having been made, Schultz's successor as CEO, Kevin Johnson, apologized to the two men and announced on ABC's *Good Morning America* that he would arrange for all Starbucks managers 'to undergo training on how to spot unconscious bias' (22). And on 29 May, just seven weeks later, Starbucks closed more than 8,000 US stores to give 175,000 employees that training (23).

Why unconscious bias training? History doesn't relate what the manager's motives were. Starbucks' reaction confirmed that they thought it was race related. But, if it was, it doesn't appear to have been terribly unconscious. On the face of it, it looked like quite nakedly conscious bias against young Black men. The police appear to have been called to deal with the apparent crime of 'Being Black In Starbucks While Not Buying Coffee'. If the Starbucks employees needed training it might have been better to teach them how not to engage in racist stereotyping. Or, more basically, just how to be courteous to all their customers whether they are buying coffee on that visit or not.

What's more, even the inventor of the IAT, Anthony Greenwald, has sounded a strong note of caution about such training to the co-host of the podcast *Blocked and Reported*, Katie Herzog, when she talked to him for a piece she wrote about the whole fiasco in The Stranger.com in 2018 (24). He said:

> Starbucks would be wise to check out the scientific evidence on implicit bias training. It appears to be the right thing to do, but this training has not been shown to be effective, and it can even be counterproductive. It will appear that Starbucks is doing the right thing, but the training is not likely to change anything. The Implicit Association Test is a valuable educational device to

allow people to discover their own implicit biases. However, taking the IAT
to discover one's own implicit biases does nothing to remove or reduce those
implicit biases. Desire to act free of implicit bias is not sufficient to enable action
free of implicit bias.

From the horse's mouth, as they say.

In all these examples we are witnessing people enacting their prejudices.
Unconscious bias training, and sibling approaches that also rely on its
questionable theoretical underpinning, has become a standard feature of
company diversity programmes, even though making us aware of bias does
not magic it away. More worrying, the evidence is mounting that it makes it
worse. Which is not really that surprising. We'd all be living in the land of
the tooth fairy if we thought that just making a wish would make it happen.
In our urgent desire to be rid of bias we are too often avoiding the hard
work and stopping at the stage of feeling guilty.

There's nothing in itself wrong with having biases. We all have them.
Mostly we've learned them involuntarily. The problem comes when having
biases and operating on them – either deliberately or without care – disadvantages other people. Some biases are perfectly innocuous – not liking
Indian food, or refusing to eat horsemeat in France. The problem comes
when we raise them above the level of personal preference and transfer them
to whole groups of people – not liking all Indian people or not liking the
French. Biases and preferences are part of the way we negotiate living. We
need to make judgements. It has always struck me as strange that 'You're
so judgemental' can be levelled as a criticism. Being judgemental is not
the problem. It's the basis for judgement that is. Bias makes the mistake of
generalizing from personal preference to a whole category of people merely
on prejudice and without the inconvenience of basing that judgement on
evidence. Saying that you don't like one person who is White, Black or
female or gay is a judgement; saying you don't like them *because* they are
White, Black or female or gay is a prejudice. And saying you don't like all
White people, Black people, women or gays is catastrophic to our ability to
live with each other in society or at work.

Notwithstanding that, unless you've met all of them, it's pretty hard to
justify that kind of judgement in any intellectually sustainable way. Not that
people who are prejudiced worry much about that, which is a large part of
the problem. If the IAT draws attention to the fact that you are behaving like
that, all well and good. But proper self-reflection combined with genuine
human curiosity about colleagues who are different from you might do that

as effectively, especially if your team and organization consciously decides to give time and space to it. But it's increasingly misleading to think that just becoming aware of biases magics them away. In fact it might even have the opposite effect.

How unconscious bias training lets everyone off

For a while the research has been flashing warning lights. At the forefront of this work have been Professors Michelle Duguid of Washington University in St Louis and Melissa Thomas-Hunt formerly of the University of Virginia, now Global Head of Diversity and Belonging at Airbnb. In one paper in 2015 they concluded:

> The deleterious effects of stereotyping on individual and group outcomes have prompted a search for solutions. One approach has been to increase awareness of the prevalence of stereotyping in the hope of motivating individuals to resist natural inclinations. However, it could be that this strategy creates a norm for stereotyping, which paradoxically undermines desired effects (25).

Their research demonstrated that 'individuals who received a high-prevalence-of-stereotyping message expressed more stereotypes than those who received a low-prevalence-of-stereotyping message or no message'.

In their experiments they gave two groups the opposite information about stereotypes – one group that they were rare and the other that they were common. And then they asked each group about how they saw women. The group that was told that stereotypes were common counterintuitively had far more stereotypical perceptions of women – more family, less career. You can see what is happening. Those people begin to think that stereotypes are incredibly common so biases aren't their problem because everybody has them and so they start to accept them more easily. You will probably have seen it in action. Once you tell people that biases that are unconscious and, what's more, everybody has them, they relax. It's an 'Oh Phew' moment. 'Oh Phew, you mean it's not just me. You mean everybody's biased?' And their responsibility for challenging it starts to diminish. The concept of unconscious bias and the associated training ends up confirming rather than challenging their views.

Michelle and Melissa go on to say not only does unconscious bias train-ing create a norm for stereotyping, but 'working professionals who received a high-prevalence-of-stereotyping message were *less willing to work with an individual who violated stereotypical* norms than those who received no message [or] a low-prevalence-of-stereotyping message'. That's the Heidi/Howard scenario in action and highlights just how very depressing the news is for those companies that have invested so much in this kind of training because it is doing nothing to challenge those biases. In fact, it may have the exact opposite effect of what is intended.

Anxiety has been further deepened about the unconscious bias approach by recent findings uncovering behaviour that researchers call 'moral licensing'. This is where people respond to having done something good by doing more of something bad. In an experiment in Taiwan one group of people were told that they were being given multivitamins and others that they were being given a placebo. In fact all of them were given the placebo. However, almost comically, the ones who thought they'd had the vitamins were more likely to smoke, eat unhealthy food and take less exercise! It's the doughnut after the gym syndrome. Iris Bohnet references an even more shocking example where 'people who were given an opportunity to endorse Barack Obama in the 2008 Presidential Election, were later on more likely to discriminate against African Americans'. She adds that 'the effect was particularly pronounced among people already racially prejudiced, raising the unsettling possibility that diversity programmes aimed at influencing the worst offenders might backfire' (26). These one-off results need further investigation, but they do raise some pretty urgent question marks.

With all the effort and training for diversity and against bias, companies could usefully look at the two main reasons that research has revealed about why it is not working.

The first suggests simply that training on its own doesn't work. One study analysed over 800 mid- to large-sized US companies over three decades to see if there was any correlation between diversity training programmes and a diversifying workforce (27). Their study concluded that 'diversity training has no relationship to the diversity of the workforce. In fact, in some cases diversity training programmes were associated with a small drop in the likelihood that certain under-represented groups became managers.' 'In firms where training is mandatory or emphasizes the threat of lawsuits', they pointed out, 'training actually has negative effects on management diversity.'

Two of the researchers further elaborated on those findings in a 2016 *Harvard Business Review* article:

It shouldn't be surprising that most diversity programs aren't increasing diversity. Despite a few new bells and whistles, courtesy of big data, companies are basically doubling down on the same approaches they've used since the 1960s – which often make things worse, not better... Those tools are designed to pre-empt lawsuits by policing managers' thoughts and actions. Yet laboratory studies show that this kind of force-feeding can activate bias rather than stamp it out (28).

Furthermore, they say, 'The positive effects of diversity training rarely last beyond a day or two, and a number of studies suggest that it can activate bias or spark a backlash. Nonetheless, nearly half of midsize companies use it, as do nearly all the Fortune 500.' As Iris Bohnet says, 'just being made aware of biases does not do the trick'.

In another piece in the *Harvard Business Review*, Peter Bregman, a leading global executive coach and author, added that 'Diversity training doesn't extinguish prejudice. It promotes it... And rather than changing attitudes of prejudice and bias, it solidified them' (29). From his wide experience in the field, he concluded that this is not the exception, it's the norm.

Why RAGE helps

Broadly speaking, you can't argue rationally with your biases because they weren't acquired rationally. They were your social education and they are very deep-seated in your way of seeing the world. To eliminate them you need to be aware of them, not in a helpless way, but actively. You must be concerned about the consequences of your biases, see the impact of your language or behaviour as significant, dislike the effect it has on others and then make a conscious effort to check what you say and do. This motivation to make that change is all important. One of the reasons that training may not be so effective is that your enthusiasm may well not be shared by all your people. Training needs to open up discussion, not close it down; offer a hand, not point a finger. It must enable your people to explore their biases openly without fear of retribution in that space, understand the effect of them on colleagues and on the business, realize the damage they cause and through that find the impetus to change. Above all they need to be given practical ways to tackle them that they feel are relevant to different situations in their lives. If it helps, here is an acronym: RAGE. **R**ecognize bias, **A**gree that it is damaging, **G**enuinely want to change it and **E**ngage actively to do so.

This is a process. You can't just outlaw bias and expect people to change their minds, preferences and decisions as a result. It won't work to try to impose diversity in a command and control way in a company. It may be fruitless for employees to participate in training unless it helps them to embrace the need to change for the good of their colleagues and the business. Otherwise, training on bias will too often prompt them in the direction of what they originally thought. Reaffirming the omnipresence of bias is in danger of reminding them that they need not worry because it's just the way things are.

The 2016 study shows quite clearly how the top-down tactic fails. While:

> it boils expected behaviours down to dos and don'ts that are easy to understand and defend… this approach… flies in the face of nearly everything we know about how to motivate people to make changes. Decades of social science research point to a simple truth: you won't get managers on board by blaming and shaming them with rules and re-education.

We all need to face our biases, and no amount of calling them 'unconscious' changes the fact that they are prejudices and people operate on them. However, it's also worth pointing out that bias can be either negatively or positively motivated even though the effect is always to limit someone else's potential and opportunities. The results of research using audit studies, where the investigators have attempted to understand how bias operates by looking at the effect of 'Black' and 'White' or male and female sounding names on call-backs for interview, are fairly tangled. MIT's significant review, also in 2016, of the various experimental methods that have been employed to measure the prevalence of discrimination is quite clear:

> Black people are less likely to be employed, more likely to be arrested by the police, and more likely to be incarcerated. Women are very scarce at the top echelon of the corporate, academic, and political ladders despite the fact that (in rich countries at least) they get better grades in school and are more likely to graduate from college (30).

One study that measured the effect of having or not having a criminal record on getting a call-back showed shockingly that 'a black applicant *without* a criminal record was about as likely to receive a call-back as a white applicant *with* a criminal record'. The data shows, with no argument, that there is disadvantage, often severe, for particular groups of people.

But the review goes on to qualify this in an important respect: 'While many in the media and public opinion circles argue that discrimination is a key force in driving these patterns, showing that it is actually the case is not simple.' There is no definitive conclusion on the causes of biased decisions. In general, the studies have not designed approaches that formally test the various theories on why differential treatment happens. Most audit studies, as they say, 'do not explicitly test which theory of discrimination has most explanatory power, even if they often informally discuss what forms of discrimination might or might not be consistent with the observed patterns in the data'. Much of that debate centres around one key dilemma: are people choosing those like them or not choosing those unlike them? The study notes that:

> Experimental evidence has shown that the assignment of people to groups, even if totally arbitrary ones and even if they do not last, is sufficient to produce favoritism for in-group members and negativity towards out-group members... While in-group love might not necessarily imply out-group hate, the same factors that make allegiance with group members important provide grounds for antagonism and distrust of outsiders.

In other words, when we recruit, promote or choose colleagues in any way, are we holding to our own or are we repelling borders? Are we, as we saw in Chapter 1 with Michael West and Jeremy Dawson's research on civility, just unconsciously favouring members of our own social groups, recruiting what my mother used to call PLU – people like us? Or are we disfavouring those who are not? The causes of these decisions that we make don't matter to those who are disadvantaged by them. They are still disadvantaged. No one should argue against the data on that. But the causes and drivers of them do matter if we are to intervene successfully to change the results of bias fundamentally and for ever.

This is not just dancing on the head of a social scientific pin, because unless we know what problem we're trying to solve then, rather obviously, we won't be able to solve it. Are we needing to counter prejudice or are we having to haul managers and senior staff out of creating comfort zones where they are all a 'better fit' with each other? It will almost certainly be a mixture of both. Neither are easy to counter, but it would help to understand the proportions of the mix of each in our own organizations and lives in order to design and implement the solutions. George Haigh & Sons denied Mahesh Upadhyaya his house in a crassly explicit way that makes us wince now. But, even if it's more 'politely' expressed nowadays and swathed in the language of unconscious bias, jobs are still being denied to people from Black and Asian backgrounds and to women, to people living with disabilities, or often to people from working class backgrounds. Whether you call bias conscious or unconscious, the data overwhelmingly tells us people from certain groups still don't get the work, the promotion or the house, which is destructive to their careers and their lives, not to mention that it results in organizations missing out on huge swathes of talent.

It wouldn't be sensible to reject altogether the idea that we carry around biases and act on them in ways of which we are not always aware. But if you really examine yourself critically, how 'unconscious' are they? If you reflect deeply on your assumptions you will probably recognize times when you have caught yourself jumping to a conclusion based on a stereotype and a preconception far more quickly than you would have done if you had slowed down, given yourself the time to reflect and made a considered judgement. Or even sought out the advice of someone who has experience of being the object of bias.

People make instant assessments even in the most serious of situations. The 2002 Nobel Prize winner Daniel Kahneman created a framework for understanding how this happens in human thinking and so how to mitigate it. This is probably best known through his book *Thinking, Fast and Slow*, which was published a decade after winning the Nobel Prize, which he shared with another economist, Vernon L Smith. Their citation read, 'for having integrated insights from psychological research into economic science, especially concerning human judgment and decision making under uncertainty' (31).

Thinking, Fast and Slow, despite being an unlikely holiday beach read, has sold over 2 million copies. In it, he introduced the world to the idea of System 1 and System 2 thinking, justifying what he wryly calls their 'ugly names', by saying: 'Why call them System 1 and System 2 rather than the more descriptive "automatic system" and "effortful system"? The reason is simple: "Automatic system" takes longer to say than "System 1"'. In the introductory chapter he explains their interaction:

> I describe System 1 as effortlessly originating impressions and feelings that are the main sources of the explicit beliefs and deliberate choices of System 2. The automatic operations of System 1 generate surprisingly complex patterns of ideas, but only the slower System 2 can construct thoughts in an orderly series of steps (32).

The nub of this thesis is that when we react to the world without sufficient consideration, we are likely to make judgements based on fallacies, commit systematic errors and perpetuate assumptions, and that if we want to avoid doing this and make better decisions, we need to be aware of these biases and work consciously to eliminate them. We make these judgements when it matters and even when it really doesn't. For instance, I began to realize that when I saw a Black guy driving past in an expensive car, I was instantly thinking, 'I wonder who he is?' But when I saw a White guy in a similar car, instead I thought, 'Nice car'. It's a bias based on a stereotype of Black men learned from television and popular culture. But I should be able to realize that and start to challenge my own judgement. The need to confront those knee jerk reactions in the less significant situations is important because, even while in that case they don't impact directly on the man driving past in the car, they reveal a tiny corner of a much larger canvas of bias that you will most likely bring to bear when it really does matter.

That pre-judgement – the etymological origin of 'prejudice' – is exactly that. Calling it 'unconscious' may try to describe how it operates. But it lets you off the hook. As Dr Lasana Harris, a neuroscientist who studies pre-judice and social learning at University College London, said in a 2019 national newspaper week-long feature on 'Bias in Britain', 'the concept of unconscious bias should not absolve people of discriminatory behaviour. If you're aware of these associations then you can bring to bear all of your critical skills and intelligence to see it's wrong to think like that. We all have the ability to control that' (33), or at least to start trying.

Bias is damaging – but it's not a character flaw, it's history

In parallel to the way anti-discrimination legislation has codified a legal disapproval of racism or sexism, or discrimination against gays or people with disabilities, there has developed, particularly in liberal thinking, a distinct inference that holding these kinds of intolerant opinions has a moral dimension for the people and not just the views. You don't just have racial bias or racist thoughts or say racist things, but you are A Racist and thus A Bad Person. This characterizes people in a way that is dangerous because it allows those people who think they are not racist or sexist – and people don't readily admit to either – to think they are Good People, to claim moral value.

But if being anti-racist, and generally anti-discrimination gives you a moral superiority, then how do you face up to the data that tells you your decisions at work have had the same effect as explicitly expressed racism or other prejudices? How do you deal with the fact that in the business you run, the department you manage, there is a steel ceiling against which certain groups of people are endlessly banging their ambition? Well, you can deal with it by calling the bias 'unconscious'. That's a much softer way of describing what is, in its effects, still pervasive prejudice. But you can continue to think you're A Good Person and that racism and sexism and the rest are only practised by certain other individuals because they are Bad People.

This matters when we are trying to effect change, because our beliefs are closely tethered to who we think we are, to our identity. Geoffrey Cohen, a psychology professor at Stanford, in his study 'Identity, Belief, and Bias', wrote that 'People may resist persuasion attempts and reject pragmatic negotiation compromises, because acquiescing to those attempts, or accepting those compromises, would be costly to their sense of identity. Long-held beliefs... can be like treasured possessions that are difficult to give up' (34). To create change at your work you need to try to understand how everyone's biases are linked to who they are, where they have lived, their culture and beliefs, and then find the best way to challenge those views in yourself and in them. Effective challenge needs empathy combined with both awareness and the desire to change. As James Baldwin wrote in his unfinished manuscript of 'Remember This House', 'Not everything that is faced can be changed, but nothing can be changed until it is faced' (35).

However, the difficulty of facing bias is compounded not just by how deep preferences are buried in individuals but also by how profoundly many of them are rooted in history. For instance, the idea of Black and White people being irreducibly separate has a long, dishonourable and profoundly mistaken tradition from the race science arguments of over two centuries ago. Then it was commonly argued among those who called themselves scientists and surgeons that each race was a separate species. In 1799 the prominent British surgeon Charles White published a volume of essays called *An Account of the Regular Gradation of Man*. In it he claimed that, based on the depth of their jaw, size of their skull, length of arms and other physical characteristics, the Europeans were 'the farthest removed from the brute creation' and that the African 'seems to approach nearer to the brute creation than any of the other human species'.

Samuel George Morton, who is said to have founded Physical Anthropology, collected skulls in the first decades of the 19th century. He claimed, using a methodology that in the light of modern scientific methods seems pretty bizarre, that by filling them with lead pellets to measure their capacity he could tell who had the bigger brain. From this curious 'evidence' base he concluded that Caucasians had the 'highest intellectual endowments', Native Americans were 'slow in acquiring knowledge... and fond of war' and that Africans were 'joyous, flexible and indolent' (36). However, to look for a more persuasive underlying reason for these theories, you only have to realize that the Native Americans had, in the not so very distant past, been almost entirely wiped out by the, according to Morton, intellectually very well-endowed Caucasians. And that the 'Africans' were at that time enslaved in the Caribbean, and in the Southern States and many of the Northern States of America, to the considerable economic benefit of White people. We can now see this work not as science, but as a shameful case of self-justification, political and economic, by groups of White people for their unpardonable actions of the enslavement of Black Africans and the slaughter of Native Americans. To stereotype all of the members of each group as 'inferior' and 'brute' was a way of making these crimes justifiable.

While slavery was officially abolished and Black people were set legally free, the stereotypes produced by this pseudo-science persisted, however. Scientific racism, as it came to be known, perpetuated the assertion that Black people were not only a separate race but also less equal in intelligence and ability. Even Darwin's brilliance in establishing that the human race is in fact a single species, couldn't lay them to rest. As the Professor of Psychology from Stanford, Jennifer Eberhardt, says in her book on 'the new science of racial inequality', *Biased*, 'Darwin's radical ideas were quickly accommodated to a racial narrative about blacks that refused to die'. As she documents, the idea of evolution mated with the prejudice of Black inferiority, and produced a damaging and lasting connection in the mind of societies. It lives on, especially in the connection made between Black people and apes.

When the patrol-car computer chats of the Los Angeles Police Department officers were made public as part of the investigations into the beating of Rodney King in 1991, they revealed messages that made precisely that link. One typically read, 'Sounds like monkey slapping time' and another, from one of the officers subsequently convicted of beating King, referred to a Black family being investigated as being 'right out of *Gorillas in the Mist*'. The list of these examples of police 'banter' is pretty long (37). It's not just the police who make the association. In 2011 an elected Republican committee member in Orange County, California, called Marilyn Davenport, sent out a group email with an image posed like a family portrait, of chimpanzee parents and child, with Barack Obama's face superimposed on the young chimp. Underneath she'd written, 'Now you know why no birth certificate' (38). And in 2016 a West Virginian women called Pamela Taylor posted on Facebook the day after Donald Trump's election: 'It will be refreshing to have a classy, beautiful, dignified First Lady in the White House. I'm tired of seeing a (sic) Ape in heels'. She was congratulated by her local Mayor, Beverly Whaling, who liked Taylor's Facebook post commenting: 'Just made my day Pam' (39). These are not isolated examples.

Eberhardt set out to test whether and how much the 'Black-Ape association' persists. In one experiment, she and her colleague, Philip Atiba Goff, a Professor at John Jay College of Criminal Justice, found that 'exposing people to line drawings of apes led them to focus their attention on black faces' (40). They further investigated the connection by adding 'a racial twist to the tried-and-true demonstration of selective attention, the well-known basketball game involving a gorilla'. If you have never seen it, take a look. It's both fun and revealing (41). It was originally designed by Daniel Simons and Christopher Chabris in 1999 and it won them the Ig Nobel Prize in Psychology in 2004, which honours 'achievements that first make people laugh, and then make them think' (42).

In the 30-second clip, six players, three in white shirts and three in black, pass their ball to those in the same colour shirt. The person watching is instructed to count how many times the players wearing white pass the basketball. Towards the end of the clip a person in a gorilla suit enters from the left, walks into the middle of the players, beats her chest, looks into the camera and then exits to the right. At the end watchers are asked, 'But did you see the gorilla?' According to Dan Simons, about half the people who see the video simply don't notice it (43).

The experiment was originally designed to test whether, when focused on one thing, people become blind to other, even very obvious, things. Like a gorilla! What the researchers called 'inattentional blindness'. In their adaptation Jennifer and her colleague wanted to test the ape connection. So they gave participants a list of names to sort through before they watched the video. Half the group was given stereotypically White names: Brad, Frank, Heather, Katie. The other group got stereotypically Black names: Jamal, Tyrone, Nichelle, Shaniqua. Philip concluded, depressingly, that 'when they watched the video, the group given the Black names was much more likely to notice the gorilla… simply bringing to mind African Americans, via the stereotypically Black names, increased the chance that study participants would see the gorilla from 45 per cent to 70 per cent' (44).

In *Biased* Jennifer details endless examples of the way in which the stereotypes of Black people are used against them across the whole range of everyday life, among them: police behaviour in stop, search and arrest; housing; electoral exclusion; the relationship between Black and White actors on TV; the likelihood of being shot by the police; the likelihood of being sentenced to death; house prices in 'Black' and 'White' neighbour-hoods; the estimated size of Black people; feelings of threat by non-Black people and their disproportionate reaction; Black student degree attain-ment; getting an interview let alone getting a job; and the rejection of their résumés.

By investigating and testing the effect of race discrimination in all of these areas of human interaction there is no avoiding the conclusion – which gives scientific confirmation of what most people already acknowledge – that bias has an unnervingly destructive effect on the lives of people of colour. The prejudices they encounter matter to their lives because of the effect. In the same way as they do to the senior women who are thought unlikeable, gay men who are thought too effete for leadership roles, people in wheelchairs who are seen only as that, the Jews whose experience of anti-Semitism that is ignored so often by those who claim to focus on racism. It is of no impor-tance whether prejudice is spoken out loud or involuntarily acted on as a result of the well-learned biases of the perpetrator. Their impact is no less.

The story that this chapter tells about bias and prejudice, the terrible material and personal shocks that it causes to people's lives and its rugged persistence in the face of multiple efforts to shift and eradicate it at work, shouldn't depress organizations into inaction. Biases exist but they clearly can be transformed. We do change. The question is what works in business? From experience and research there are two clear lines of attack.

Engage employees to listen to each other and find solutions

The first step is to stop hiding from responsibility for bias by calling it 'unconscious'. This just shields people from the reality of their own pre-judice. But it doesn't afford those affected by bias that luxury. If you are the object of prejudice, its nature is of little or no comfort. The helpful response to your own bias is not guilt or blame – even if they may be the first port of call for your emotions – but rather the spirit of genuinely heeding and understanding what other's lives feel like. Be curious and listen and start the process of conscious change.

When Reni Eddo-Lodge wrote 'Why I Am No Longer Talking to White People about Race' in 2014, it was because when she and other Black people did talk to them:

> you can see their eyes shut down and harden. It's like treacle is poured into their ears, blocking up their ear canals. It's like they can no longer hear us. This emotional disconnect is the conclusion of living a life oblivious to the fact that their skin colour is the norm and all others deviate from it (45).

So it is with all prejudices that affect a whole range of different people's opportunities at work. Organizations and managers are often deaf to those voices, discounting them as grumbling or self-victimization. So, when someone who is not like you and has a different life experience is telling you about that, don't make them do the work. Don't assume that your norm is their norm. My mother used to describe two kinds of personal taste: her taste and bad taste. Don't be like that.

As crucial as it is to find a way to listen meaningfully to individuals, organizations also need to listen to groups of employees. They tend to do this with staff surveys, with responses calibrated on scales that range from Agree Strongly to Disagree, A–D or 1–5. These can be useful barometers. But, as the best of the practitioners in the field always acknowledge, they need to be analysed with care. As I wrote in the introduction to a report I co-authored with the IPA (the Involvement and Participation Association) in 2015 called 'Diverse Voices' (46):

> Like all good questions the ones that this report investigates were a lot easier to ask than to answer. At their root lay a challenge to an assumption. Employers, with good intentions, are often asking their staff questions about work and the organization and then trying to understand the answers in terms of the large identity groups, the protected characteristics. When in reality people's lives and experiences are far more diverse than that and their group identity bears on their experience of work mainly when there are questions of, on the negative side, persistent bias or, positively, shared cultural or sub-cultural affiliation.
> In other words, go ahead and ask all the staff about their level of satisfaction about the café but be careful of any real significance in the result if statistically you find out that gay people like it less than women.
>
> Of course, if you find out that physically disabled people like it less than able-bodied people, you may have discovered something very helpful about access. But beware using the big categories as if they are always the right tool of analysis and basis for the solutions.

How do we best listen to our employees and understand both their experience in groups and as individuals? You need to be clear when the group is a salient factor in their experience and therefore the right tool of analysis. Then you have to understand their individual situation, ambition and life experience. In the work that we have done at Diversity by Design over the last decade, my business partner, Roy Hutchins, has been the main influence in developing an Insight tool that we have used with organizations in a novel way. A great example of how it works involves a story about shoes and dresses, and a boss and a PA.

We were working in a very sizeable department of a large retailer. Its director was gripped by the need to transform his department to deliver a reorganized set of strategic goals responding to considerable changes in consumer behaviour. He also has young daughters, which by the way is often a significant catalyst for fathers in seeing the value of diversity. As they take in the constant stream of data from across the economy that speaks of gender pay gaps and glass ceilings and the culture that envelops women at work, they look at their girls and realize that these intelligent and talented young women-to-be will more than likely have blocks put in the path of their ambitions in ways that will not happen to their sons or any of the girls' male school friends. That they too will have to face Heidi's trade-off between competence and likeability.

This director had a sense that women in his department were not having a good time at work and asked us to investigate. We used this very simple, yet highly engaging and revealing tool. Everyone in the department was asked to answer five simple open questions and to write down their responses in their own words:

> My individual skills, way of working, personality, background and experience
> (i) are valued in my current team, (ii) would be valued if I went for promotion,
> (iii) mean that I can be ambitious at work. And (iv) as an organization we value
> individual skills, ways of working, personalities, background and experience
> and as a result we have diverse teams that work effectively; (v) my diversity i.e.
> my age, ethnicity, disability, sexual orientation, sex, faith, educational or social
> background – does not act as a barrier to my opportunities and ambition within
> the organization.

We monitored the answers for men and women and for part-time and full-time employees. We then analysed what the respondents had written into four themes: Progression, Culture, Men & Women, Senior Management.

When we took it to the departmental Executive, we just read out the feedback. No actors, no role play. We stopped after each theme and asked them to discuss in pairs or threes, not what they thought, not what should be done about the issues raised, but what they *felt* about what their people had written. As managers they are trained, and by habit they default, to finding solutions. It's what they are good at. But it lessens their engagement. Asking them what they feel is a way of absorbing them emotionally as individual leaders. This is what your people say about working here. You're their leaders, how do you feel about it?

The experience of the women in this department could only be described as 'weary'. There was a sense of resignation shot through all the comments. Drip-drip sexism of the kind that masquerades as banter was rife in the culture. There were some egregious examples of offensive behaviour, but mainly women were putting up with endless remarks about things like their appearance rather about than their work. One woman wrote that her boss commented every day on her dress and her shoes. When we got to the end of reading the section that included her story, one of the exec team raised his hand. 'I am that man... the dress and the shoes... she is my PA'. He was upset. He was brave to volunteer. He never imagined that he was doing anything other than complimenting her. But she didn't experience it as a compliment. There followed a discussion about compliments, which many men find very problematic these days, post #MeToo. But after a while they got the point. A compliment is defined by how it is received not by how it is intended. Our survey revealed that women generally found that these kinds of remarks detracted from them being treated as colleagues. When you read what they had said in response to our five Insight questions, it was clear they wanted men to talk to them about their work, not their clothes; what they did, not how they dressed. If the men wanted to compliment women in the department, they should talk about that.

The result of this discussion was that the director asked his exec to present our Insight findings themselves to the next level of management down. And to identify one habit, one way of talking or behaving on which they wanted to be challenged by anyone in the department. Eventually they drew up a code of conduct. But the important thing was not developing a set of rules. Rather, through really listening and responding emotionally to what their people had to say, they had opened a conversation between all their colleagues about behaviour and language between men and women in order to improve working lives for both.

What matters in these situations is emotional engagement, not just being aware of bias but getting to the stage where you mind about the effect of your behaviour and decisions on others. Organizations need then to offer opportunities to their employees to put that concern into action by focusing on not just endless restatements of the problem but on ways forward. This has become very clear recently in training aimed to prevent sexual harassment, which 40 per cent of women and 16 per cent of men say they have experienced at work. That figure appears not to have changed much since the 1980s. A study in 2020 (47) that assessed whether the programmes to tackle sexual harassment were working, used the measurement of whether fewer women leave as a result of sexual harassment from organizations that undertake such training. It concluded, adjusting for other influences, that when companies create mandatory 'forbidden behaviour' training programmes, the representation of women in management drops by more than 5 per cent over the following few years. The research reveals that this kind of training is mainly flawed for the twin reasons that it is mandatory and it focuses on forbidden behaviours. The message from that is that men need to be forced to pay attention and they need fixing. Once they get defensive, they are less likely to want to be part of the solution. What is needed are actions that engage both men and women in tackling the issue together and that also make women feel safer.

What the research suggests will be most effective are two specific kinds of training: bystander-intervention training and training managers to support those interventions. These have been piloted by the University of New Hampshire's Prevention Innovation Research Center in their Bringing in the Bystander programme. They are based on the premise that those on the course are allies working together with women to solve the problems of harassment and assault rather than just potential perps (48). So, if you see something happen, intervene. Say or do something. The manager training operates on a similar basis. It frames the issues as something that all managers have a responsibility to deal with, whether it's their people involved or another manager's. They are trained to know how to see, intervene and prevent harassment.

Engaging your people like this in a common endeavour to find the solutions is critical. The Old Vic Theatre in London faced allegations in relation to the conduct of their then Artistic Director, Kevin Spacey. The theatre's immediate challenge was that none of these alleged incidents, with the exception of one, had been raised in any way directly with the management.

So firstly they had to investigate and establish what they could from events, all of which were historic. The Executive Director of the theatre, Kate Varah, with the Board made a very particular and carefully considered decision. They avoided any public comment. They did this to underline that something rather obvious was needed to ensure the integrity of any such investigation, but which is too often overlooked in the inevitable social media frenzy that can surround these things, that first of all the facts needed to be securely established. Each case then needed to be dealt with in an appropriate way.

Their next responsibility as an organization was to look to the future and set about creating a change in the culture so that these kinds of incidents would not happen again. Or, if they did, there would be confidence in their people to speak up and a route for them to follow to deal with the situation. As Joanna Down who runs the programme said, 'Our priority was to support and listen to those who had something to say. Then we commissioned a privileged investigation by Richard Miskella, a partner at the law firm Lewis Silkin'.

The theatre, recognizing that this kind of abuse of power was spread across all industries, then originated and developed the Guardians Programme, which is now some 50 organizations strong.

The programme has three stages. The first is a discussion with all the employees, similar to our Insight discussion with the retailer. This is to give them the opportunity to explore the distinction between two kinds of behaviour: actions that are simply unacceptable (or even criminal) and others that make some people feel uneasy, or they think are inappropriate, even when that was not the intention. The first has be agreed on and will often have a clear disciplinary route. The organization needs to be very clear in these cases that they will support people to be heard and that there is a trusted process through which evidence can be looked at and a course of action can be settled upon. An example of the second category in The Old Vic's case might be that the theatre world can be very affectionate and tactile. But not everybody feels at ease with that. To some people it feels distinctly uncomfortable. They need to be able to express that. Whether it's in response to lighter moments or to serious sexism, racism or offensive language, employees need to be able to draw boundaries around colleagues' behaviour.

Having explored those boundaries over several workshop discussions with all the employees, The Old Vic then moved them on to deciding an accepted way of signalling discomfort with someone's behaviour in an everyday situation. They settled on 'OK/Not OK'. It is now part of the way that they all behave with one another. Without either sanction or debate, one person can say to another about their behaviour: 'That's not OK with me.'

Thirdly, they identified Guardians in the organization. These are volunteers, trained to listen. Their role is just that. To listen and, if the person wants to explore options to take the issue further, to advise them what those options are. In these kinds of cases, it can often feel to the person who experienced the unwanted behaviour that the formal process is running away from them. They can end up feeling as if they are standing outside the process, rather like the victim in a court case, watching as the system determines a verdict without reference to them. The presence of a Guardian helps to keep it in their control.

These two examples, our Insight tool and the Old Vic's Guardians scheme, are active and effective ways of engaging your people in a process of meaningful expression and listening to each other. Of exploring differences and understanding differing attitudes and life experiences in order to find solutions together when the stakes are high and prejudices, biases and damaging outcomes for people are ever present. They rely on communicating feeling and experience, really listening and giving an emotional response that can then be transformed into an organizational solution.

Change the context for your people to interact more deeply

Perhaps the most persuasive of all the models that have been developed to inspire change in individuals' habits, views and biases about others is what has become known as Contact Theory. A particularly eye-catching example illustrates rather brilliantly how it can work. In 2017, Heineken produced their 'Worlds Apart' TV advertising campaign (49). They partnered a feminist with someone who described their political views as on 'the new right'; a climate change denier with an environmental activist; and a transgender woman with a man who said 'Transgender is very odd. We're not set up to understand or see things like that.'

Each pair was filmed separately. They were given a flat pack and a set of instructions. Working together they assembled what turned out to be a drinks bar and two stools. Then they were asked to describe to each other 'what it is like to be you in five adjectives' and list three things they had in common. The conversations developed swiftly to the personal. One of the participants said to her pair, 'We know each other better than people who've known each other for ten minutes should.'

They were then asked to watch a video of what they had each said before they met about the key issue on which their opinions were divided. 'Feminism is man hating', said one. His pair said, 'I would describe myself as a feminist, 100 per cent.' 'We're not taking enough action on climate change,' said another, while his pair stated rather firmly, 'If someone said to me that climate change is destroying the world then I'd say that is total piffle.' And so on. Then they were given a choice, they could leave or they could stay and discuss their differences together 'over a beer'. (It was a Heineken commercial after all.) They all stayed and wanted to talk. 'I've enjoyed working with you', said one. 'I've been brought up in a world where everything is black and white', said another, 'But life isn't black and white.' That pair exchanged mobile numbers.

This is not just an ad person's fantasy. The development of the campaign was based on a study led by Goldsmiths University on 'the science of common ground' (50) and a partnership with The Human Library (51), which 'uses conversation to challenge stereotypes' and describes itself as 'a safe space for dialogue'. A 'library of people', they host events where readers can 'borrow human beings serving as open books and have conversations they would not normally have access to'. Every human book from their bookshelf represents a group that is 'often subjected to prejudice, stigmatization or discrimination because of their lifestyle, diagnosis, belief, disability, social status, ethnic origin' and so on.

Originally ideas about contact theory emerged in the 1930s. None of those early researchers were suggesting that you just needed to sit people down and magically they'd join hands and start singing *Kumbaya* together. There had to be some preconditions that would make the process work. One of the first to set them out was Robin Williams Jr in a book called *The Reduction of Intergroup Tensions* published in 1947. He listed 102 propositions under which contact might or might not prove positive. This was refined a few years later by Gordon Allport, one of the biggest figures in social psychology in his book *The Nature of Prejudice*. He slimmed down to four the optimal conditions for an effective improvement in intergroup relations. Prejudice is most likely to be reduced, he argued, when contact entails: equal status between the groups in the situation; common goals; intergroup cooperation; and the support of authorities, law or custom.

There is a feeling of common sense to these. You can see them in the Heineken ad. The participants came together pretty much as equals because they had no prior knowledge of the experiment or of each other or of their contrasting views. They were given the same instructions. Then together they built a flatpack bar. Finally, they were given the opportunity to talk. As a joke, one of the participants pretended to leave. But clearly there was every incentive and gentle social pressure to stay.

Allport's thesis has been much tested. In 2006, Linda Tropp, a contact-theory expert at the University of Massachusetts Amherst, worked with Thomas Pettigrew, a well-known social psychologist at the University of California Santa Cruz. They ran the largest ever study of (all the) studies of contact literature. The results were very positive. They concluded that contact between groups did indeed produce positive reductions in bias and that was even true when just some, rather than all, of Allport's conditions were met. That's largely the case because the four conditions work together and encourage each other. Jesse Singal reported on their meta-analysis, in the *New York Magazine* and quoted Linda as saying that their research suggested that 'every little bit helps, and the more we're able to approach those optimal conditions... that takes us a good part of the way'. It was worth being pragmatic and 'rather than worry about having everything on that checklist, let's do what we can to move in this direction' (52).

The practice of contact theory is not a magic wand. It can go wrong. Members of minority groups can come away feeling patronized or condescended to, even by well-intentioned attempts to reach out by a majority group member. If members of the majority group deny the existence of inequalities, that can stymie progress. Conversely, minority group members may be misled by positive contact with majority group members and so feel less need to work with other minority colleagues to tackle group injustices or inequalities.

Whatever the pitfall in these encounters, though, the evidence is increasing that if people are given the chance to form meaningful relationships across divides through joint efforts in a common cause, there is a good chance that they will open up to the differences in each other, begin to dissolve stereotypical views they have been harbouring and be able to have good conversations not despite their differences, but because of them.

A striking example of how the contact model can achieve change in the interaction between groups was the introduction of civil partnerships in the UK in 2004. Many of those who since then have gone to such 'weddings' – and they are, as was predicted at the time the law was passed, almost always called 'weddings' – may well never have imagined themselves doing such a thing. But what might have seemed strange, unnatural, sinful even to some parents or family members, feels very different when what they actually experience is an event that looks very much like all the heterosexual

weddings they've ever been to. Civil partnerships provided a formal occa-
sion for families and friends to participate and engage in the celebration of
lesbian and gay relationships and of love. The question for the parent or
sibling with rather more old-fashioned views was then no longer, 'Do I
approve of homosexuality', but rather, 'Is my son/brother/sister/cousin
happy?' The opportunity to participate was key to the change in attitude in
the way that endless arguments about the rights and wrongs of same-sex
relationships never could be. Meaningful engagement with people who are
unfamiliar to you, even those about whom you might hold a prejudice, in a
joint enterprise changes your relationship with them. It is the catalyst for a
change in attitude.

There is quite a body of research, particularly in behavioural economics,
that shows that behaviour changes thinking, not the other way around. We
are not rational but habitual. Biases are not decided upon. They are learned
through a process of social osmosis. Towards the end of the 2010s, 'nudge'
became a buzzword as governments sought new ways of trying to change
people's behaviour in society other than just by punishment. It has become
increasingly clear that creating new norms, giving us opportunity and social
backing to change our behaviour, has a powerful effect on changing what
we think. In business that involves engaging your people to collaborate with
those who are different from them so that, by sharing those differences, they
experience unfamiliar framings of the world and hear about different life
experiences, all of which challenge their attitudes through action rather than
through instruction.

At the end of 2012 Bradford's remaining synagogue was facing closure.
The roof leaked and the walls were damaged. They were having to sell up.
But a year later they had won a lottery grant and the renovations were starting. The people who helped them raise the money and make the application
were, surprisingly, Muslims whose Mosque was nearby (53). Their paths
had crossed entirely accidentally. Zulficar Ali owned the Sweet Centre res-
taurant, which was just a few doors away from the synagogue. He was
opposing planning permission for another curry house in the area. He
knocked on the synagogue door to ask Rudi Leavor, the chairman of the
synagogue, for their support.

Over the year other shared connections emerged. Zulfi Karim, secretary
of Bradford Council of Mosques, discovered that the mill where his father
worked after emigrating from Pakistan in the 1960s was run by a Jewish
descendant of Joseph Strauss, the rabbi who founded the Bradford synagogue in 1880. The first conversation, reinforced by the coincidental

historical interweaving of their communities, eventually led to the Muslims helping the Jews to raise money and save the synagogue. Now the two communities have started a new tradition where the Jewish congregation invites local Muslims and Christians to Shabbat, the Friday night dinner. Muslims return the invitation for a Ramadan feast. This all happened not because they sat through interminable training about how they should get on with each other, but because they worked together on something of common interest that was of importance to both local communities. Ten years before, Rudi had taken down the sign on the synagogue because someone leaving had been spat at by two Pakistani men driving by. Now they break bread together.

These are simple stories. If you are curious about life and explore enthusiastically the experiences of others, they will resonate with you and enliven your understanding of difference in a hugely positive way that will lay a basis for challenging and eliminating bias. It will awaken an awareness of your assumptions and create bonds between those you work with that will give you reason to care about the effect of your behaviour or language. The simplicity of these stories can, however, mask the barriers and potential resistance from individuals and from organizations. Changing that requires conscious effort. Because however curious, however adventurous you think you are about others, research and data show that you will so often be driven towards your own – by culture, income, class, sex, sexual-orientation, religion and, yes, comfort. People prefer it and find it easier. Creating teams of difference in businesses requires a determined effort to design those teams and the working environment that will take your people out of that zone to enjoy both the discomfort and, more importantly, the long-term rewards of embracing diversity.

You can harness the Power of Difference to confront bias honestly and equip employees to overcome it effectively by exploring:

- what bias exists in your business even if the social attitudes of your people seem more liberal;
- the effect on the person who experiences bias rather than whether the bias is conscious or unconscious;
- whether your recruitment and promotion suffers from a 'someone like me' or 'not someone like you' bias;
- that Good People can also be biased;

- employees' experiences of bias in their own words rather than percentages and surveys that average it out;
- how you can engage your management colleagues emotionally in the feelings of your people;
- how you test the subjective experience of employees against evidence in order to find a solution that is supported by all;
- how you can create the situations that are most likely to reduce prejudice where contact entails:
  - equal status between the groups in the situation;
  - common goals;
  - intergroup cooperation;
  - the support of authorities, law, or custom;
- how you can give people a safe opportunity to:
  - recognize bias;
  - agree that it is damaging;
  - genuinely want to change it;
  - engage actively to do so.

If it helps, there's an acronym: RAGE.

05

Ditch the superhero

Al-Amarah is a city south-east of Baghdad about 50 kilometres from the Iranian border. One of the final centres of resistance to Saddam Hussein, the British arrived in 2003 but soon came under frequent attack by local militias.

In the early hours of 1 May 2004, a 24-year-old corporal in the Princess of Wales' Royal Regiment was driving a warrior armoured vehicle through the city at the head of a convoy sent to rescue a platoon that was trapped by enemy fire. His vehicle was ambushed and hit six times by rocket-propelled grenades. The platoon commander and the gunner were both wounded and concussed. The corporal, with no means of communicating with anybody or any other vehicles, decided his only option was to drive through the ambush. They were hit again. This time the vehicle caught fire and filled with smoke. So, he opened the hatch and stuck his head out to get his bearings.

Through the fumes, he saw another rocket-propelled grenade heading directly towards him, so he jerked the hatch down with one hand and managed to swerve the vehicle with the other. The blast of the explosion ripped the hatch out of his hand, further wounded the gunner and destroyed the armoured periscope. So now he had no option but to drive the thing another 1,500 metres with his head poking out of the top, dodging bullets, one of which lodged in his helmet. He managed eventually to get to the comparative safety of an outpost and came to a halt. Then, he twice returned to the burning vehicle, while still under fire, to rescue the wounded. Once they were safe, he went back a third time, jumped in and moved it so it couldn't be captured by the enemy. He finally immobilized the engine, disabled the weapon system, activated the fire extinguishers and jumped into another warrior. Where he collapsed.

Just over a month later, on 11 June, he did exactly the same thing all over again. Only this time as the ambush started, he received a serious head injury from a grenade that exploded on the front of his vehicle. But before he passed out, with blood pouring down his face, he managed to reverse out of range, enabling soldiers from the other vehicles to come to the rescue of his crew. He was in a coma for the next five weeks on the edge of life and death. 'No-one thought I'd make it. But, hey, I am here. I've been in pain for six years but life goes on,' he said in 2010. 'Because I've got life.'

The corporal is Johnson Beharry. The details of these two extraordinary acts of heroism come from the citation for the Victoria Cross, which he received on 27 April 2005 (1). In 2011, when I was Chairman of Sussex University, we made him an Honorary Doctor of Engineering to recognize his involvement with our engineering students. Meeting him at the ceremony, what struck me was his steely modesty. Courage of that degree doesn't require boasting. His story carries its own moral authority. Reflecting on that first ambush, Johnson simply said, 'If I stayed there, I was blocking everyone else behind me and the whole platoon was going to die. 30 soldiers. At that point I realized that someone had to lose their life for the 30 soldiers to live. And I decided I was going to take that part.'

We have an enduring need for heroes because they tell a bigger story than their own. They tell us of what we might achieve as human beings, what we might do for each other. But when we hear of their actions, how many of us say to ourselves, 'I couldn't have done that'? We put them outside of our own capabilities. Then we overload them, we endow people who have done heroic things – saving lives or fighting for freedom – with superhuman qualities. I have been lucky enough to meet and spend time with a number of people who are heroic. Among them, two groups stand out: several of the ANC leaders of the struggle against apartheid and some of the trade unionists who were the backbone of the National Federation of Sugar Workers in the Philippines. I first came across them through my involvement in the 1980s with a charity that worked in the developing world.

What struck me was the ordinariness of their lives. These people got up, fed their kids, took them to school, went out and risked their lives and then came back home again. While the mythical heroes of Greek legend or characters in 'Black Panther' are superhuman, the people I have met are not. They are decidedly human. They are us. They just make particular choices in life and through them inspire us to do the same. Their experience may seem out of the grasp of our comprehension, but their individual humanity is not. They dig deep into who they are to rise to a challenge.

Despite this unassuming demeanour of many heroes, we fall easily into hero-worship. This reaches deep into many areas of life. In business, particularly, unreal expectations and power are placed far too readily into the hands of single individuals – the CEO, the tech entrepreneur, the many-millions-of-pounds-super-rewarded chairperson – each of whom apparently 'turned the company round'. Their achievements are set up as super heroic. In so doing all agency is surrendered to them, erasing anyone else's part in the success. In business these superheroes are too easily created. They may inspire, but really they just take all the credit.

The man who coined the phrase 'hero-worship' was the Victorian writer, Thomas Carlyle. Despite the great success of his book about the French Revolution he fell short of cash. So he planned a series of lectures that he called *On Heroes, Hero-Worship, and the Heroic in History* (2). Between 5 and 27 May 1840, at 17 Edward Street, Portman Square in London, his lectures defined 'the hero' into six categories: divinity, prophet, poet, priest, man of letters and king. Had he been writing today, he could propitiously have added a seventh: the CEO – with sub-themes of the vice chancellor, star manager, rugby coach, salesperson of the year, founder of Facebook, Google, Amazon, Uber… you can add your own business idol category.

Carlyle was the foremost proponent of the 'great man' view of human history. Heroes were:

> the leaders of men, these great ones; the modellers… and in a wide sense
> creators, of whatsoever the general masses of men contrived to do or to attain;
> all things that we see standing accomplished in the world are properly the outer
> material result, the practical realization and embodiment, of Thoughts that
> dwelt in the Great Men sent into the world (3).

Carlyle's reputation has not had a great trajectory. It reached its nadir when his ideas became associated with the authoritarian and totalitarian personality cults that brought European civilization to the brink of destruction in the Second World War. In 1945, Goebbels wrote in his diary that Carlyle's *History of Frederick the Great* was Adolf Hitler's chief source of solace during his final months in the Berlin bunker (4).

But, while his notion of the heroic came to be associated with dictators and despotic rule, his idea of the great and good man continues to hold us in its grip. Churchill won the war, Mandela freed South Africa, Gandhi liberated India, Martin Luther King ended segregation. It's shorthand, yes. And it's often not their own view of themselves. But it endures as a lens through which much of society sees achievement. In business it's peculiarly distorting. There will always be extraordinary leaders and brilliant people. But, as Jim Collins said in his now legendary book, *From Good to Great*:

the 'Leadership is the answer to everything' perspective is the modern equivalent to the 'God is the answer to everything' perspective that held back our scientific understanding of the physical world in the Dark Ages... Every time we attribute everything to 'Leadership', we're no different from people in the 1500s. We're simply admitting our ignorance (5).

The 'hero' CEO

In the later 20th century, hero-worship of the all-accomplishing-chief-executive started to become a business story because of Lee Iacocca, the Chairman of Chrysler. His autobiography, published in 1984, was called, with a lack of elaboration but an abundance of ego, simply *Iacocca*. It remained in the *New York Times* bestseller list for 88 weeks. Iacocca was acclaimed by endless column inches, and even more so by himself, as the man who 'saved' Chrysler. Taking over the car company, which was losing over $150 million a quarter, he oversaw the slashing of costs and the launching of new models. He fronted the company's TV adverts ('If you can find a better car, buy it') and negotiated $1.5 billion in loan guarantees from the US government. The company rode high for a while having returned to profitability and popularity.

In a scholarly demolition of both the academic business theories that inflate the myth of the all-achieving leader, and of Iacocca's reputation in particular, Professor Bert Spector from North Eastern University noted that people unanimously acclaimed him as 'a folk hero who had helped lead the United States out of the economic abyss of the 1970s stagflation' (6). But he concluded after examining the data, which many academics and business-people who were swept along on the tidal wave of hero-worship had failed to do, Iacocca's 'success' was not sustained: 'Chrysler quickly fell behind its competitors as the decade continued and faced a second near-bankruptcy crisis in 1991.'

But nonetheless, his brilliance at self-promotion, the albeit not long-lasting but swift revival of Chrysler and the wish-fulfilling adulation of Americans desperate to be rescued from the gloom of the economic slump of the 1970s, made him the point of inflection in the image of the CEO as business superhero. In turn he gave rise to a lineage of such big beasts as Murdoch, Dyson, Branson, Jobs, Musk and, reaching a chilling apogee of empty self-promotion and pointless and destructive vanity, Trump.

This phenomenon of the superhero all-achieving leader pervades organizations and companies still and has filtered down the hierarchy of businesses to create not just the idea of superhero CEOs but superhero managers as well.

Of course leadership matters. But it is not what achieves success on its own and it's of no particular use unless you've got the right people to lead. Jim Collins is now famous for saying in his book that it's who you 'get on the bus' that really matters:

> We expected to find that the first step... would be to set a new direction, a new vision and strategy for the company, and then to get people committed and aligned behind [it]. We found something quite the opposite. The executives who ignited the transformation from good to great did not first figure out where to drive the bus and then get the people to take it there. No, they *first* got the right people on the bus... and *then* figured out where to drive it.

The question, if diversity matters and is going to deliver a dividend, is who are the *right* people? If business follows the superhero route and vests all its faith and expectations in the achievements of single individuals, it logically ends up always trying to appoint and promote 'the best person for the job'. This is a phrase that drives recruitment and promotion. But it does so to the great disservice of businesses. It might seem unarguable that what businesses need is always the 'best person'. But, despite someone's personal brilliance and the manifest skills they may bring to a role, very little is achieved in organizations by someone on their own. People excel when they collaborate. That's how diversity adds strength. It may seem counter-intuitive, but what businesses need is not the best *person* for the job. What they need is the best *team*. What makes a strategy real in a company and puts it into action is deploying the right combination of different types of people, who are led in such a way that they work together effectively, complementing each other in teams and groups.

Business needs to 'ditch the superhero'. Instead it needs the ability of real heroes – in other words your people – to bring, through who they are, their diversity of abilities, backgrounds and experiences to rise to the challenges that face your organization. How do you do that? Whom do you choose? Whom do you combine? And how do you make sure that they are the right combination?

Murderous chickens and open heart surgery

Margaret Heffernan, in her book about the value of collaboration *A Bigger Prize: Why no one wins unless everyone wins*, describes a scary experiment that is a Brothers Grimm-like warning about the dangers of thinking that, in order to get great results, you just need to put the 'top performers' together (7).

She tells of William Muir, who is a geneticist at Purdue University, and his experiment that involved chickens. He observed two sets of birds. The first were the most productive *groups of hens*. The other the most productive *individual* hens. He then watched them for six generations. As Margaret relates:

> The free flocks were still full of plump, fully feathered hens and egg production had increased dramatically over the course of the experiment. But the second group, supposedly a super-group of hens, were shockers. After six generations, only three hens were left; the other six had been murdered. The three survivors were nearly bare of feathers, having plucked each other mercilessly.

Margaret recounts that when a biologist colleague reported the experiment to some of his fellow academics, showing a slide of the ragged super-hens, 'a professor exclaimed, "That slide describes my department! I have names for those three chickens".' Catastrophic results like this are not that uncommon in teams.

The lesson at this point is not about a failure of management, but the stark truth that, as she says, 'collecting outstanding soloists doesn't yield highly productive systems'. Science, which was what Margaret was particularly examining when she used the illustration of the murderous chickens, counter to our popular image of the solo genius, is in fact a highly collaborative exercise. To produce great results you have to 'stand on the shoulders of giants', as Isaac Newton self-effacingly put it. Significant discoveries and advances rely on the cumulative effect of a number of different smaller discoveries and contributions from a range of people working together either in the same place or across different geographies. This is true within teams and also between them.

Stars, the super-achievers, at work are only of any real value to the organization if they are the impresarios of other people's talent. Many of us had great teachers. What marked out the two that I especially remember was the care they took to inspire us in ways that resonated with our ability and enthusiasms rather than with their own cleverness. What made them so motivating was not their brilliance but their capacity to see ours. Their curiosity in us rather than their satisfaction with themselves was what enabled us to shine. To create teams not of superheroes but of collaborators of difference, who behave like those great teachers in recognizing the talents of others, is what serves businesses best. Virtuosity is mostly far richer interacting with an orchestra or a band than it is going its own way solo. People at work who think they are the best rarely know the ways in which they aren't. In life we seek friends and, most fundamentally, a partner or a spouse. We are always almost 'better together' as the phrase goes. Yet at work we can easily forget that. We continue too often to reward people with individual bonuses and incentives, flying in the face of what we know, which is that what achieves the best outcomes – and frequently the most enjoyable times at work – is not knowing something, then asking others and then teaming up and creating something even greater together.

Medicine relies on this kind of deep collaboration and provides us with another eloquent example of how teams, the diversity they embrace and the way they operate, are fundamental to the achievement of success. Not many of you will be involved in open heart surgery – either as practitioners or, I hope, as patients – but this example makes the point eloquently.

As the name would suggest, open heart surgery involves cutting open the chest. It is then levered apart with a rib retractor, named the Finochietto retractor after the Argentinian physician who invented it in 1936. The success rate is high, but the results are painful and the recovery long. A technology company, seeking to reduce both the pain and the length of recovery, developed a process of 'Minimally Invasive Cardiac Surgery' (MICS). Rather than ratcheting open the chest, this technique gives access to the heart through a small incision in the ribs. It changes the standard way of operating quite fundamentally.

Professor Amy C Edmondson, a considerable innovator in the field of collaboration and diversity, for her book *Teaming* researched 16 teams that were adopting MICS to see how successful they were (8). She discovered that what determined their success was not their brilliance (although they all were), nor their status, nor the support from their hospital. Rather, as she says, it was 'differences in how the project was framed by each project leader [which] gave rise to different attitudes about the technology and the need for teamwork'. She describes four examples, two that succeeded and two that did not.

The leaders of the two successful ones recognized that the new technology required a team approach, where 'they emphasized their own fallibility' and that 'without working as a team, the minimally invasive routine would be nearly impossible to choreograph'. Operating in such a small space, through the slit in the ribs, the surgeon required team members to report on data from other monitors and images and thus to treat them as integral to the process. Surgeons are treated as gods in the hierarchy of health services, so leading like this is somewhat counter to that tradition. But working together in a way that underlined how much the team was dependent on each other was crucial for the new technology's success. She quotes one of the leaders of the two effective teams as saying, 'The whole model of surgeons barking orders down from on high is gone. There is a whole new wave of interaction.'

In contrast, the approach and attitudes of the leaders of the two teams that eventually had to abandon the adoption of MICS, 'communicated that other team members were not playing a significant role in implementing the new technology'. One framed the exercise as simply a new technological approach and saw only the need to 'train the team'. And the other sounds like he was built to the specification of the old fire spitting chief surgeon from the *Doctor in the House* movies of the 1950s, Sir Lancelot Spratt. Amy quotes one of the nurses involved in his team being told, 'he was the captain of the ship, he's the chairman and that's how he runs the show'.

The significance of the leadership in the two successful projects was the recognition that the input of the people who were non-surgical was none-theless crucial in a surgical procedure. They were constantly communicating 'to assess and guide placement of surgical components during the [new form of] surgery'. They were fully empowered to voice observations and con-cerns. As Amy says, a noteworthy contributor to the success in implement-ing MICS by those teams was that 'other participants besides the lead surgeon were viewed as partners, valued teammates, and essential resources for overcoming new challenges'. To lead a project to success you must value the different contributions that all the members of the team can make to its success and also tell them that you do. Valuing difference matters to the efficacy of teams.

Complexity needs diversity

In the last decades, as organizations and businesses become increasingly global and complex, there has been a huge upswing in team working. In 2016, in a piece called 'Collaboration Overload', the *Harvard Business*

Review estimated, according to data the researchers had collected over the past two decades, the time spent by managers and employees in collaborative activities has ballooned by 50 per cent or more (9).

This is not surprising when you look at what managers and colleagues are having to face. Flicking through some recent job sites for managers and picking a random sample, people at work right now can be faced with anything from understanding the brain or creating robots, to designing and managing complex supply chains, managing logistics (often in the face of intemperate expectations about the speed of delivery of products ordered online), understanding and delivering on the increasingly pervasive internet of things, tackling climate change technologically (let alone politically), developing or implementing or just working within new global legal frameworks for regulating and holding international companies accountable, to reducing obesity in rich countries and hunger in poor ones.

Then, most recently, has been added the global experience of trying to understand, contain and cure, or at least vaccinate against, a pandemic infection and simultaneously care for those who got sick and do that under the extraordinary pressures that health workers in hospitals have experienced. And for those of us confined to our homes we've all had to discover how to carry on working in entirely new ways in wholly different circumstances. Managers have simultaneously had to learn at lightning pace to manage in this completely changed landscape. The complexity of all this is bewildering. The speed of change is exhilarating.

It seems axiomatic that no one person, no one group of people, at work can possibly understand or solve these issues of the modern world on their own. They demand combinations of knowledge and skills, insights from growing up in different contexts and backgrounds, diverse identities that shape what people know, overall a range of lived experiences and different approaches to problem solving. Scott E Page makes the observation, next to what he confesses is an 'incomprehensible' diagram titled 'Obesity Knowledge Structure', that the disciplinary understandings required to confront that epidemic cross 'economics, nutrition, physiology, sociology, biology, media studies, advertising, transportation and infrastructure, and genetics' (10).

All of these are big ticket issues and may feel a long way from our everyday grasp. But their complexity will touch many aspects of work through interactions with technology, supply chains, changing expectations and demographics of customers and the nature of the sectoral and industry challenges and so forth. This will be the case whether what you do is: organizing nursing capabilities in a brand new hospital; aiming to close the gap between mental health provision and Black people in the UK, a well-researched flaw in current provision; re-booting a building society's offer to compete digitally in a ferociously cut-throat financial services sector; building a new drought prevention pipeline; aligning services in a local authority so it can provide access to support for people and local businesses to fulfil their potential; developing the breadth of lived experience in TV commissioning teams to find the stories that describe the Britain of today; or recruiting the breadth of lived experience and technical skill to create artificial intelligence algorithms that without bias reflect accurately the range of human experience and identity.

All of these are among the challenges that, even in our pretty small operation at Diversity by Design, we have worked on with our clients and their people over the last few years to produce diversity-based solutions. The changed context of their work now requires organizations consciously to create a combination of difference in their teams to meet the shifting demands of transforming markets, sectors, supply chains and consumers combined with technological disruption, the pressure to decarbonize and shifting global trade patterns.

Putting together these teams requires very significant focus. Who would ever just throw ingredients into a pan without thought and expect a great meal? Recipes are there for a reason. Cooking is alchemy. It turns base metal into gold. In order to do so, recipes specify the relative proportion of ingredients, the order of preparation and the right length of time for cooking. The ingredients alter when combined to produce something more than the sum of the parts. Diversity is a similar alchemy. So why would creating teams at work need any less focused consideration? Why would you not want to spend time creating the right recipe of people to achieve your organization's or department's goals? Why would you not want to understand exactly how to achieve the dividend that can come from the right kind of diversity?

Creating diversity doesn't happen accidentally

In starting to build an approach to reap these dividends it's important to recognize something most pithily put by Scott E Page, 'a person cannot *be* diverse, but a person can *add diversity*'. Diversity is not a quality, it's a function. How many times have you heard people say, 'We've got several diverse candidates.' Actually, what they usually mean is that they're interviewing some Black or Asian people. In so saying though they are reinforcing the idea that diversity is about adding minorities. The baseline is White and male and straight, so Black people, women and gays are 'diverse'. This way of thinking needs to shift, because to create diverse teams and get the bonus from that, you need to create a mix. You need to bring together the people who can bring a new perspective, a different background, a fresh approach to problems and combine them with others in the team to create new solutions. You are not adding 'sparkle' to the norm, you are changing it.

Scott defines what we bring to work as 'repertoires' and sub-divides them into: information, knowledge, tools, representations and frameworks. And from that he concludes that: 'A team's diversity can be measured by the lack of overlap in members' repertoires.' Therefore measuring someone's rightness for a team requires you to know what range of 'repertoires' the task requires, which of those repertoires are already covered in the team and therefore which you need to add. At Diversity by Design we call this 'The Virtuous Circle of Selection'. *What is the team for? What's the job for? What combination of difference would enhance the team's ability to achieve what it's for? Who have you got? So, who do you need to add to fulfil what the team is for?*

It is important at this point to note something quite crucial. Diversity bonuses are not possible for all tasks or in every situation. There are some tasks that are just not amenable to these bonuses because of the nature of the task itself. For instance, flipping burgers is not the kind of thing that improves the more diverse the group of people doing it. There may be a great deal more fun to be had at work if you're in a really mixed bunch, and even a social dividend from gaining greater knowledge about different cultures or finding friendship or romance across different identities. But there is no improvement in the speed or efficiency of the cooking and handing over of the burger and the bun and the fries that comes from a group of employees that embraces a range of ages, both men and women, gays and straights, a mix of ethnic backgrounds or of skills and attitudes to problem solving. Similarly, some operations simply need the combination of 'the best'. Like a relay team. To create the fastest team, you just need the four fastest runners. That's it. There is no extra benefit to their race time from any of them adding some kind of diversity.

So far, so clear. There are tasks that are capable of delivering a bonus from diversity and there are those that are not. You need to know which is which. Scott divides the types of jobs people do into four categories: manual routine (burger flipping), manual non-routine (care working), cognitive routine (sales) and cognitive non-routine. The last category is where the greatest diversity bonuses arise. These are lawyers, scientists, financial analysts, managers of organizations and teams, people who solve technical problems, people leading HR and organizational development, programmers and the like. In the modern economy this is the fastest growing category of jobs (11). These are the people involved in designing and managing how to tackle the kinds of issues I listed earlier. The reason that the teams of these people require diversity is because the complexity of challenges they face is increasing and therefore the range and amount of knowledge needed to do them simply cannot be acquired by one person. As Scott says, 'Any one person can master only a small slice... Even the most accomplished person relies on outside help. That outside help need not be smarter, but it must be diverse. It must possess different knowledge or skills to add value.'

Professor Katherine W Phillips, who wrote an interestingly provocative commentary at the end of *The Diversity Bonus*, expanded that argument in an important way when she tackled the question of the benefits that flow from *identity* diversity. The first is that 'identity is a source of *cognitive* diversity' (12). In other words what you know is to some significant degree shaped by who you are, by your life experience. How you see the world is formed not by just what you learned but where and how you learned it.

When I have spoken at conferences, I often ask women to raise their hands if they have taken maternity leave and returned to work after having their children. Many hands go up. I then ask them whether, when they came back, in effect the organization asked them, 'What have you forgotten?', for instance by providing lots of 'catch-up' opportunities. Most hands stay up. But perhaps a much better question for organizations and businesses to ask these returning mothers is: 'What have you learned... about priorities, time management and stress?' After a recent event where I asked these questions, a woman came and told me her story. She had twins who were six. After she had gone back to work, she said that her career had skyrocketed. She explained, without in any way being flippant or dismissive, that she now 'managed everyone as toddlers'. She said that what she had learned from being a new mother was exactly what she needed to know in order to respond to her high-performing and demanding team. Being a mother of twins taught her how to manage demands on her time, when to realize that one of her team was really needing attention and when it was just a squall at sea, how she now prioritized things at work even more effectively than before and how to balance her personal and work life to greater effect than ever. All of this came from her being a new parent.

She had learned it much more effectively through coping with young children than through thousands of pounds being spent on training courses or MBA modules. I now suggest to managers that when a woman takes maternity leave, they ask her to capture what she feels has changed in her view of work, so that when she returns she can have a conversation about what she has learned rather than just what she needs to catch up on. What makes her and her experience so valuable is what she will bring to the business through being a mother that is new. It's not just what the business can give her but what she can give to the business. Lived experience can enrich people's ability to work and thus a business's level of performance, often more so than technical skills.

The second benefit that Katherine identifies is that 'simply seeing differences on the surface makes people assume that there are more cognitive differences there in the group, prompting them to seek out this information'. The very presence of people different from each other, if they are curious and open, will remind them that their framing of the world is theirs and is not the same as everyone else's. How you organize your view of the world depends on who you are. Difference in a team opens up opportunities to question and explore goals and the routes to their achievement by making you aware that those goals and solutions look different when seen through someone else's eyes.

This is an urgent reminder of how people need to be triggered out of their desire for similarity with others. What Professor Sheen Levine of the Naveen Jindal School of Management calls 'the siren call of sameness' (13). As General Patton is reported to have said, 'If everyone is thinking alike, then somebody isn't thinking.' If you are too similar on a Board, in an Executive team or in a department leadership, you are more likely to share blind spots and collude with each other in groupthink. What you need is difference of approach around the same table, in the same room, at the same time, listening to, responding to and building on each other's ideas.

The sameness often comes not from being all men or all women for instance, but from the fact that you may all – Black, White, female, male and so on – have very similar experiences if, say, you're all graduates, or you all, despite your origins, now consider yourselves middle class. Or if you're all heterosexual, married and have children. Of course you're not all the same, you're all individuals. But unless there is a conscious effort to discover the differences between you, it is easy to slip without challenge into the same framework in which to see and analyse the challenges you face.

It's good business to be nosy: so, go on,
find out the differences between you and others

At the start of sessions with management teams or Boards, I ask them to talk in pairs and 'to identify two or three differences between you that come from your background or identity and which affect the way you work and the contribution you make'. The conversations are very revealing. Some recent examples are:

> I've worked with him for 12 years and I had no idea that his father was a single parent, which was very unusual when he was a child. I had no idea that it had affected his passion for change so much.

and:

> When I came to this country, my father was a diplomat for Pakistan, so I led a very comfortable life. But X, who I was paired with, came here from the same part of the world as me but with no money at all and was poor till she managed to get to university. We are passionate about the same things but we see life chances very differently.

Sometimes, it's that one person grew up in care, their pair in a stable and comfortable family. Other times it's just that they come from different parts of the UK and being Scottish, Irish, from Yorkshire, from a city, from the country has in each example had a different and often profound impact on the way they see the world and their work. What has now ceased to surprise me, as people say it so frequently, is that often they have simply never had these conversations with each other and that, now they have, they feel a door has opened for them to work better together because they know a bit more who the other person is, how they each work differently and what motivates each of them.

This is borne out by the research that Katherine Phillips and two other academics, Margaret Neale and Gregory Northcraft, did when they conducted an experiment, which sounds fun to have been involved in (14). They set groups of three people – some with two White and one Black person and some with all White members – a murder mystery to solve. The groups had a shared set of information and then each member was given something that only they knew. So they had to share clues with each other in order to solve the crime. The groups with racial diversity significantly outperformed the mono-racial teams. They got the answer right 75 per cent of the time while the homogeneous groups only managed 54 per cent. Significantly they had very different experiences. The more successful groups had far more debate and discussion and felt exposed much more to the complexity of the case.

Samuel Sommers from Tufts University made a similar discovery in his studies of racial diversity on jury decision making (15). He compared two groups of jurors, one with six White jurors and the other with four White and two Black jurors. He found that 'white jurors in diverse groups raised more novel case facts, had fewer factual inaccuracies in their discussion of the case, and identified more missing evidence during the deliberation than whites in homogeneous juries'.

In another experiment Katherine Phillips discovered a number of significant behaviours that flow from identity diversity or the lack of it. She found that people assume there is more likelihood of agreement if they are in a group of similar people because they don't think to look for the differences. They are also more irritated by disagreement from people who are like them when they are in a homogeneous group. However, if the group is more diverse then a member of a majority identity is more able to express a dissenting view.

Further studies have shown that these effects are not just exhibited in relation to race but to a wide range of other differences. The key insight from the research on this is that, as Katherine says, 'Simply adding social diversity to a group makes people believe that differences of perspective might exist among them and that belief makes people change their behaviour.' When it comes to diversity seeing really is believing in the possibility of other worldviews. It opens you up to curiosity about the way other people frame issues and problems. Identity not only clearly produces cognitive diversity, but the presence of difference in a group enhances people's awareness of it. The issue is how, when you see difference, you can respect, enjoy and value it and combine it to practical use.

Stoves, codes and bankers: how diversity saved cooks, almost won the war and could have prevented the crash

For thousands of years women have been cooking on 'three stone fires' using wood or anything else that will burn. As Caroline Criado Perez points out, this is disastrous for their health because of the fumes (16). They are exposed 'in an unventilated room to the equivalent of more than a hundred cigarettes a day'. Because of the inefficiency of these stoves, women are subjected to these fumes for 3 to 7 hours in 24, 'meaning that, worldwide, indoor air pollution is the single largest environmental risk factor for female mortality'.

There have been multiple attempts to tackle this issue. Most of them however have been about trying to change the stoves women cook on or the kind of fuel they use. All the attempts ended in failure with the women abandoning the whizzy 'High Efficiency Cookers' (HECs), going back to their three stones and continuing to inhale the equivalent of five packs of Marlboro a day.

Finally, the people in one field study in India in 2015 decided to increase the repertoire of tools that were being used to solve the problem. They widened the diversity of the people involved in tackling the issue. But they didn't employ more people to do this. Instead they did something which, on reflection, you might think falls into the category of the staggeringly obvious. They talked to the women doing the cooking.

The solution that emerged was not to fix the women by urging them to use different types of stove, or getting them to chop wood or use different fuels altogether. But, with the advice of the women, to fix the stove. They came up with a simple and original solution. It is called a *mewar angithi*, an uncomplicated metal device that was 'engineered to be placed in a traditional chulha in order to provide the same airflow mechanism… as occurs in the HEC stoves' and redirect the fumes. Furthermore, it's made from scrap metal and so is very cheap. That way the women could continue to cook in the way that they wanted but without the damage to their health or to their working day by having to chop more wood or gather different fuel. This long-sought solution came through, what an academic study might call, 'the diversity bonus of adding an identity-based perspective'. In other words, getting another person's slant on the problem.

Differences of identity and in the range of disciplines in a team underpin the likelihood of reaping a diversity dividend. The founding inspiration of Sussex University, Asa Briggs, was a code breaker in the Second World War. The first of his family to go to university, he graduated in history from Cambridge in 1941 and joined the Royal Corps of Signals. Not long after his 23rd birthday he was recruited to Bletchley Park, the Allied code-breaking centre. The breaking of the German's Enigma Code was a process of inspiration combined with dogged, methodical work and, remarkably, was kept an absolute secret by all the people who achieved such a notable contribution to winning the war for the statutory 30 years until the 1970s. When they did tell their stories it emerged that these code-breakers were an idiosyncratic mix of men and women with an unsuspected range of intellectual disciplines. This was key to their ability to identify and decode the 'cribs' in the Enigma. Cribs are the repeated sections of text that code-breakers anticipate will be included in the signals that they are intercepting. As Asa remarks in his book, *Secret Days*:

> Historians could make excellent 'cribsters' since they were usually well-read, drawn to lateral thinking and taught to get inside the mind of people totally different from themselves... They were capable of imagining what their German opposite numbers were like by tracking their habits and styles... Many what might be thought of as 'hunches' were genuine insights (17).

Cracking codes is not just a 'technical' or mathematical challenge. Despite the scientific brilliance of Alan Turing and the others who paved the way for modern computing through their ground-breaking work at Bletchley, what was also required were insights from other disciplines.

Breaking codes is about spotting the cribs and then having that 'hunch' as to what they might mean. That way you can start to assign letters to regularly occurring words and phrases and begin to understand the code. As Asa recounts, 'Germans liked to incorporate the names [and] ranks... of the senders and receivers', almost always signing off with 'Heil Hitler'. Through familiarity with German military jargon and the communication habits of the operators, it was the historians and other non-mathematicians who were able to see that the patterns were peculiar to German and Nazi style and routines – this constant use of rank, for instance, and the robotic repetition of Heil Hitler. With that information the mathematicians could then compare the 'cribs' and, using Turing's mechanized invention called the 'bombe', do it at vastly increased speed and capacity. It may overstate the case, but while diversity didn't win the war on its own, it made a pretty significant contribution. An example of social and intellectual exuberance trumping the fascistic illusions of those who believed in mono-cultural supremacy and a master race.

For there to be the possibility of a diversity dividend, the problem has to be complex and the diversity of the team complementary. The members have to add difference not similarity. A few years after Lehman Brothers collapsed in 2008, one of the precipitating events in the global crash, Christine Lagarde, head of the IMF from 2011, commented, 'As I have said many times, if it had been Lehman Sisters rather than Lehman Brothers, the world might well look a lot different today' (18). She was taking the not unreasonable view that the banking industry was too dominated by one group of people (remember the FTSE 100's John, David, Andrew and Michael). But her comment, while rhetorically useful, contained a flaw. What would possibly have made a difference is if the bank had been not just Lehman Brothers or Lehman Sisters but Lehman Brothers *and* Sisters. Once again it would have been a combination that could have delivered the dividend.

It's not men per se that create the groupthink, when it occurs, within banking and industry. It's the preponderance of men. More significantly, it's not the fact that they are men, it's the likelihood that people who get to the top – who mostly are men – and dominate Boards and Executive committees typically inhabit the same networks and have had almost identical training, career paths and routes to the C-Suite. Groups like that are not so much 'the best' as they are 'the same' and so run the considerable risk of always sharing similar approaches to framing problems, approaching challenges and seeing solutions. It is that which leads to groupthink, to a blinkered view of possible risks, and the fact that, as The Queen politely enquired of an economist at the LSE, after reportedly losing £25m of her personal wealth in the crash, 'why did no-one see it coming?' (19).

However, just adding women isn't enough on its own. Many of the women who are considered 'eligible' are likely, in terms of training, approach to finance and banking, and their route to the top, to be more of the same. But it is a start. As we have seen, at least the presence of difference in groups alerts their curiosity and makes a material change in their perception of what is possible and of how to seek out what they don't know. In order to achieve this kind of team composition, where difference is seen, valued and deployed, you need to make some quite fundamental changes to the way businesses and organizations put them together – the way you recruit and promote people.

The Virtuous Circle of Selection

So let's return to The Virtuous Circle: What is the team for? What's the job for? What combination of difference would enhance the team's ability to achieve what it's for? Who have you got? So, who do you need to add to fulfil what the team is for? As Scott E Page's research shows, the logic of the diversity bonus, where each person has to bring difference, means that 'no [single] test can be applied to individuals so that we are guaranteed to select the most creative group'. Furthermore, he says, 'we cannot evaluate

people individually and determine an optimal group'. This is a quite fundamental change to the idea that one, apparently 'objective' test will, when
used across all appointments, guarantee the best choice of people. High
performing teams need individuals who are different from each other. You
need to construct recruitment and promotion along that principle. There is
a key assumption that underpins this. All recruitment is relative. Every time
you do it you need to decide whom you invite to apply, what you value in
the candidates who do and on what basis you choose the successful one.

To follow this through and demonstrate how a new approach would
work I am going to use 'selection' to cover both recruitment and promotion
and 'team' to cover all groups of people who work together – whether that
means an Executive team (at organization or department level), a permanent team or one brought together around a specific project. They do all
have different dynamics. But the new process of selection is driven by the
same underlying principles. You can then adapt the illustration to your
specific situation. The process is called 'Recruiting for Difference' – RfD.

What's the team for?

When Diversity by Design has asked managers to discuss 'what their team is
for' – what it's in business to achieve – it often feels like the question is a
welcome relief for them from the unremitting pressure of the day-to-day.
Many of them enthusiastically welcome having even just a small amount of
time to reflect. The targets and objectives that they have been set are very
often short term, almost abstract, rather than related to any overarching
purpose for the business. So some managers even seem to have forgotten the
long-term point of what they are doing, it's been such a while since anyone
asked them what it was or gave them the impression that it mattered. Despite
their enthusiasm for the question, they occasionally look temporarily
stumped. They need time to regroup and gather their thoughts. Others jump
straight in with articulate enthusiasm. One of these was a senior manager in
a water company we worked with. I won't say which as the example I am
going to give you touches on regulatory issues that you will know, if you've
ever worked in a utility, are very delicate. But I can tell you they were working on a sizeable infrastructure project involving several hundred kilometres
of pipeline.

When I first met him, I fell into the trap of making an immediate assumption about him. I thought, 'Here's a classic middle-aged, male engineer who

won't be at all interested in diversity and is only here because the HR director made him come and he thought he ought to show willing.' Even if you spend every day thinking about diversity, it is still far too easy to make instant judgements based on personal bias. The only thing you can do is to be constantly on the alert and check your assumptions as fast as you can. I did and discovered how wrong I was. He was the most thoughtful of managers.

He had coined this phrase to describe the work on the project: 'If we *don't* build a pipeline we'll have failed. But, if we *only* build a pipeline, we'll also have failed. This is a "change" project.' Water companies are regulated in what they borrow, what they can spend and what they can charge the customer. Their margins come, therefore, while delivering water as safely and as economically as possible, from the ways they can innovate, mainly through technology, their products, processes, planning and implementation. For instance, these days, instead of building a pipeline and then effectively making a 'snagging' list, they build the pipeline virtually, stress test it virtually, iron out the bugs and only then build it for real. The manager was clear therefore that what he needed in his project management team was not just their technical skills but, even more importantly, their ability to innovate. The discussions we had about recruiting them led to him describing a combination of difference, grounded in his desire to put innovation at the centre. One part of the recruitment advert read:

> We are clear that this Leadership Team will only build the pipeline and make the change we want if it has a combination of people with different personal and professional backgrounds, approaches and life experiences. So are you someone who really takes to heart that the more diverse we are in our backgrounds, identities and ways of working, then the harder we will need to work to understand and listen to each other and therefore the better and more original the decisions we will make?
>
> So we are looking for a combination of people with different technical skills and approaches to work that come from both your professional and life experiences (whether the latter are because of your sex, your ethnicity, that you live with any kind of disability – visible or not – your sexual orientation, class background or education), and from the particular route to success at work you have followed.

Expressing who he was looking for in this way came in part from a conversation in which he and the others in the room had shared the experience of two engineers they worked with who had very different routes into engineering. One had left school and had worked their way to the top of their profession through first being an apprentice. The other had taken the graduate path. Apparently, they argued frequently about approaches and solutions. Our client said that as long as he could ensure that their disagreements were calm and constructive, it was the best partnership he had in his department. In short, a combination of different backgrounds, in this case education and probably class, led to an engineering dividend. It's not just what you know, it's how you learned it.

The thing that is striking about so many of these discussions is how little time managers seem to have to reflect. They are driven by their diaries. The demands on them are constant. It must be a certain sort of hell because they are so often forced just to react rather than shape what they do in terms of a larger purpose for their team in the business. This is despite the fact that, while thousands of pounds have often been spent on developing 'strategies', 'missions' and 'values' in companies, too often managers' performance is still judged by senior leaders against top-down targets that do not reward the longer-term achievement of any of those higher-minded 'strategies', 'missions' and 'values'. That militates against progress because just setting targets for diversity that are divorced from its purpose in the business drives tokenism and disappointment. A change in this approach can't come too soon because leading people by developing a common purpose is crucial to them embracing diversity as an approach to talent. In the situations where diversity can deliver a bonus it can only do so when that common purpose is defined. Only then will you have a chance to analyse exactly what differences you need to fuse together in the team in order to realize its goals.

What's the job for?

We are often faced with a similar experience when we ask managers what the job is for? Not what it was for last time they recruited it. But what it requires now in *this* context, for *this* team to achieve *this* set of objectives. Over the years working with clients I have read many, many job descriptions. More often than not they consist of pages and pages of unintelligible bureaucratese that has accumulated as a result of arid hours spent around negotiating tables compromising on issues like grading and salary spines. It is surprising how little they tell anyone about what the job actually requires. Oddly what job descriptions very rarely do is to describe the job. Likewise, the person specification frequently, for example, asks candidates to be 'good communicators', 'able to work well with others', 'able to be proactive in taking decisions' and 'demonstrate an adherence to the values of the organization'. These kinds of phrases so lack definition that they brook very little contradiction and don't give you much of an idea about who you really are looking for.

Not only do the job description and person specification not usually tell a candidate – or the recruiting managers – much about the job, but they are rarely altered in any significant way between recruitments. But if you are following the logic that there is 'no single test' and that all recruitments are relative to the team, then it will pay to spend some time considering what you will need the successful applicant to do at this precise moment, in this set of circumstances, for this particular one of your teams. Taking time also challenges one of the great enemies of diversity – the desire of managers to want the recruitment to happen yesterday. It's never quite clear why this is so often the case. It feels that perhaps demonstrating this kind of urgency makes them and what they are doing seem more decisive, more urgent, more important. But speed is no help when you are trying to think clearly.

One of the NHS Trusts we work with built a new hospital, bringing all its services into one location. One of the divisions wanted to recruit a Head of Nursing. In the session we had with them they started to talk quite conventionally about who they wanted. 'Experienced nurse', 'a number of years in leadership', 'specialist in their field'. The conversation changed tone when we asked them what the job was for in this new context? They started to talk about the excitement of the new hospital, how bringing all the various functions, clinical and non-clinical, under one roof would open up new ways of working, how there were possibilities for more integration in the way clinical and non-clinical colleagues worked together towards the common goal of the patients' needs.

They fast realized that, of course, they wanted a skilled nurse. That wasn't the main point. The emphasis of the role in these new circumstances was not just about a high level of nursing skills, but all about a certain quality in their ability to lead. For the advert they came up with a distinctive phrase: 'You will need to both stabilize and innovate'. They emphasized that 'our people have been through a sustained period of change leading to our move to the new hospital'. So the Trust was 'really interested, not just in your clinical excellence, but also your ability to lead people by understanding their feelings and their situation and taking them with you to embrace this change and enjoy the responsibility of making it all work brilliantly for the patient'.

They set the clinical standard they wanted. But the emphasis of the role was on their ability to lead successfully through change. This process is not dissimilar to what many employers sometimes call 'values-based recruiting'. However, the main difference is that, in shifting the emphasis of what the role requires from candidates' 'technical' skill towards their personal capabilities, they should not be assessed against a generalized set of 'values', but against a quite specific list of what is required of them personally in the particular context and that particular role.

What combination of difference enhances team performance? Or why more diversity keeps us safer in our beds

This is where the idea of recruitment being relative starts to be made operational. We've established that a dividend from the diversity of teams is possible but not guaranteed. We also saw that, nonetheless, the mere presence of difference adds to a team's ability to think freshly, frame differently and be more dissenting with each other. To reap those benefits of diversity you do need to discuss and agree how the achievement of the team's objectives can be enhanced by diversity and by what type of diversity.

In order to answer that you need both Scott E Page's 'repertoires' – information, knowledge, tools, representations and frameworks – on the one side of the ledger and, on the other, a diversity of identities. These overlap because the research – and personal experience – tells you that the repertoires, what you know and how you apply it, is influenced by who you are and the life experience you've had. In academic terms, cognitive diversity is influenced by identity diversity. Diversity should be understood as being about both *who* you are at work and *how* you are at work. It is your style and approach (repertoires) and your identity – not just the box you tick, but what you bring through who you are. Like the mother of the twins.

Working in GCHQ is a curious experience. You are both cut off from the outside world because you have to surrender your phone, laptop, iPad and any other electronic devices, yet at the same time you are in a place that is more connected to the wider world than probably anywhere else on earth. We used to start every session we did with them by saying, 'if greater diversity in GCHQ will not lead to us sleeping in our beds more safely tonight, then please will you go back to your desks and spend your time more usefully defeating the threat of terrorism'. We meant it. In reply they were very clear. They considered that diversity was crucial to their ability to keep the UK safe from threats. And they meant it.

They have the largest digital spy system in the world, a product of collaboration after the Second World War between the UK, the United States, France and later, somewhat ironically perhaps because of GCHQ's origins in Bletchley Park, Germany. In their IT division they need employees whose history and longevity in the organization give them the understanding to keep that system working. In addition, because terrorism is mostly cooked up and communicated these days in deep and to most of us inaccessible parts of the Web, they need people who have the skills to challenge and adapt GCHQ systems to penetrate that. The combinations of 'repertoires' they need are broadly consolidation and disruption – two very different approaches to IT. They also need, as Bletchley did, to engage colleagues who have a range of intellectual and analytical frameworks, including a profound understanding of the countries from where the threat of terrorism emanates and of the cultures, languages, religions, ideologies through which it is expressed. They also have to be British citizens. To protect us and the UK they need a combination of who and how. They need diversity to equip their technological weapons against terrorism, not only so they can penetrate the complexity of information they are required to analyse but also to give them the insights they need to understand the enemy and how they are planning their attacks.

The consequences of a team without these differences could be seen when 9/11 happened. The Americans, and especially the CIA, were not only shocked and scared but they were deeply traumatized by the fact that they had been invaded, their 'second Pearl Harbor' as one security expert put it. Furthermore, they had been attacked by terrorists who were led by a man with a beard, dressed in simple clothes and issuing threats from a cave. As Richard Holbrooke, one of President Clinton's most senior officials exclaimed, 'How can a man in a cave out-communicate the world's leading communications society?' Easily. Because, as Matthew Syed pointed out, to the US security services Bin Laden seemed the essence of backwardness. But his simple clothes showed that he modelled himself on The Prophet; since Mohammed's vision of the Koran happened in a cave, caves are holy places; and Bin Laden frequently communicated to his followers in verse, which to them is a holy form (20).

As Matthew says, 'the very images that desensitized the CIA to the dangers of Bin Laden were those that magnified his potency in the Arab World'. The dearth of diversity in background and cultures, verified by the CIA's own diversity data that showed just how White and Protestant and male it was, is one of the factors that prevented it from having the collective insight to see the threat. In 2017, Carmen Medina, a former deputy director in the CIA who worked at their HQ in Langley for 32 years, put her finger on it, 'The CIA has not met its own diversity goals. If the composition of the US national security community is such that almost everyone has one world view, we are not in a position to understand our adversaries and anticipate what they are going to do'. Matthew pungently summed it up, 'The CIA were individually perceptive but collectively blind'.

It's not enough to be clever as an organization. Lived experience is often a more insightful tool for understanding how to approach a challenge than a university degree. The Financial Conduct Authority explains its mission as follows:

> Parliament has given us a single strategic objective – to ensure that relevant markets function well – and three operational objectives to advance: (1) Protect consumers[,] (2) Integrity – to protect and enhance the integrity of the UK financial system [and] (3) Promote competition – to promote effective competition in consumers' interests (21).

When we worked with them, they had just done a very comprehensive report on complaints. They had spoken to a representative and a large sample of people who had complained about their treatment by the financial services. Effectively, they had spoken to 'everybody who complained'. However, with an eye to the first of their three 'operational objectives', consumer protection, we asked them, did you speak to anyone who didn't complain? Because they are the very most unprotected from mistreatment by the financial services. If you complain, you should experience an effective process in dealing with your issue. But those who are so disengaged that they do not have the confidence, the means or the ability to complain don't even get that far. They are the consumers receiving the least protection. The answer was that they hadn't spoken to them.

The people we were working with had a very open response to our question and wanted to ask themselves why they hadn't thought to include that group. After a discussion they realized that internally they were not giving any real value to the experience of any employees who had grown up poor and they weren't recognizing how much that could contribute to the FCA's work. This is valuing the contribution of what many charities who work with people who are disadvantaged call 'experts of experience'. For the FCA lived experience could contribute very significantly to carrying out the first of the three missions given to them by Parliament. They have in subsequent years taken advantage of their location in East London to recruit and employ more local people and more non-graduates.

The answer to the question of how diversity will enhance what you're doing is important for two reasons. It focuses you away from the tick-box, the abstract target. It makes diversity functional rather than tokenistic. It also engages your people in a much more interesting way. To ask scientists how diversity will enhance chemistry, engineering or genetics is to engage them in a discussion about a subject they love. To ask marketeers and sales-people how diversity will improve what they do is to tap into their desire to exceed their performance targets. I once asked the 40 leaders of a global car manufacturer the question and we ended up discussing the relationship between facing up to climate change, car design, automation, their production processes and diversity. They didn't expect to have the discussion. When it started they didn't expect to enjoy it. But once they were clear that it was another approach to thinking about talent and technology in the future of the car industry, they engaged in a very animated way.

These are all examples of discussions at a fairly high level about the effect of diversity on the realization of the purpose of an organization, but the anatomy of those conversations can be applied much more locally to individual teams. I urge you to try it. Just for 45 minutes. The richness of the conversation may surprise you.

Who have you got?

This is a more complicated question than the simplicity of its expression suggests. The purpose of it is both to identify the diversity deficits and also to relate them to what you decided in the previous section about the particular kind of diversity you needed. In addition to that, while you are assessing those deficits in the team and the dividends that can arise if you add appropriate diversity, you will also need to think of that diversity in terms of both the *who* and the *how* of the existing team members.

There is no need to recite the manifold deficits in the UK and US workforces. The data is clear. When you look at most teams, the more senior you go in an organization, the more they lack sufficient participation of women, people from Black and Asian backgrounds, people living with disabilities, people open about their religion or people who are lesbian or gay. The Equality Act in the UK and anti-discrimination legislation in many other countries alert us for good reason to these groups of people. On the face of it they are the most likely to experience discrimination in not being hired or promoted. There are exceptions. Certain segments of the senior workforce are well represented with women, for instance. But, while some albeit slow progress has been made in female representation, at a higher level it is hard to find similar advances for people of colour and the other groups highlighted in law. These diversity deficits may not occur in every part of every company. But when they do, they matter keenly to individuals because they block their talent, and to your organization because they reduce the talent pool and with it your ability to choose who you really need.

It's also worth pointing out that one of the most significant bases for exclusion in the UK is social class, which was removed as a ground for discrimination by the incoming Conservative government who inherited the draft Equality Act from the outgoing Labour government before it passed into law in 2010. It is a significant omission. In *The Class Ceiling: Why it pays to be privileged*, two academics from the London School of Economics, Sam Friedman and Daniel Laurison, recently showed that 'the higher ranks of prestigious occupations are drawn almost wholly from the upper classes – and that even when people from working-class backgrounds manage to break through into those jobs, they earn ten to fifteen percent less than their peers', which they estimate is about £6,400 annually. It also should be said that this situation is considerably worse for working class people of colour. 'Black British working-class women have average earnings in top jobs that are £20,000 less per year than those of privileged-origin white men' (22).

Part of the reason to make fundamental changes in the processes you use in selection is not just to put together the right diversity for the tasks at hand but also to open up the talent pool, to widen opportunities to those frequently excluded from them. In assessing who you haven't got in a team, and therefore who you want to add, you need also to send the right message to those in excluded groups who you already employ lower down in your organization. You want to signal to them that they can have the opportunity to fulfil their ambition. In actively seeking to rebalance your teams you are drawing on the widest existing talent and also investing in the development of future talent by flagging up possibilities in your organization to the next generation. If you don't, they may well leave.

By taking this approach to redesigning your selection processes you are able to remedy the deficits in such a way as to create a diversity dividend. What you are looking for is not just an arithmetic rebalancing of teams, but adding difference that new employees can bring through who they are. Often recruiters will be under pressure from higher up the company to recruit 'more women'. But that is an abstract demand. As I've emphasized earlier not everyone in a group is or thinks the same. You may wish to try to equalize the gender balance of the company. The question still remains though, what do you want those women to bring to the team? Any recruiting manager put under the expectation of 'more women' should always question: why? What are we trying to achieve in recruiting more women? Which women? What do you want them to bring? How do you want them to alter the mix? Because a team should always recruit women who will, through a combination of particular life and work experiences, skills and approaches, bring a particular enhancement to the work. This goes for any recruitment. You have to combine solving the deficits with realizing the dividends.

Asking these questions also challenges the idea that the reason you are bringing in people whom you need but are currently not in your team is because they bring 'the woman's point of view' – whatever that might mean – or that they are helping you to open up particular markets or fulfil particular diversity functions. As Scott E Page notes, 'Limiting identity's expected contributions to knowledge-based bonuses has the undesired effect of siloing diverse employees in identity – and diversity – related jobs... To assign people jobs limited to their own identity groups skates on the edge of exploitation: come and tell us about your people so we can sell them more soap'!

In our work we have often seen that taking time as a manager to identify 'who' your existing team currently is, helps with the conversations that managers can often find difficult. In making diversity functional to the task at hand it gives them a chance to explore with team members who they are, to find out more about what they bring to work through their life experiences, to open up the variations of the personal histories in their team. I encourage managers always to take time with their teams to tell personal stories, to chat with each other and understand more about each other, to discover the differences. This really helps to transform diversity into a practical realization of the power of difference rather than just 'complying with company policy'.

In assessing 'how' people are at work, organizations use a huge variety of ways from psychometrics to sheer guesswork or by drawing on insights from managers about their experience of working with team members. Many of you will at some stage have been classified as an ENTJ or ESTP or another combination of four letters in, the now rather disparaged, Myers Briggs or a Fiery Red or an Earth Green in Insights Discovery or belonging to one of the Belbin clusters of behaviour as a Specialist, a Plant or an Implementer. For our work we have put together a composite framework that represents the fundamental dynamics that underpin high-performing teams. For your recruitment you need an adaptable model that you think will give you an understanding of how the team's various cognitive differences and style of working relate to its purpose. Choose the one that best suits your organization. Then enhance it by telling each other your stories.

So, who do you need to add to achieve the team's goals?

You can now start to describe who you want to select in the round. What becomes significant here is the way that you express this as you search for suitable candidates. Our research and work has shown that large numbers of applicants have become all but immune to the typical strap lines about diversity. 'We are an equal opportunities employer', 'We are committed to promoting a diverse and inclusive community' or, most commonly, this type from one of the world's best-known brands: 'All qualified applicants will receive consideration for employment without regard to race, colour, religion, gender, gender identity or expression, sexual orientation, national origin, genetics, disability, age, or veteran status'.

These statements expressing a commitment to non-discrimination are of course perfectly reasonable. But they are the opposite of what the research, the logic and our experience demonstrates if you want to realize a dividend from diversity. The crux of the necessary change in selection is that you no longer recruit 'without regard to', you recruit precisely *with regard to* how those differences bring a bonus. In the future you should recruit FOR difference, not DESPITE it.

That has led us to compose adverts so that diversity was not a final add-on but described as intrinsic to the high performance of the team. Working with the Linguistic Profiling for Professionals (LiPP), an analytical language project at Nottingham University, they analysed the effect of many of the adverts that we've developed with clients (23). What this showed was that writing them this way 'fosters active inclusion to a higher degree than traditional recruitment templates... they successfully embed inclusion within the job adverts that goes beyond tokenistic gestures to EDI practice'. LiPP added that the adverts 'address a wider range of protected characteristics… as dimensions of experiential value to recruiters… and frame the application process as a… conversation between employer and prospective employee'.

We have to *design* out the bias: it won't happen on its own

So, one final set of comments on how you can make the process of selection as fair as possible and likely to produce the diversity in the team that you want. Much of the good work done by moving through the Virtuous Circle of Selection to develop the criteria against which you will recruit the right person to add the difference, can all be for nothing if you don't also adapt the way you frame the questions for applicants, how you review their answers and how you structure the 'interview' or assessment day.

In 2015, the 'Nudge' Unit, formally the Behavioural Insights Team of the UK government, published the results of a trial they had run with Avon and Somerset Police (24). They were seeing how they could 'increase the success rate of applicants from a black or minority ethnic background'. The numbers had told them that while these applicants were applying there was a disproportionate drop off in those getting through to interview. To investigate this they drew from the substantial amount of research, started in the mid-1990s, that defined an observable phenomenon called 'stereotype threat'. This operates through the cues that remind people of the negative stereotypes about the social group they belong to. For instance in one experiment, three groups of Asian girls aged five to seven were each asked to colour in a different picture before doing a maths test. One group had a picture of a girl with a doll, reminding them they were a girl; the next group's picture was of Asian children eating with chopsticks, reminding them they were Asian. The third group was given a picture of a landscape – the control group. Those reminded that they were girls did worse than the control group and those reminded they were Asian, did better. Each conformed to a widespread perception about the stereotypical skills of their group (25).

The concept of 'stereotype threat' has come under some criticism more recently. However, the Nudge Unit still decided to test whether there might be a way of priming minority candidates so that they could do well rather than badly. They therefore framed the questions in the application as Situational Judgement Tests. For instance, 'You're a police officer outside a pub at 11 pm and there is a fight. What would you bring from your skill and personal experience to deal with the situation?' The effect of this was to legitimate the applicant in the job. Questions in this form produced significant improvements. The analysis of the trial suggested that candidates from Black or minority ethnic backgrounds, having been primed by the premise of the question that they could be a police officer, were more likely to have confidence in themselves, trust their own experience and so provide better answers. The results showed a 20 per cent increase in the probability of candidates from these backgrounds getting through to interview.

At Diversity by Design we work with clients to develop the criteria on which they've decided into these kinds of real scenarios for the application. This is because not only will these types of situational questions test what you actually want to know about a candidate's suitability for the role, but the research also suggests overwhelmingly that they are a much stronger predictor of future job performance. Educational qualifications, length of service, reference checks and other traditional CV metrics that are often used are significantly less reliable predictors. Much more effective are General Mental Ability tests, whose overall predictive power is, as Iris Bohnet points out, 'maximized when… [they are] combined either with a work sample test [very directly measuring the skill required to perform the job], integrity tests, or… with a structured interview' (26).

We need to get the right shape and structure of the questions to get the best out of the candidates. Not only is it more effective to use situational judgement or work sample tests to predict performance, but the questions should also be designed so that they emphasize that the personal background and identity of the applicant are really valued by the selectors, that as a prospective employer, you want to know what the candidate can bring to the role and the organization through their experience, through who they are. Having done that, the issue is how to then assess their answers so as not to undo this positive effect with our own biases.

As we have already established, we make very quick judgements about people, but these are rarely based on facts. We do it the moment we see them. This is true whether that means 'seeing' them in person or in the form of a CV. We make these judgements based on information we pick out because we like or don't like what it says about them. What school they went to, where they previously worked, their age, even their hobbies. These impressions, for they are that inexact, can be based on prejudice either against some groups of people or in favour of others. Or they can simply be qualities, experiences or skills that chime with our own. As we read through a single CV, we become subject to the 'halo' effect. The term was coined by a US psychologist called Edward Thorndike in 1920 (27). It describes the way in which, if you like one thing about someone, you start to like other unrelated things about them too. The opposite is also the case. I call it the 'eclipse' effect when you dislike one thing about them and that builds into an overall negative view. However hard we try, it's very difficult not to do this.

Consequently a few organizations have now stopped using CVs as part of any assessment at all. But, more commonly, many others have merely 'blinded' them. The latter, by removing identifying details such as name, age, university or school, and certainly taking off pictures, is thought to help to reduce the way in which selectors will make prejudicial judgements. The results on experiments to test this are slightly mixed. In 2010 the French public employment service involved about 1,000 firms over ten months to compare résumés that were either transmitted anonymously or non-anonymously (28). The experiment discovered two rather contradictory conclusions. Women got higher call-back rates with anonymous job applications, at least if they were competing with men. But migrants and residents from deprived neighbourhoods got lower call-backs. The explanation given was that 'participating firms tended to interview and hire relatively more minority candidates [when using standard résumés]. The anonymization therefore prevented selected firms from treating minority candidates more favorably during the experiment'. Anonymization was hindering positive action. Round about the same time a similar German experiment concluded that anonymization led to less discrimination against minorities in the rate of call-backs. (29)

Anonymizing CVs certainly can help in trying to minimize bias. However, it doesn't go far enough. As we have seen, not only is the information they typically contain a poor predictor of success in a role, but also the way we read them means that we pick and choose the information we want from them according to our own preferences. Even when they're blinded we can still decode them. Recently I experimented on myself in a recruitment process for new trustees of a charity I volunteered for. They agreed to blind CVs rather than drop them completely. Try this for yourself, but I very soon felt, even against my better judgement, still being drawn to look for what I wanted to see. Even with all the identifying information removed, there is a strong possibility that you'll still form an impression about the person based on your personal preferences rather than any evidence about their suitability for the role. It's very hard not to. The form of the information in front of you – reading one person's complete information – encourages you to let in your biases about the person, rather than to make as fair an assessment as you can of their skills and ability for the job.

Looking for a solution to this, Iris Bohnet and her colleagues undertook an experiment designed to mimic real hiring decisions (30). The participants had to select a candidate for either a stereotypically male task, a maths problem; or a stereotypically female task, a word assignment. The participants were asked to do this in two different ways that Iris termed 'joint' and 'separate' evaluation. In other words, selectors were given a single candidate and asked to score them. Or they were given two or more candidates and asked to compare them and then score. In short, they discovered that 'when evaluators looked at candidate profiles individually, men were more likely to be hired for the math task and women for the verbal task, including those who had performed below par'. However, 'when the evaluators were exposed to more than one candidate… [the intervention was] able to overcome these stereotypical assessments. Comparative evaluation focused evaluators' attention on individual performance instead of group stereotypes. When candidates were evaluated comparatively, the gender gap vanished completely and all evaluators chose the top performer'.

Over the years of working with Diversity by Design clients we have adapted and developed this idea into a system. The criteria that emerge from going around The Virtuous Circle, form the application. They are turned into scenarios and those are the only questions that candidates are asked to answer and the only information the selectors see. CVs are excluded from the assessment. These criteria and the scenarios in this redesigned process are constructed to elicit from candidates what they can bring to the role through who they are, emphasizing that the selectors are as interested in what they bring from their background as much as they are in their technical abilities. Skill may be neutral, but its application is not. How you work, what you bring from your background tells volumes about your suitability for that role in that team at that moment in the organization.

After the closing date the candidates' evidence is sorted for the selectors so they can see all the candidates' answers against the first criterion/scenario, all of them against the second and so on. To start with they never see all the answers from one candidate. That way selectors get to make a direct comparison between the evidence and each criterion, without being interrupted by the noise of their own preferences that blasts in when they read all the way through each person individually.

Lastly, it's worth saying just one thing about interviews. They are a lousy way of assessing people for jobs! We persist with them despite the fact that evidence piles up that the unstructured interview opens the door allowing a gale of biases to sweep through the process. Not only will they more likely lead you to choose someone like yourself, but they have very little chance of predicting whether or not they'll be any good in the job. As Iris – once again the doyenne of insight on this – says most emphatically, 'the data showing that unstructured interviews do not work is overwhelming' (31).

There are two main problems with them. The first is that if interviews lack a structure through which each candidate can be tested against a set of agreed criteria, then the conversation will in all probability just head off down the path of shared enthusiasms and similarities. Each candidate will, in effect, be assessed entirely differently. Most organizations now realize this. Most senior and middle management are recruited in a far more rigorous way than just for their clubability. All sorts of psychometrics and other apparently scientific methods are applied. But hiring continues to rely on the kinds of encounters, usually at the end of the process, that illustrate their second flaw, which makes them equally unreliable – the panel interview.

To mitigate bias, company after company insists that it will ensure 'we will have diverse panels for all our interviews'. Except, as anyone who has even been on a selection panel with someone more powerful than themselves knows, it is not easy to raise a countervailing view nor to sway the group to make it stick. Diverse panels are of little or no use unless the whole panel is fully involved in determining the criteria and the metrics from the start, that all panel members are given equal voice and that there is no circular discussion. The last is particularly what removes the illusion that 'diverse panels' produce a diverse outcome. Put bluntly, never mind how diverse the panel, if the discussion is unstructured, they are easy to manipulate if you are the most powerful or most articulate member. Just visualize that you are a Black female nurse on a panel faced with a middle-aged, White Senior Consultant, who is determined to have his preferred candidate appointed as another Consultant. You are a member of the Staff Cross Cultural Network drafted into the interviews in an insurance company for the next Head of Regulation to make the panel more diverse. Walk in their shoes for an imaginary moment and ask yourself how easy it would be to speak up? How easy would it be to break the pattern of a discussion that, as it moves from person to person round the table, inevitably therefore zeros in on a consensus as each following person is swayed to echo the previous speaker? Most of us have watched it happen. These two examples are ones that I have seen.

One promotion round described to me by a banking client was the worst example I've encountered. But the fact that it was so extreme helps us to see the problem because it brings it into very high relief. It was operated by partners bringing their nomination to an Executive Committee meeting. They simply spoke, usually with the kind of brevity that revealed their lack of respect for any need to bother to make a case at all, and put the name of their preferred candidate on the table. The discussion then went round the other members. What happened rather inevitably was that momentum simply gathered behind the candidates of the most powerful people in the room. This is a form of group confirmation bias in operation. Imagine if you were the person appointed to such a panel to 'make it more diverse', what chance would you have to intervene against the tyranny of this kind of lack of structure operating in a palpable hierarchy?

We have found however that if you stick to the following rules you've got more than a gambler's chance of making the outcome fair and evidence based:

- The sole purpose of the interview is to test the suitability of the candidate for the job in terms of the criteria you've outlined, assessed on the metrics for each criterion you've agreed.

- Ask the same questions in the same order. But that doesn't mean that you can't follow up with each candidate on their particular answer, if it will help to test them against the criteria.

- Score a candidate's answers strictly against the metrics you've agreed.

- Each member of the panel should score each answer separately.

- Panel members should not compare scores with each other.

- Scores should be collected and added up by a third party.

- If you have set the right criteria and properly discussed and agreed the metrics for scoring, the discussion should in the first instance only be about any divergences or anomalies between individual members' scores.

There will more than likely at the end be a discussion that weighs up the balance between two candidates. Following these rules makes it far less easy for any one member of the panel, even the most powerful one, to steamroll the others, because you've got the criteria, the evidence, the metrics for assessment and the scoring to refer to.

The logical extension of this approach is that interviews are simply not the best form of assessment at all. If we take the success of the situational tests to its conclusion, unless sitting in a chair opposite a panel of people on the other side of a table is actually what the job you are applying for involves, then why are you testing candidates' ability to do that? Might we not get more accurate and reliable assessments by devising situations, role plays and other methods of evaluation that test candidates' ability to do what's actually required? Some organizations have ditched interviews in favour of just giving applicants work-based tests. But organizations and hiring managers hang on tightly to the habitual comfort of doing interviews. We are used to them. And we think we make good decisions. But at this stage in our examination of more effective approaches to diversity, we ought to know better! We need to redesign the way we reach conclusions about other people to enable us to make better decisions. Having the evidence more clearly identified helps us to do that.

In one NHS Trust, where Governors who are elected from the local population appoint the Board, we had worked to get a strong pipeline of women to apply. Only 2 out of 11 of the current Board were female. There were four candidates for interview: three women and one man. The women had all scored better than the man. However, the Governor, also male, continued to insist that the man was the best candidate. Observing from the side, it looked and sounded clear to me that the male candidate just appeared to the Governor to conform to the kind of professional experience and type of person that he expected to be right for the Board of an NHS Trust. He persisted in arguing the case until the rest of the panel simply went back to the criteria, the metrics and the scores, where the three women were ranked higher, and asked him directly to explain in what ways he thought the man was the better candidate. He was unable to do so. All he could do was allow himself the luxury of his own preferences with language like, 'I just feel he's a better fit'.

Despite appearances, blind CVs and diverse panels will not ensure a greater diversity of candidates or appointments.

There are many issues that affect attempts to widen the diversity of appointments. There are sectors where the pipeline of applicants has historically been very unbalanced – men and engineering for instance. There can be a failure in the language used to try to attract applicants that actually puts them off. Some groups of people have had their confidence to apply for certain types of jobs significantly damaged. Headhunters, recruiters and managers simply don't try imaginatively enough to plug into networks where they might find really suitable applicants from underrepresented groups. As we saw with BHP Billiton, if you work to transform substantially what management speak calls your 'employer value proposition', you can dramatically change the pipeline of applicants. So there is much to be done in deliberately setting out to attract a wider range of talent. But when you do get their attention and they do apply, what you need to do is to make sure that you assess them as fairly and reliably as possible for the role.

Drawing on all this research and working it through with clients as a redesigned approach to recruitment produces encouraging results. In the case of the recent selection of an Engineering Professor, for instance, in a sphere where women are highly underrepresented, the applicants were 15 per cent female. The eventual shortlist was 35 per cent female and they appointed two women. One of the best moments of feedback was from one (as it happens unsuccessful) applicant who said, 'I felt I was invited as a woman to apply but that I had been assessed as a scientist'.

Here are some examples of how you might express this method in action:

A Professor in Engineering:

> We believe that diverse teams deliver the highest quality teaching, research
> and student experience. So, to achieve the Faculty of Engineering's vision of
> being top ranked in all areas for Research and Knowledge Exchange as well
> as Education and Student Experience, we are seeking applications from high
> quality people whose backgrounds, experience and identity can contribute to
> our understanding of how to broaden and enhance the diversity of our existing
> team. The Faculty is committed to creating opportunities for people from
> groups traditionally underrepresented in Engineering.

A Nurse Practitioner in an occupational health service in a large corporation:

> We believe that, for the team to support our people really well, we need
> the widest combination of people who can understand the wide range and
> increasingly complex health needs of our employees. We want to see applicants
> who have got expertise from their background and experiences at home and at
> work who can particularly *bring insights into the health needs of* [my italics]
> men, Black colleagues, those people who are religious, those younger people
> under the age of 40 and who are LGB or T.

Commercial Partner in a law firm:

We are looking for a senior partner with expertise in commercial law who:

- has the breadth of experience in working collaboratively with colleagues from a wide range of cultural and socio-economic backgrounds;
- can evidence how they can create and manage teams where relationships between men and women are respectful and fulfilling;
- will build a team where difference is valued as the partners believe that this will build the firm's ability to develop stronger solutions for our clients;
- can draw on the strengths of their team to deliver new business to the firm and solutions for clients that will give us a competitive edge in the legal marketplace;
- can develop business in hitherto untapped markets.

HR People Solutions Partner:

Do you have the experience, from your personal or your professional life, to get under the skin of why people might leave the hospital and why they stay? There are many different reasons why people move on or are off sick. We are delivering the service across a culturally diverse (in all senses of the word) group of people. We want you to bring, through your own personal background, experience and difference, an understanding of that range of people's motivations. We are particularly keen to see you if you can bring in ideas from outside the team to solve problems in unconventional ways. We want the broadest range of insight into the needs of different groups and individuals in our people, particularly men, those over 40 and colleagues who are open about being LGB or T and those who come from a socially deprived background.

Head of Climate Change in a large city council:

We are as interested in what you can bring to this role through your personal background, lived experience and future vision as we are in your knowledge of ecological and sustainability issues.

We are particularly keen to hear from you if you can bring insight into businesses run and staffed by people from Black, Asian and Minority Ethnic communities and those from socially deprived backgrounds and engage with the widest variety of communities in the city and surrounding areas that our services do not currently reach.

You can harness the Power of Difference to redesign your recruitment and promotion to create the most effective teams by exploring:

- how you can recruit 'the best team for the job' rather than 'the best person for the job';

- how your business can combine an individual's brilliance, skills and life experience with others so teams can excel when they collaborate;

- how your business can respond to the challenge that no one person or group of people can understand or solve the business issues facing the modern world on their own;

- how you can slow down the process of recruitment enough to give yourselves time to think carefully about what the job requires now and what you really need the successful candidate to bring;

- 'The Virtuous Circle of Selection'. What is the team for? What's the job for? What combination of difference would enhance the team's ability to achieve what it's for? Who have you got? So, who do you need to add to fulfil what the team is for?

- how you can highlight to potential candidates that you see their background and life experience as significant contributors to their ability to do the job, as well as their technical skills;

- how you can recruit people who show that they have a commitment to increasing diversity and have some ideas about how to do it;

- how you structure the criteria, the metrics for assessment and the 'interviews' so they are both fair and also test the candidate rigorously and reliably for the role;

- how you can transform the criteria you have decided on into practical and likely scenarios in the job, which will place the candidate in the role and test what they can actually bring to it.

06

Diversity isn't harder to manage

You only think it is

Derek Black was brought up White Supremacist royalty. In the mid-1990s his father, Don, launched Stormfront in the United States with its strapline: 'White Pride World Wide'. His mother's first husband and his godfather is David Duke, described by the Southern Poverty Law Centre (SPLC) as 'the most recognizable figure of the American radical right, a Neo-Nazi, long-time Klan leader and an international spokesman for Holocaust denial'. By the time he was 13, Derek was running the Stormfront children's page. At 19, he was introduced as 'the leading light of our movement' at a secret conference in Memphis of Ku Klux Klan leaders and prominent neo-Nazis, whose agenda read bluntly, 'The fight to restore White America begins now'. He was a key part of the Far Right's attempt in the United States to make its politics more palatable to voters. Never mentioning White nationalism, instead he framed his appeal in a local political election in Florida in 2008 as a fight back against political correctness, affirmative action and unchecked immigration. He won. Yet in 2013 he wrote a public message to the SPLC disavowing the beliefs of his upbringing:

> I can't support a movement that tells me I can't be a friend to whomever I wish or that other people's race require me to think of them in a certain way or be suspicious at their advancements... The things I have said as well as my actions have been harmful to people of color, people of Jewish descent, activists striving for opportunity and fairness for all. I am sorry for the damage done.

He continues to speak out against White nationalism.

What changed his mind? In fact, his life. Two people played a crucial role. The first was Matthew Stevenson, an Orthodox Jew who went to college with Derek and was in the same dorm. They met when Derek was playing Country and Western songs on his guitar and Matthew liked to sing along with him 'very badly'. The other was another fellow student, Allison Gopnik.

Realizing that he'd be ostracized by other students if he owned up to who he was and to his racist ideas, Derek kept his beliefs to himself. Despite studying at what he describes as one of the 'most pot-friendly, most gay-friendly', liberal colleges in the United States, he started to make friends. However, in April 2011, the inevitable happened and his cover was blown. Someone posted who he was on the student message board. The reaction was immediate and hostile. There were over 1,000 messages. Some students wanted him expelled, others urged people on campus 'not to make eye contact or make him feel acknowledged at all. Make him as irrelevant as his ideology.' But one wrote: 'Ostracizing Derek won't accomplish anything, we have a chance to be real activists and actually affect one of the leaders of White supremacy in America. This is not an exaggeration. It would be a victory for civil rights.' And another asked, 'Who's clever enough to think of something we can do to change this guy's mind?' One person was. Two days after students had shut down the college in protest, Matthew invited Derek to the Shabbat supper he held in his room every Friday. Derek accepted.

Allison was not happy about the invitation. She loved the suppers and the time it meant spending with friends. But she just didn't want to sit down with Derek. She stopped going. 'People on campus were saying that by being friends with this person you are supporting his ideology.' But she missed the suppers and went back a few weeks later. Derek puzzled her. 'He kept coming to supper week after week. I didn't understand his behaviour. It didn't measure up. One of his close friends was a Peruvian immigrant.' Politics was off-limits at the suppers. But her curiosity continued to grow about why he believed what he did. They'd meet and she'd ask him about his beliefs: 'What was the evidence? What were the pillars? What do you base it on? What do you make of the counter-arguments? In order to argue against it,' she says, 'you had to understand it.' Derek was equally puzzled:

> Usually I would say that I didn't want to talk about it and they would change the subject and we'd move on. Allison wouldn't let me talk about other things. That was very new. It was a personal, private way of disagreeing. There were no points to win with Allison. I'd start explaining with my 'evidence' and she would come back with evidence which showed how badly I was abusing the statistics.

Allison says that 'he was producing "evidence", rather than just saying he had a gut feeling that he didn't like Black people. I am not sure I could have worked with him just saying that. He had reasons but they were misusing science and logic. I was pretty sure we could deconstruct that.' When asked why he engaged with Derek, Matthew draws on his own upbringing:

> It wasn't as though he'd come to this ideology on his own as an adult. He had been born into possibly the most pre-eminent White Nationalist family. I think if I was raised in that same family, I don't know that I could say that I wouldn't have those exact same views. I can see how my own parents shaped me.

They had indeed shaped him. In a very different way. His father said when they spoke about Derek, 'reach out and extend the hand no matter who is waiting on the other side'. His mother was very involved with Alcoholics Anonymous. Even as young as 10 years old he had heard stories there 'of personal redemption where people had done a 180 degree turn to become forces of positivity'. Also Matthew felt that the response of some students had gone too far, even suggesting violence towards Derek. 'I felt that was unacceptable because even if someone who I disagree with holds what I feel are absolutely repugnant views, it still doesn't give you a right not to treat that person with human dignity.' Movingly he describes the obligation he felt to give Derek the chance at least to meet the kind of people his ideology despised. 'We're not obligated to complete the work, but we're not free to desist from it. We have to push the rock, not necessarily move the rock' (1).

From Shabbat supper to managing difference

These are exceptional young people. Fortunately there are more stories like this in the world. They are very inspiring. Often when I have heard them through The Forgiveness Project, I have retold them and described the people involved. When I've done so, the response from those listening is almost always the same. 'I just don't think I could do that', or 'It would be far too hard', or 'I wouldn't know where to start'. That seems true of Derek and Matthew and Allison's story too. It began in a place of extreme difference that was potentially incapable of transformation because of the distance between them and the degree to which Derek's beliefs were enmeshed with his family, his upbringing and the whole of his social circle throughout his childhood and adolescence. But despite it seeming impossible, together they did achieve change. What these three people who became friends accomplished, while being extraordinary, actually describes the anatomy of the management of difference in many ordinary situations and particularly managing the differences that will inevitably exist in a team at work. You can sum up the shape of how to meet the challenge in three Cs: context, curiosity and change.

Matthew through his invitation to supper provided the context. By coming together as friends rather than adversaries Derek encountered the kind of people that he had never met before. He knew they were appalled at his politics, but also, he says, 'they were people that I knew. I respected them. I took classes with them. I knew how smart they were,' which was like neither the anonymous hate mail he was used to getting online nor the hermetic monoculture of his family. Matthew's invitation brought him into a different context where he was not challenged on his views and forced to defend them, but instead where he encountered new people and their ideas socially, allowing them to discover each other as human beings. Then he could see his views in a new context. Managing difference needs to start with what is possible given the differences between people, rather than with what seems impossible because of them.

Allison pursued her curiosity. She was trying to understand and when she did, she quietly argued rather than condemned. She felt that if Derek 'engaged genuinely then I had an obligation not to walk away from it'. Why people believe what they believe or behave as they do will have many origins and explanations. So before judgement therefore has to come curiosity. The attempt to understand needs to precede the rush to make assumptions. Only through discovery provoked by curiosity can you work out how to motivate different members of a team.

Derek himself of course was the most significant change and the catalyst for it was that he listened. Both the new context and Allison's curiosity gave him that chance. They gave him an opportunity that he'd never had before. Those two elements won't always create the change, but without them there's not even the possibility of it. They are pre-conditions, but without Derek's willingness to question there would have been no movement. It's like the old joke: 'How many psychiatrists does it take to change a lightbulb? Just one. But the lightbulb has to want to change.' We are only able to encounter difference meaningfully when we are given the best opportunity to do so. When Derek was asked how he would set about changing someone who held the views that he did, significantly he identifies that as only being possible in those who 'see themselves as someone who doesn't want to cause other people harm'. There has to be a seed from which to grow common ground.

There have been myriad theories of management since Frederick W Taylor published the four principles of his 'scientific management theory' in 1909. They stretch from his efficiency-based micro-management through Fayol's 14 principles, Weber's bureaucratic theory, Mayo's human relations theory, systems theory and many others all the way up to some of today's HR orthodoxies of 'wellness', 'happiness' and 'mindfulness'. But whatever tools and frameworks you use to manage your people, there is certain good sense and simplicity in the American Management Association definition that management is 'the act of getting things done through others and having them do it willingly'. To manage well is to be able to motivate different people to work together towards a common goal.

To see difference, value it and be able to combine it well in pursuit of that common goal managers need to provide the context where people can explore their differences and exchange their perspectives in order to collaborate productively. They have to give rein to their employees' curiosity and to their own. Finally, they have to understand what motivates each one of their people to be able to contribute through their work. When Allison describes how she went about discussing with Derek what he believed, to try to change it, she found a way to enable them to talk. She says, 'to start with I didn't know the science and the answers so I had to find out. At one point I even googled "what are the best arguments against White nationalism?" Which was not a particularly helpful google search!' Curiosity by definition involves acknowledging what you don't know in order to understand it. Management is not precise, it's an exploration.

Consequently, being an effective manager is a considerable challenge. It's pretty complex to see and understand the differences in every employee in order to know how to motivate them. It's not much of a surprise that managers think that complexity is reduced and made much easier to deal with if their people all seem the same. But the reality is that despite appearances, no group of people is the same. Sameness is an illusion. Managers are always managing difference. But the research shows that they think managing visible difference is much harder than managing groups of people that appear homogeneous.

Diversity perceived as conflict

Katherine Phillips at Columbia Business School, whose research, as we saw earlier, helped to establish that the mere presence of diversity delivers a dividend, set out to examine this negative perception. She and her colleagues ran a series of experiments in which 'every participant either read the same exact transcript, watched the same video interaction, or listened to the same discussion among a group of four members. The only thing that changed was the racial composition of the group' (2). The homogeneous groups were either all-White or all-Black. The diverse groups were made up of two White people and two Black people. Participants were then asked to report on how they saw the group interact and, on that basis, allocate budgets to them.

The conclusions were striking. 'When reading a transcript with pictures revealing the group's composition, racially diverse teams were perceived as having more relationship conflict than homogeneous ones.' To be sure it wasn't that the transcripts were sparking the participants' imagination and affecting their interpretation, they then hired actors to recreate the transcripts in videotaped discussions for the participants to watch. She ensured that content, tone and behaviour of the actors was identical across the videos. It produced the same result. 'Diverse groups were perceived as having more relationship conflict, and because of this, financial resources were less likely to be given to them than to homogeneous groups.' This discord was not perceived in the all-White groups and the all-Black groups. It was only the diverse groups that were thought to have greater relationship conflict. Furthermore, the perception of the diverse groups was not that they argued more about the task in hand, but that they just conflicted more with each other. Even though they didn't.

Getting over this negative perception of the interaction of people who are different from each other is vital at work because diversity is, and always has been, a given in teams. It's not as if human difference was suddenly invented in the third quarter of the 20th century. The richest aspect of human relationships has always been the differences people have with one another and how they manage to combine them towards a common goal. What is new is the explicit attempt to acknowledge those differences, embrace them, call that 'diversity' and deploy it to the benefit of your organization and your employees. The campaigns for equality in the last decades have certainly increased visible diversity. With more women working, lesbian and gay people out at the office, a much richer ethnic and cultural mix among colleagues and disabled people less confined by assumptions about their ability, the workplace looks far more diverse than in previous eras. But teams have always, often despite their appearance, been full of individual difference. If managers haven't noticed it and consequently have just managed everyone the same, their organizations have been missing out. We now know, as a result of the work of Scott E Page and many others, that the application of diverse groups to complex tasks, when well managed, will lead to greater innovation, richer solutions and even increased productivity. If you want to reap those dividends then you have to manage the diversity in your teams effectively. There may be more visible diversity at work, but that will only seem harder to manage if you've been ignoring people's differences all along. It's not managing difference that's harder; it's managing well.

How diversity might have saved RBS from collapse

Diversity doesn't mean manufacturing the appearance of unity around a common goal. It means forging real partnerships between employees to achieve something willingly together. Otherwise, what managers produce is a false consensus that looks like everyone has been motivated into a single, magnificently performing team or organization, but actually employees are a seething morass of insecurity and unease. The Royal Bank of Scotland (RBS) under the reign of its former CEO, Fred Goodwin, is a pretty good example. In his book *Shredded* about the rise and fall of the bank, Ian Fraser describes Goodwin, not without good reason, as 'a sociopathic bully, whose achievements had been massively over-hyped' (3).

RBS appeared to be a great alliance of thousands of people in an ambitious project to create a 'world-class' Scottish bank. But the seeming success certainly didn't come from any idea of valuing difference. In fact dissent was all but forbidden. A colleague who worked there at the height of the Goodwin bubble, described to me how the rallying call was that 'we were all part of "the winning bank"'. But they went on to say that, if you dared to suggest any disagreement with or question Goodwin and his team's direction of travel, 'you were just labelled a loser'. Nick Cohen, the political journalist, wrote that 'anyone who raised doubts... heard managers call them "Business Prevention Officers"... the hierarchy would mark them as fifth columnists' (4). The HR Director at the time said that Fred the Shred, as he became known, 'cared deeply about people's feelings'. But, as Ian Fraser rather acidly comments, 'not their feelings generally, just how they felt about The Royal Bank'.

How the bank stumbled and almost fell is widely known. As is the fact that it nearly brought the UK economy down with it. The catastrophe had an entropic effect on the financial state of Britain, more locally on the lives of those who lost their jobs, and on the health and happiness of the bank's remaining employees. The near collapse of RBS was the direct result of an egotistical failure to recognize that difference and discussion are strengths not weaknesses. That it is diversity of views that delivers success, not enforced unanimity.

Goodwin's plan was that RBS would buy a Dutch bank called ABN AMRO as part of a three-way consortium with Santander and a smaller Belgian bank called Fortis. Pulling off the deal was to be the peak of Goodwin's ambition. However, when he deftly slid the issue onto the Board's agenda, they hardly discussed at all whether the deal was solid, sensible or sustainable. They were so swept along by the unexamined momentum of the bank's apparent success, that they just considered the detail. No-one questioned whether the deal itself was the right thing to do. They were after all 'the winning bank'. As Ian reports, there was only one Director who 'raised serious objections... However his concerns related more to the complexity of what was being proposed than its wisdom'. Ian continues, 'the RBS Board got so mired in a discussion about the practicalities of a consortium bid that they did not even discuss whether a three way carve up bid made any sense' in the first place. In the absence of any meaningful challenge and airing of difference they discussed only the detail not the substance.

As a result, without substantive debate, RBS was tied into a deal that soon turned so sour that it caused what one former senior employee characterized darkly as the 'carnage and horror that came about'. Alfred P Sloan, the famed President, Chairman and CEO of General Motors until the 1950s, is reputed to have said after one of his Board meetings, 'If we are all in agreement on the decision – then I propose we postpone further discussion of this matter until our next meeting to give ourselves time to develop disagreement and perhaps gain some understanding of what the decision is all about'. Making good decisions relies on good management that explores and cherishes the differences that are essential to human interaction, allowing them to release their full creative tension. Understanding risk, investigating what you don't know – the Rumsfeldian 'unknown unknowns' – can only be done through managers valuing difference and pursuing curiosity (5). Whether on Boards, in Executive Committees or teams you manage, the presence of the right kind of diversity will be the trigger to that.

It's not just the people in these teams who will be different, managers also need to understand the unique relationships between them and the varied situations the team is facing – another three 'c's: casting, connectivity and challenges. In the 1970s many orchestras introduced blind auditioning by putting a curtain between those playing and those listening. That way they could, unencumbered by any preconceptions provoked by the appearance of the candidates, just listen to how they played and choose the best musicians. Over time it has had some effect on the mix of men and women in orchestras – the casting. However, those who were successful didn't automatically enhance the performance of the orchestra, just because they were best of those who auditioned. The conductor has then to create a relationship between all of the individual musicians in the orchestra to produce a unique sound. They have to create a connectivity between the players.

In 1999, two great friends, the Israeli pianist and conductor Daniel Barenboim and the late Edward Said, the Palestinian academic, created the West–Eastern Divan Orchestra. Barenboim said they were not creating a political orchestra but simply a way to promote dialogue, starting with its own members. In 2018 he described that process to a journalist:

> I sat them together, so you had a Syrian cellist and an Israeli on the same stand. What do they do? First of all, they tune to the same 'A'. So they have to listen. Then they try to play the same way, with the same bow strokes. They do that for six hours a day, and then they eat in the same dining room. Their attitude changes… I always say to them: 'I expect all of you to agree on how to play Beethoven, I don't expect you to agree on the other side's narrative. But I do expect you to try to understand it and respect it' (6).

Ten years earlier he had commented, 'When it started, after the first summer, Edward said to me, "You will see, we will learn more from them than they from us." If I stand in front of the Staatskapelle in Berlin and I say to the oboe to play a phrase in such and such a way, he can do it.' But Barenboim continued:

> In the Divan, they ask why? And therefore it forces me to try to understand why I want something in a certain way. I can teach them. I can inspire them. I can animate them. But they are the ones who make the sound. Conductors have to remember that. And the musicians also have to remember that they don't just sit there and wait to be animated. They have to contribute. The Divan does that like no other orchestra in the world (7).

Understanding the difference you have 'cast' in your teams gives you a way to manage them to achieve great results together.

Creating the space in teams and organizations where that connectivity can happen lies at the core of managing difference. In the case of the Divan Orchestra it's the dialogue between Israelis and Arabs. In your team it may be the collaboration between people from different class backgrounds, different cultures, different kinds of personal relationships and how they relate to each other. For diversity to be a reality in teams it is not enough to simply 'get more women/Black people/gays'. As we've seen, managers also need to be aware of the way in which different groups of people, and the individuals within those groups, interact with each other and what is produced by that interaction. Different business situations each require specific combinations of difference. You may be able to build that diversity specifically for a project or you may be working with the people you've already got. In either case the diversity of the group will vary in nature. Understanding that diversity and the interrelationship between the people is what will produce the dividend. Perhaps if Goodwin and his colleagues hadn't bullied their employees into the illusion of a consensus around the 'winning bank' and instead worked out how to give them the framework to create it together through their different contributions, if they'd understood how to enable diverse people to combine, collaborate and challenge, maybe RBS would have succeeded and Goodwin would still be *Sir* Fred.

Guerrilla warfare, tanks, and fast and slow thinking

The third test that faces managers are the differences in the kinds of challenges they encounter. A few years ago, I attended a seminar at the Ministry of Defence about what men could do to support women in the workplace. (How the army has changed since my father joined in 1934!) Afterwards, a Lieutenant Colonel called John Kendall, with whom I had exchanged some ideas in the discussion, took me aside and started writing on the flip chart. He mapped out three different kinds of scenarios that his experience in the army had revealed required different kinds of leadership. There was the situation you'd encountered before and knew how to deal with; there were situations that looked like ones you'd seen before but which, deceptively, were not; and, finally, there were entirely new situations that you'd never met before. While business is not war, it struck me that the difference between the three scenarios highlighted how much collective and collaborative leadership is needed in today's complex business situations in order to interpret and understand them correctly.

The first type of scenario is where the situation is what you think it is and you do indeed just have to approach it in the same way as before. The second type is, for instance, what the Americans encountered with fighting the Viet Cong, which looked like conventional warfare but wasn't. For ten years they tried to bomb the Viet Cong into submission. But the Viet Cong outfoxed them by fighting a hit-and-run guerrilla war. They avoided the bombs by sheltering in underground tunnels, used their intimate knowledge of the jungle to avoid being targeted and then set ingenious and highly effective traps for the US troops on the ground. What failed the US Army was facing a fresh situation with old tactics and an inflexible and inappropriate leadership approach

In the third scenario, the wholly unknown, John's example was the impact of tanks on the outcome of the First World War. They were a decisive innovation because they were able to drive into the hail of bullets, supported by infantry behind them, and overwhelm the enemy defences. His modern example of such a game changer is the suicide bomber. They are not just a wholly new and unorthodox tactic in a guerrilla war against military targets, but a horribly effective means of terrorizing and instilling fear into civilians. Dealing with them entails a wholly new and different set of military and intelligence tools. The insight and approach required is miles from the deployment of traditional leadership.

In business, as in the military, it will be the very rarest of leaders who possesses the insight, the ability and the analytical expertise to equip them for all three sets of circumstances. To decide the right course of action in a business will need three-dimensional leadership and management, engaging with a breadth of personal and professional perspectives to understand accurately the context in which you and your business find yourselves. You may not be under fire from bullets, as John has been in the army, but failing to understand what your team is facing can be metaphorically fatal for it. So, what are the Types One, Two and Three of business scenarios?

The ever-present personal challenge of managing people is that you always have to balance the self-assurance to make decisions with the curiosity and openness to investigate what you don't know or understand. It is often easier though to pretend that you do know what to do. But that is precisely the time when it is easiest to make completely wrong assumptions, diagnose the context entirely mistakenly and so make the worst decisions. The danger always lurks in management of overconfidence in your own judgement. This is not new. As Adam Smith wrote in *The Wealth of Nations* in 1776, 'The overweening conceit which the greater part of men have of their own abilities, is an ancient evil remarked by the philosophers and moralists of all ages' (8). It is easy to convince yourself that decisions are rational, considered and based on evidence and experience when despite that, or sometimes precisely because of that, they are still wrong for the situations you are actually facing. It is all too common to believe in hindsight that you did understand something before it happened, when actually you didn't, and mistakenly take the same course of action the next time.

John settled on these three dimensions of leadership by applying Daniel Kahneman's theories about 'thinking fast and slow' – which we encountered in Chapter 4 – to his own leadership experience in the army (9). As we saw in that chapter the value of Kahneman's insights into human judgement has meant that a considerable number of people who are engaged in diversity have become very familiar with his work. They find it far more effective than the flawed notion of 'unconscious bias' in helping to explain why humans make snap judgements about people and situations, rather than allowing their rational and analytical minds to engage with what they see and hear in order to draw more considered conclusions.

Kahneman's framework helps in management because, put very simply in a way that's not going to win me any Nobel Prizes, what he called 'System 1' is how you jump to conclusions and 'System 2' is how you make a conscious and careful effort to reach them. The automatic versus the thoughtful. According to Kahneman they constantly interact. System 2 thinking can overrule the habits that have become ingrained in System 1. But it would be easy to kid yourself that a decision is free from bias just because it involves taking time to consider what to do. The problem with apparently rational conclusions is that they draw from the habits that have become in-built to System 1, which contain all the preferences and biases that you have absorbed along the way in your life. It's worth adding that Kahneman agreed with Adam Smith, once telling an interviewer that 'if he had a magic wand that could eliminate one human bias, he would do away with over-confidence' (10).

The challenge with managing people is that mostly you'll think of yourself as this rational human being who makes reasoned choices about your people and their abilities, how they interact and the situations your team or organization is faced with. Whereas too often you'll actually make decisions, influenced not by evidence and enquiry, but by the pressure of time, demands from your own boss or simply because what you've decided to do is what you and your team are used to doing and have always done before. You are more likely to be using System 1 thinking, where through practice, decisions have become intuitive, swift and accessed without effort, often rationalizing them as being based on your experience. Decisions that are automatic in this way can perpetuate biases with ease.

Just as Socrates is credited with saying about life that the unexamined one was not worth living, the unexamined decision is not worth taking. To eliminate unintentional preconceptions from decision making you have to examine your assumptions in both modes of thinking. John Kendall's three dimensions help because they can act as a warning, when faced with any situation in business, to challenge and be challenged in how you are managing and make decisions about it. So, how best to deal with each of the scenarios?

Defining something as a Type One situation in work does not necessarily mean that it's not what you think it is. Often things really are exactly the same. It turns out that you do indeed need to run a process just like you did the last time or manage a team to tackle a project in exactly the same way that they tackled the last one. But, of course, the danger is that you'll mistake the situation you're facing for a Type One when in fact it's a Type Two or Three. Only constant vigilance and questioning will save you from that.

Type Two is more of a trap obviously. People often quip: 'If it looks like a duck and quacks like a duck…'. But, frequently in the complex world of human management, actually it isn't a duck! Consider for instance a classic Type Two situation – the challenge faced by what's known as Generation X in managing the next generation down, the so-called Millennials or Gen Y. At the start of the 2020s that could mean someone around 45 managing someone who is in their mid-20s. That manager could well operate on an assumption that the 25-year-old is pretty much like they were at that same age and has many identical responsibilities and aspirations. So, they set out to manage and motivate the younger person in ways that worked for them at that point in their life. However, the research suggests that they'd be quite wrong. Gen Y values very different things at work from Gen X.

There is, of course, a caveat to grouping people by generation and then generalizing. It may be that the difference between the two groups is more about the life stages they've reached. The cliché is that every generation thinks the one below them is different and probably less robust, hardworking and engaged. You often hear people say something like, 'The children now love luxury; they have bad manners, contempt for authority; they show disrespect for elders and love chatter in place of exercise,' which you may think was muttered by your grumpy, complaining parent or grandparent. But it is in fact attributed to Socrates (again) in the 4th century BC.

Extensive studies do however support the existence of real generational differences, rather than life stage differences, specifically between Gens X and Y/Millennials, particularly in what they want from work. And even more pronounced is what Gen Z may be seeing as valuable in their jobs.

It is well worth exploring and testing these deeply etched generational differences with the age groups in your people. There is definitely a very useful discussion to be had between the generations. But generations as much as groups (see Chapter 2) won't all think alike. So you'll also need to tease this out, understanding group and individual differences. In the light of what you discover, there will be some profound implications for how you manage those different generations of employees. A number of factors underlie these differences not least the march of technological change. If you were, say, 23 when mobile phones started to become an everyday part of life, your 25-year-old Millennial employees were just 3 years old. You can still imitate the sound of 'a telephone ringing'. They can only make the sound of *their* phone ringing. You would have been 22 when the dot-com boom happened. They were 2 years old – you get the idea.

However, not just through the explosion of digital but also via a whole series of other societal shifts, Millennials have come to have a significantly different attitude to work. Adam Kingl, in his book, *Next Generation Leadership*, asked Millennials from 44 different countries how long they expected to stay in their jobs (11). Some 90 per cent of them said they'd stay for only between one and five years. During their lifetime, he estimates, they'll have between 15 and 16 employers. This contrasts with Gen X who will have half that amount. So, retaining a Millennial for an average of three years or so is a realistic expectation and you'll need to think what will keep them that long. In 2016 Gallup surveyed both Millennials and Gen X and reported that 59 per cent of Millennials said that 'opportunities to learn and grow are extremely important to them when applying for a job'. This compared with 30 per cent fewer Gen X and 35 per cent fewer Baby Boomers (b.1943–1964) who said the same. Gallup concluded that 'Millennials assign the highest importance to this job attribute, representing the greatest difference between what this generation values in a new job and what other generations value' (12).

This matters because if that's what will motivate or retain your younger people, you need to understand it and find ways of meeting that need in order to keep them engaged and working to the full. However, Gallup's insight is that companies are not living up to Millennials' expectations. They reported that 'only 39% of Millennials strongly agree that they learned something new in the past 30 days that they can use to do their jobs better'. And less than 50 per cent 'strongly agree that they have had opportunities to learn and grow in the past year'. Not only do Millennials want managers to find ways to invest in their futures and hone their skills, but they want it starting today. In their eyes, 'development shouldn't only come through tenure'. Adam Kingl also suggests that 'side hustles' are as important to the Millennials as the job you are employing them to do. 'What better way [for them] to have career insurance than to cultivate career options and nurture them before those options are required.' Rather than think of these endeavours as distractions, he warns, 'think of them as opportunities for professional development and engagement'.

Whereas security and longer-term prospects matter more to Gen X, what Millennials really want is a sense of purpose, for themselves and also for the company. In a twist on JFK's famous challenge in his 1961 Inauguration speech, 'Ask not what your country can do for you – ask what you can do for your country', Millennials are more likely to say to their manager, 'Ask not what I can do for the company but what the company can do for me'. The examples are legion. In France, for instance, the campaign group 'Pour un Reveil Ecologique' – Ecological Awakening – published a manifesto in 2019 in which they wrote 'We want to take advantage of our power as students by turning to employers that abide by the demands set out in this manifesto' (13). So far just over 32,000 have signed up, pledging only to work for environmentally conscious companies. In 2018 over 1,000 Googlers in Tokyo, Singapore and Dublin staged a lightning midday walk-out demanding, not higher wages, but transparency and public commitments to action on sexual harassment and inequality at the company (14). While no-one wants to be paid less than they're worth, Millennials are prepared to take a pay cut to move to a better job. By which they mean an 'improved "quality of work life" – such as career development, purposeful work, work/life balance, company culture', according to a study by Fidelity Investments in 2016 (15).

When it comes to Gen Z, about whom we rather obviously don't know very much as a consequence of them having only been born since the year 2000, Adam Kingl nonetheless identifies some emerging markers. He argues that, reacting against the 'spend now, pay later' Millennial philosophy, they may well be far less interested in the idea of ownership, bringing with it as it does considerable financial obligations. They will also be 'more accepting of the limits of resources… and considerate of the trade-offs between con-suming and wasting… with a fair degree of anxiety in relation to privacy, sustainability and community'. All of this he thinks will create 'a more stable equilibrium between employer and employee, with both parties recognizing a twenty-first century approach to living and working that transcends… the Industrial Age'. So, they won't own a flat or a car, they'll consequently be far more mobile in the job market. They will belong to communities that share their values and be much more demanding and adaptable about working flexibly both where and when and that will require managers to feed back to them with much greater regularity. Keeping an eye on this emerging set of generational values will help to manage your younger people better and with more insight.

Technology: HMV and Covid-19

So we come to Type Three. The biggest revolution in working lives in the last decades has, of course, been the internet. While it has greatly affected where and how people work and so how to manage them successfully, it has also had a wide and very fundamental impact on organizations, their models, their products and their people. The wrong strategic response by managers, Executives and Board members have in some cases laid waste to companies and also whole areas of commerce. Equally, where they've recognized it as a fundamental challenge to their business model and made the right decisions on how to adapt and transform, it has opened up vast new horizons. A num-ber of very well-known companies completely failed to see its significance. In 2002 HMV, the record store, floated on the stock market at a £1 billion valuation with a share price of £1.92. Philip Beeching, who for 25 years ran the agency that handled their advertising account, wrote in 2012 how, not long after that stock market listing, he had been asked to re-pitch for the business (16). He gave a presentation in which he said, 'The three greatest threats to HMV are, online retailers, downloadable music and supermarkets discounting loss leader product'. He then suddenly realized that 'the MD had stopped the meeting and was visibly angry. "I have never heard such rubbish", he said.'

Ten years after that stock market float the share price was a little above 30p and the company was valued at £15 million. Philip brusquely describes the reasons for that as, 'Hubris, arrogance, a feeling of invincibility'. HMV was riding high on the wave of its own success, but they didn't have the perceptiveness to see that the online challenge was to sell the content not just the things that carried it – records, CDs and games. Philip says that he and his colleagues 'could clearly see what was developing with the internet, yet HMV's efforts were at best a token gesture'. It's worth asking that, if they'd had the right kind of diversity to give them the insights they needed around their Board and Executive table – particularly across generations who might have better understood the impact of the internet – would they have realized they were facing a Type Three challenge and risen to it? Instead the internet blew up their model.

Similarly it has upended traditional ways of working and therefore presents quite a challenge to the way you should manage how people are able and want to work now. Adam Kingl acutely observes that 'when Generation X-ers and baby boomers talk about "work/life balance" to them that is a "when" question. For Gen Y it's a "where" question.' The flexibility Millennials aspire to is to work, not just when they want, but crucially where they want. While being present was the sign of hard work and application to an older generation, being absent, in the best sense of getting on with it without needing to 'come into the office', is the way a younger generation now frequently wants to work. However, without recognizing that difference explicitly, it is easy for an older generation to misinterpret what is happening, breeding mistrust on both sides. The trouble will start when your younger people think they're working and you think they're slacking. So constantly check up on them.

With so many employees forced to work at home rather than in offices, the Covid-19 pandemic has given a graphic demonstration of this failure of trust. In April 2020 a team led by Professor Sharon K Parker, the Director of the Centre for Transformative Work Design at Curtin University in Perth, Australia, surveyed over 1,200 remote workers in 24 different countries in industries ranging from manufacturing and science to real estate, education and financial services (17). She discovered a profound lack of trust by managers. Almost 80 per cent of them lacked some degree of confidence in managing employees remotely and over half felt that remote workers usually performed worse than those who worked in an office.

She concluded, 'Altogether, the picture is not a rosy one, suggesting a substantial number of managers have low confidence in their capability to lead remotely, have rather negative views about this work practice, and distrust their own workers.' One of the strongest reasons for this is that distrust is passed down the line. If you're being micro-managed by your boss, you're more likely to micro-manage your people. What makes that even worse are the snooping and supervising possibilities that technology now offers in the service of that micro-management.

Although the focus of their research was specifically on employees being forced to work at home as a result of the lockdowns, and not the question of flexible working generally, it nonetheless reflects that mistrust always grows from organizational culture and management habits, expectations and practices. Failing to modify that culture and your management approach to embrace what may well be a more permanent shift in working practices, made possible by the internet and already preferred by Gen Y, will affect your business considerably. Building trust in managing people who are working remotely is an imperative to creating a sense of belonging, which is especially a challenge when they are much of the time physically somewhere else. Without adapting to a new and different situation, and understanding the generational difference, managers will be in danger of building up a lack of confidence between the age groups, which in the long run will be corrosive. Not to mention the pressure we have seen that working at home puts on women who have children, nor the effect on your people's mental health. All of which requires very different kinds of support from managers.

Just as the German enemy was overrun by the tanks, so managers will be in danger of being undermined by remote working if they don't respond imaginatively and positively. As the new and the different mount up, it's not business as usual. Grace Hopper, who before she died in 1992 was the oldest commissioned officer in the US Navy and one of the early developers of the business programming language COBOL, once said, 'The most damaging phrase in the language is "We've always done it this way".' It's worth putting that up on your wall.

Managing difference, in individuals, in the way they interact with others and in the wide array of situations in which your team or business will find itself, is a bewilderingly huge task. But, if you dwell on how difficult it is, then demoralization will harden into inertia. Instead, you will need to brace yourself for the challenge, enjoy the diversity it offers and, never mind how demanding the practice of good management is, it is, as the make-up people would say, 'worth it'.

Why 'safe spaces' damage diversity

The constant theme of this book has been that there are considerable advantages to be reaped by consciously recognizing difference because only then can you leverage it to create dividends. Furthermore, recognizing difference, as we've seen, is the everyday of good management not the exception. Identifying and therefore being able to manage difference well is what helps teams to grow their innovation and performance, it's what enables difference in perspectives to reframe problems and it's what ultimately supports your people to work more productively and happily.

An underlying necessity in order to achieve all of that is the ability of managers to create what Amy C Edmondson calls, 'psychological safety'. She defines it as 'a climate in which raising a dissenting view is *expected and welcomed*' (my italics). It's all about creating the atmosphere where you feel you can speak up. That making a mistake doesn't lead to scorn or ridicule. Where, she says, quoting the MIT professors of organizational development, Edgar Schein and Warren Bennis, 'people feel secure and capable of changing... are free to focus on collective goals and problem prevention rather than on self-protection' (18).

The idea of 'safe spaces' is being dangerously misused at the moment. Language that might offend is being equated with actions that actually do. Hurt is equated with harm. Demands with Rights. But in groups at work where differences are explored, offence will be given and taken, upset and comfort will co-exist, anger will erupt and happiness will break out. Spaces only become safe when trust is built. And trust is only built through the understanding that comes from exploring and experiencing differences. Managers and their people have that exciting challenge when they work together to take those steps into what feels like dangerous territory. It is pretty scary to tackle the deep divisions that are in society and that therefore bleed into work. But the result of not doing so means that people then retreat into their separate corners, refusing to encounter each other unless there's a guarantee of protection against the very differences they are setting out to explore. That is a work environment where trust will never be created. Managers have to hold the risk and encourage their people to take it.

At the start of the chapter we saw in Katherine Phillips' experiment how diverse groups are thought to have more personal conflict. However, that perception should not be confused with the existence of productive conflict about the goals of the team, or ways of solving problems and meeting business challenges. The first is individual competition that leads to self-protection. The second is what Dorothy Leonard-Barton, the Professor of Business Administration at Harvard, called 'creative abrasion' (19). This is not dancing on a pin. Where humans are involved in any joint enterprise, conflict is inevitable. But for it to be constructive it needs to be about a shared goal not personal advantage.

Amy C Edmondson adds that psychological safety creates 'a climate that supports people in taking the interpersonal risks necessary to pursue high standards and achieve challenging goals... Conflict must be moderated by psychological safety to enable a learning climate of discussion and innovation'. This can only be created by 'the frames and behaviours of leaders and the interaction among peers working together'. In other words, it needs the explicit expression of difference from team members and the explicit support for that from their manager. This deployment of difference that, through discussion and disagreement, leads to an agreed plan of action is the most fruitful way to manage and lead teams. To reemphasize, safe spaces must be safe *for* disagreement *not from* them to achieve the best and most satisfying results.

In his presciently titled book, *The End of Diversity As We Know It*, Martin Davidson of the Darden School of Business in Virginia, describes a wealth management firm he worked with (20). The MD of one of the divisions wanted to see how she could grow the client base. She had realized that younger clients would have career paths that would mean that they'd build wealth differently from their parents. So she put together her team 'meticulously... recruiting a strategically diverse set of leaders of varying age and industry experience'. To sell wealth management to different generations of clients she wanted a team similarly spread in age. Once she had assembled it, she managed the team quite explicitly around that variation of ages. In one of their 'raging meetings' one of the team members proposed that they apply their generational difference to recruiting clients across whole families. That way they'd win business from one generation and the next. Through experience they discovered that certain households were predisposed to this more than others. By concentrating on them they grew their clients and revenue considerably. Where the MD had so significantly succeeded was in explicitly designing the team to include different generations and then leveraging that diversity to sell more of their services across families.

Not all teams are permanent. Some groups of people are just scheduled to work together, like surgical teams. It turns out that even the smallest gesture at recognizing difference, when that is the case and they don't know each other at all, can make a disproportionate difference to their effectiveness in working as a team. Atul Gawande is a celebrated surgeon and writer who in 2006 was asked by the World Health Organization to lead a group of people to tackle the fact that as the volume of surgery increased in the world 'a significant proportion of the care was so unsafe as to be a public danger' (21). Learning from the construction and airline industries he led the group to develop the Surgical Checklist as a way of tackling this. The hospital where he works in Boston has 42 operating rooms and more than 1,000 employees. So, as he says, they are virtually always adding strangers to their teams.

One of the elements on the checklist is disarmingly simple. Before starting any operation everyone introduces themselves by name and role. It turns out that people who don't know each other's names don't work together as well as those who do. In his book, *The Checklist Manifesto*, he recounts how two psychologists at Johns Hopkins in Baltimore tested this. They asked surgical colleagues coming out of operations two simple questions: how they would rate the level of communications during the operation and what were the names of the other members of colleagues involved? They found that the communications ratings jumped very significantly when they knew the names. Most importantly to the effectiveness of operations, 'when nurses were given a chance to say their names and mention concerns at the beginning of a case, they were more likely to note problems and offer solutions'. The researchers concluded that, 'giving people a chance to say something at the start seemed to activate their sense of participation and responsibility and their willingness to speak up'. It is now a feature of the checklists in hospitals across the world.

This simple idea is worth applying beyond the surgical experience, not only because it encourages people to contribute but because it gives them permission to challenge. As airlines discovered the two factors that enable co-pilots and other employees to speak up when a flight is in trouble are the checklist and the extent to which the captain is open to dialogue. Atul Gawande discovered that crews working with 'decisive' pilots, who did not routinely have open exchanges with their crew members, are less likely to speak up *even when they have information that could save the plane.* That's in italics because what that means is that they'd rather die than speak up. Your meetings might not have life or death consequences like that. But, unless you demonstrate all the time that you genuinely want to hear challenge, then your people will not give it, for fear of punishment, of damaging their relationships with you or with colleagues or from just feeling powerless. It's worth developing your own simple checklist, starting with, for instance, everyone saying their name at a meeting (or if they all know each other already, ask them to contribute something about what they've done recently or that day or whatever). This just ensures that from the start you open up the meeting to all of the participants.

Of course not everyone, even if the checklist has 'brought them into the room', necessarily will contribute in the same way or to the same extent. One of the reasons for this is that the world is made up of introverts and extroverts. I admit to being one of the latter. I always say that inside me there is a shy person. But he's trying to stay in there. The fact is that extroverts can easily dominate. Leigh Thompson, a Professor at the Kellogg School of Management, concluded that in a typical six-person meeting, two people do 60 per cent of the talking (22). Neatly summarized by the author Devora Zack, 'Introverts think to talk, and extroverts talk to think' (23). Each reflects and reacts to others in a totally different way. Extroverts throw out ideas, their verbal flow spinning possible approaches to issues, exploring the options out loud. Introverts meanwhile are often silent, evaluating what they've heard and what they think before they commit (sometimes in writing afterwards rather than verbally at the time). One is not better than the other. It's not necessarily the case that one resents the other. That will only happen if their difference is not acknowledged and valued. But they simply work differently. The methodology of the checklist is a way of ensuring that everyone has a voice and that challenge upwards is always on the cards, however and whenever it comes.

One of the techniques to achieve the right kind of balance for different styles in meetings is the 'golden silence' developed by Amazon, which Jeff Bezos has described as the 'weirdest meeting culture you ever encounter' (24). Before a meeting one of the people attending is asked to write a six-page memo that is 'narratively structured... has real sentences and topic sentences and verbs... not just bullet points' summarizing the issue under discussion. The meeting then starts with silence for at least 30 minutes so that everyone can read it. This opens up the opportunity for each person to turn over in their mind what they think about the issue. Then they discuss. The most senior person always speaks last.

Creating discussions through the positive recognition of difference not only helps to galvanize the contributions of the range of people in the team but it can also help to reframe the problem you're trying to solve. It is also part of good management to ensure that their team is not just engaging everyone but also, once engaged, they are not stuck in analysing it from the same old perspective.

Caroline Criado Perez jokingly called one of her chapters in *Invisible Women*, 'Can snow-clearing be sexist?' One of the more 'PC-has-gone-mad' types in the Council in Karlskoga in Sweden had scoffed that at least snow-clearing was something the 'gender people' wouldn't be able to get their hands on. But his (I am assuming) comment instead got the women think-ing. The snow had always been cleared from, in order of priority, the main arterial roads, the smaller ones, the pavements and then the bicycle paths. It turned out this affected men and women differently. Men drive more and typically have a twice daily commute. Women are more likely, with caring, kids and shopping to deal with, to make a series of interconnected shorter trips. Once they realized this, the Karlskoga Councillors swapped the order of priority to clearing the snow from pedestrian and public transport routes first. They figured it was easier to drive a car through three inches of snow than push a buggy through it. This also, as it turned out, saved the public purse a considerable amount of money because in icy conditions pedestrians are injured three times more often than motorists. It is estimated they saved £3.2m on healthcare costs and productivity that wasn't lost. Caroline reports that in Stockholm they now clear the 200 km of joint cycle and pedestrian lanes with special machines, and accidents have declined by 50 per cent.

Start from how it might be, not how ghastly it is

An intriguing incident of reframing an issue was recounted by David L Cooperrider and Diana Whitney, who, in 2001, jointly developed the five principles of an approach called Appreciative Inquiry (AI) (25). Essentially, AI seeks to transform the way that organizations see issues. Instead of per-ceiving them as problems, AI, according to their colleague Gervase Bushe, 'advocates collective inquiry into the best of what is, in order to imagine what could be, followed by collective design of a desired future state that is compelling and thus, does not require the use of incentives, coercion or per-suasion for planned change to occur' (26).

They had been approached by a consultancy who for two years had been working with a Fortune 500 company on the problem they were having in their organization with sexual harassment. Whatever the consultancy did, the problem continued to get worse. Participants in their workshops left feeling less able to talk to members of the opposite sex, less trusting of those work relationships and the women were making no more headway up the company. The consultancy wanted to know what to do.

David and Diana thought about it and called the head of the consultancy back. They asked her what she wanted to learn and achieve for the company with her intervention. She replied, rather obviously, that she wanted to reduce the sexual harassment. When David and Diana pushed her, she said that what she really wanted was the kind of modern company in which men and women modelled great working relationships with each other. David and Diana started with that. They asked people in the company to nominate themselves 'as candidates to study and share their stories of what it means to create and sustain high quality cross-sex relationships in the workplace'. From this positive reframing of the issue in terms of an inquiry, they built the momentum to make a huge impact on the working lives of the men and women in that business.

It takes bravery and imagination to reframe issues, particularly ones so damaging and personal as sexual harassment. But as David recounts, when they offered the invitation to be part of the inquiry, 'A waterfall was experienced. Stories poured in – stories of achievement, trust building, authentic joint leadership, practices of effective conflict management, ways of dealing with sex stereotypes, stages of development and methods of career advancement.' Rather than seeing the difference between men and women in the company negatively, by stigmatizing the men and making victims of the women, they instead developed the best experiences they'd had. They were able to combine the different experiences of men and women working together in the company to model great future relationships between the two sexes.

There are many words one can use to describe the quality needed in a manager or a leader to achieve this enjoyment of difference and to illustrate the ability required to create an atmosphere that enables challenge, ease, constructive disagreement and the engagement of the whole team by setting store in their differences. In his blog, The Red Hand Files, in 2019 the musician Nick Cave explored the rather old-fashioned term 'mercy' (27). What he wrote resounded with humanity. It is a warm and optimistic place to end our adventure through the Power of Difference. He wrote:

Mercy is a value that should be at the heart of any functioning and tolerant society. Mercy ultimately acknowledges that we are all imperfect and in doing so allows us the oxygen to breathe – to feel protected within a society, through our mutual fallibility. Without mercy a society loses its soul, and devours itself. Mercy allows us the ability to engage openly in free-ranging conversation – an expansion of collective discovery toward a common good. If mercy is our guide we have a safety net of mutual consideration, and we can, to quote Oscar Wilde, 'play gracefully with ideas'.

You can harness the Power of Difference to enjoy managing diversity by exploring:

- how your business can recognize what a challenge it is to be an effective manager;

- how, despite appearances, no group of people is the same, so managing well is always managing difference;

- how you can create agreement about common purpose in teams and organizations through the creativity of difference;

- how you can create an environment where raising a dissenting view is expected and welcomed;

- how you can always check whether you're using System 1 or System 2 – the automatic versus the effortful – to analyse which kind of scenarios you and your team/business are facing. Is it:

    o Type one – often things really are exactly the same;

    o Type two – 'If it looks like a duck and quacks like a duck...' in the complex world of human management it often isn't a duck!

    o Type three – remember Grace Hopper: 'The most damaging phrase in the language is "We've always done it this way".'

- how you can make sure you recognize a situation is new and think afresh about how then to manage people;

- how you can develop your self-assurance to make decisions with the curiosity and openness to investigate what you don't know;

- how you can frame issues at work in terms of possibility rather than problems;

- how you can find the best of what is, in order to imagine what could be.

REFERENCES

Introduction

1 Pits and Perverts gig [accessed 2 April 2021] When Miners and Gay Activists United: The Real Story of the Film *Pride* [Online] www.theguardian.com/ film/2014/aug/31/pride-film-gay-activists-miners-strike-interview (archived at https://perma.cc/6ZSE-LYXH)
2 The title of the benefit originated as a headline in the British tabloid *The Sun*: 'Perverts Support the Pits' [accessed 2 April 2021] [Online] https://justiceforworkersblog.wordpress.com/2016/02/03/coal-miners-and-gay-activists/ (archived at https://perma.cc/9W45-LFL5)
3 Day, K and Keeley, G [accessed 2 April 2021] My Father, RD Laing: 'He Solved Other People's Problems – But Not His Own' [Online] www.theguardian.com/ books/2008/jun/01/mentalhealth.society (archived at https://perma.cc/ EVL3-C62E)
4 Laing, RD (1967) *Politics of Experience and The Bird of Paradise*, Penguin, London
5 Stanford University [accessed 2 April 2021] *Encyclopaedia of Philosophy* [Online] https://plato.stanford.edu/entries/hegel-dialectics/ (archived at https://perma.cc/9XLT-VTXW)
6 Prejean, H (1993) *Dead Man Walking*, Penguin, London
7 Halpern, S [accessed 2 April 2021] Sister Sympathy, *New York Times Magazine*, 9 May 1993 [Online] www.nytimes.com/1993/05/09/magazine/sister-sympathy.html (archived at https://perma.cc/82KM-AFED)
8 Steinmetz, K [accessed 2 April 2021] Kimberlé Crenshaw: She Coined the Term 'Intersectionality' Over 30 Years Ago. Here's What It Means To Her Today, *Time Magazine*, 20 February 2020 [Online] https://time.com/5786710/ kimberle-crenshaw-intersectionality/ (archived at https://perma.cc/52XL-VNRP)
9 Foreman, A [accessed 2 April 2021] Sylvia Pankhurst by Rachel Holmes: Review – Finally Having Her Moment, *The Sunday Times*, 20 September 2020 [Online] www.thetimes.co.uk/article/sylvia-pankhurst-natural-born-rebel-by-rachel-holmes-book-review-d0mqclndc (archived at https://perma.cc/ HS74-PJ9B)
10 Verkaik, R [accessed 2 April 2021] Gays Win the Same Rights As Married Couples, *The Independent*, 10 October 2011 [Online] www.independent.co.uk/

news/uk/crime/gays-win-the-same-rights-as-married-couples-733103.html
(archived at https://perma.cc/25U9-WFKS)

11 Terry Sanderson's Media Watch, *Gay Times*, June 1986 [Online]
https://gtmediawatch.org/1970/12/01/gay-times-93/ (archived at https://perma.cc/
2WN3-8QML)

12 Lovelock, M [accessed 2 April 2021] Fifty Years of Gay Rights But Some in the
British Media Are Peddling the Same Homophobia, 25 July 2017 [Online]
https://theconversation.com/fifty-years-of-gay-rights-but-some-in-the-british-
media-are-peddling-the-same-homophobia-81465 (archived at https://perma.cc/
54RE-NLV6)

13 Mills, R [accessed 2 April 2021] Terry Sanderson's Media Watch, *Gay Times*,
October 1986 [Online] https://gtmediawatch.org/tag/ray-mills/ (archived at
https://perma.cc/N39X-NRS7)

Chapter 1

1 Kearns Goodwin, D (2019) *Leadership: In turbulent times*, Penguin, London,
pp 211–43

2 Douglass, F (1876) [accessed 2 April 2021] *Oration in Memory of Abraham
Lincoln* [Online] https://teachingamericanhistory.org/library/document/
oration-in-memory-of-abraham-lincoln/ (archived at https://perma.cc/DH9Z-
M8EK)

3 A Lesson in Core Values from Steve Jobs, A For Adventure, 2 February 2016
www.aforadventure.com/blog/2016/2/2/a-lesson-in-core-values-from-steve-jobs
(archived at https://perma.cc/N6LM-ZGHD)

4 Shakespeare, W (1606) *Macbeth*, Act 5, scene 5, lines 16–27

5 Press Association [accessed 2 April 2021] H&M Apologises Over Image of
Black Child in 'Monkey' Hoodie, *The Guardian*, 8 January 2018 [Online]
www.theguardian.com/fashion/2018/jan/08/h-and-m-apologises-over-image-of-
black-child-in-monkey-hoodie (archived at https://perma.cc/KCD2-84YL)

6 Wright, J [accessed 2 April 2021] '& Other Stories Used a Racial Slur for the
Internal Name of a Hat: Employees are furious, *CNN Business*, 5 August 2020
[Online] https://edition.cnn.com/2020/08/05/business/and-other-stories-racism/
index.html (archived at https://perma.cc/9KGN-2MYX)

7 Wong, JC [accessed 2 April 2021] Snap to Stop Promoting Trump's Content in
a Move That Adds Pressure to Facebook, *The Guardian*, 3 June 2020 [Online]
www.theguardian.com/technology/2020/jun/03/snap-stop-promoting-donald-
trump-facebook (archived at https://perma.cc/5F89-N6A6)

8 Microsoft blog [accessed 2 April 2021] Change in Ourselves Helps Drive
Change in the World, 5 June 2020 [Online] https://blogs.microsoft.com/

blog/2020/06/05/change-in-ourselves-helps-drive-change-in-the-world/
(archived at https://perma.cc/7QMV-3Q4S)

 9 Palmer, A [accessed 2 April 2021] Read the Email Tim Cook Sent to Apple
Employees About George Floyd, CNBC, 31 May 2020 [Online] www.cnbc.com/
2020/05/31/apple-ceo-tim-cook-email-to-employees-about-george-floyd.html
(archived at https://perma.cc/46Y6-C3DY)

10 Rooney, K and Khorram, Y [accessed 2 April 2021] Tech Companies Say They
Value Diversity, But Reports Show Little Change in Last Six Years, CNBC,
12 June 2020 [Online] www.cnbc.com/2020/06/12/six-years-into-diversity-
reports-big-tech-has-made-little-progress.html (archived at https://perma.cc/
P8UE-QQFG)

11 US Census [accessed 2 April 2021] [Online] www.census.gov/quickfacts/fact/
table/US/PST045219 (archived at https://perma.cc/UN83-CT55)

12 Bursztynsky, J [accessed 2 April 2021] Here's What Tech Companies Have Said
They'll Do to Fight Racism in Wake of George Floyd Protests, CNBC, 12 June
2020 [Online] www.cnbc.com/2020/06/12/george-floyd-protests-tech-
company-responses.html (archived at https://perma.cc/ZS8M-KNAQ)

13 Yurieff, K [accessed 2 April 2021] Airbnb CEO Brian Chesky: 'We Could
Have Done So Much More' on Race, CNN *Business*, 11 June 2020 [Online]
https://edition.cnn.com/2020/06/11/tech/airbnb-brian-chesky-boss-files/index.
html (archived at https://perma.cc/C4GT-C9AT)

14 Johnson, T [accessed 2 April 2021] When Black People Are in Pain,
White People Just Join Book Clubs, *Washington Post*, 11 June 2020 [Online]
www.washingtonpost.com/outlook/white-antiracist-allyship-book-clubs/
2020/06/11/9edcc766-abf5-11ea-94d2-d7bc43b26bf9_story.html (archived at
https://perma.cc/593X-JQKA)

15 Ritschel, C [accessed 2 April 2021] Alexis Ohanian: Reddit Co-Founder
Resigns, Urging Company to Replace Him With Black Candidate,
The Independent, 6 June 2020 [Online] www.independent.co.uk/life-style/
gadgets-and-tech/alexis-ohanian-reddit-resign-cofounder-black-candidate-
serena-williams-a9551896.html (archived at https://perma.cc/AFP5-QFCU)

16 Reichert, C [accessed 2 April 2021] Reddit Appoints Michael Seibel As New
Board Member After Alexis Ohanian Resignation, C-Net, 10 June 2020 [Online]
www.cnet.com/news/reddit-appoints-michael-seibel-as-new-board-member-
after-alexis-ohanian-resignation/ (archived at https://perma.cc/6DFC-MJEH)

17 Harper, SR [accessed 2 April 2021] Corporations Say They Support Black
Lives Matter: Their employees doubt them, *Washington Post*, 16 June 2020
[Online] www.washingtonpost.com/outlook/2020/06/16/corporations-say-
they-support-black-lives-matter-their-employees-doubt-them/ (archived at
https://perma.cc/VZ6T-GE6C)

18 Energy & Utility Skills [accessed 2 April 2021] Workforce Renewal and Skills
Strategy 2020–2025: Response and refresh [Online] www.euskills.co.uk/about/

energy-utilities-skills-partnership/skills-strategy-2020/ (archived at
https://perma.cc/QG8G-2DXT)

19 Diversity UK [accessed 2 April 2021] BAME Population [Online]
https://diversityuk.org/diversity-in-the-uk/ (archived at https://perma.cc/
L7TJ-FMZQ) and England NHS [accessed 2 April 2021] *NHS Workforce Race
Equality Standard 2019 Data Analysis Report* [Online] www.england.nhs.uk/
wp-content/uploads/2020/01/wres-2019-data-report.pdf (archived at
https://perma.cc/GN7G-Y699)

20 Seeley, R [accessed 2 April 2021] *NHS Figures, NHS Women on Boards
Report* [Online] www.nhsemployers.org/-/media/Employers/Publications/
NHS-Women-on-Boards-report.pdf (archived at https://perma.cc/AJ9Y-MP9Y)
and National Health Executive [accessed 2 April 2021] Only a Quarter
of Key NHS Leadership Roles Are Held By Women [Online]
www.nationalhealthexecutive.com/Health-Care-News/only-a-quarter-of-key-
nhs-leadership-roles-held-by-women (archived at https://perma.cc/Q3FZ-DSCE)

21 Rooney, K and Khorram, Y [accessed 2 April 2021] Tech Companies Say
They Value Diversity, But Reports Show Little Change in Last Six Years,
CNBC, 12 June 2020 [Online] www.cnbc.com/2020/06/12/six-years-into-
diversity-reports-big-tech-has-made-little-progress.html (archived at
https://perma.cc/P8UE-QQFG)

22 Universities UK [accessed 2 April 2021] *Black, Asian and Minority Ethnic
Student Attainment at UK Universities: #Closingthegap NUS & UUK Report
2019* [Online] www.universitiesuk.ac.uk/policy-and-analysis/reports/
Documents/2019/bame-student-attainment-uk-universities-closing-the-gap.pdf
(archived at https://perma.cc/DFW5-623E)

23 Adams, R [accessed 2 April 2021] Fewer Than 1% of UK University
Professors Are Black, Figures Show, *The Guardian*, 27 February 2020 [Online]
www.theguardian.com/education/2020/feb/27/fewer-than-1-of-uk-university-
professors-are-black-figures-show (archived at https://perma.cc/RQZ8-ZY78)

24 Adams, R [accessed 2 April 2021] Fewer Than 1% of UK University
Professors Are Black, Figures Show, *The Guardian*, 27 February 2020 [Online]
www.theguardian.com/education/2020/feb/27/fewer-than-1-of-uk-university-
professors-are-black-figures-show (archived at https://perma.cc/RQZ8-ZY78)

25 Adams, R [accessed 2 April] British Universities Employ No Black
Academics in Top Roles, Figures Show, *The Guardian*, 19 January 2017
[Online] www.theguardian.com/education/2017/jan/19/british-universities-
employ-no-black-academics-in-top-roles-figures-show (archived at
https://perma.cc/LS74-VXLU)

26 Cheek, S [accessed 2 April 2021] Number of Female Managers Stagnates as
Funds Universe Balloons, Portfolio, 4 March 2020 [Online] https://portfolio-
adviser.com/number-of-female-managers-stagnates-as-funds-universe-balloons/
(archived at https://perma.cc/J2GE-X46C)

27 Catalyst [accessed 2 April 2021] Women in Financial Services: Quick Take, 29 June 2020 [Online] www.catalyst.org/research/women-in-financial-services/ (archived at https://perma.cc/KFW6-S64P)

28 Catalyst [accessed 2 April 2021] Women in Financial Services: Quick Take, 29 June 2020 [Online] www.catalyst.org/research/women-in-financial-services/ (archived at https://perma.cc/KFW6-S64P)

29 McKinsey [accessed 2 April 2021] *Gender Diversity: A corporate performance driver*, 1 October 2007 [Online] www.mckinsey.com/business-functions/ organization/our-insights/gender-diversity-a-corporate-performance-driver (archived at https://perma.cc/SVC8-CTCJ)

30 Page, SE (2017) *The Diversity Bonus*, Princeton University Press, Princeton, USA

31 Page, SE (2008) *The Difference*, Princeton University Press, Princeton, USA

32 Credit Suisse [accessed 2 April 2021] Gender Diversity is Good For Business (updated 2019) [Online] www.credit-suisse.com/about-us-news/en/articles/ news-and-expertise/cs-gender-3000-report-2019-201910.html (archived at https://perma.cc/UT79-LLM8)

33 Hunt, V, Layton, D and Prince, S [accessed 2 April 2021] *Why Diversity Matters*, 1 January 2015, McKinsey [Online] www.mckinsey.com/business-functions/organization/our-insights/why-diversity-matters (archived at https://perma.cc/VM8F-6SRQ)

34 Hunt, V, Yee, L, Prince, S and Dixon-Fyle, S [accessed 2 April 2021] Delivering Through Diversity, January 2018, McKinsey [Online] www.mckinsey.com/ business-functions/organization/our-insights/delivering-through-diversity (archived at https://perma.cc/4JPK-LLTJ)

35 Bourke, J and Dillon, B [accessed 2 April 2021] *The Diversity and Inclusion Revolution: Eight powerful truths*, Deloitte Review [Online] www2.deloitte.com/ content/dam/insights/us/articles/4209_Diversity-and-inclusion-revolution/ DI_Diversity-and-inclusion-revolution.pdf (archived at https://perma.cc/ J6WK-L3EB)

36 *Evening Standard* [accessed 2 April 2021] Census Data Shows 100 Different Languages Spoken in Almost Every London Borough, 30 January 2013 [Online] www.standard.co.uk/news/london/census-data-shows-100-different-languages-spoken-in-almost-every-london-borough-8472483.html (archived at https://perma.cc/22UY-LPAE)

37 Fanshawe, S (2018) [accessed 2 April 2021] Diversity: The new prescription for the NHS [Online] https://diversitybydesign.co.uk/wp-content/ uploads/2018/05/Diversity-The-New-Prescription-for-the-NHS-FINAL-version.pdf (archived at https://perma.cc/HZ26-DKD2)

38 Dawson, JF *et al* (2011) [accessed 2 April 2021] Why organizational and community diversity matter: representativeness and the emergence of incivility and organizational performance, *The Academy of Management Journal*, **54** (6), pp 1103–18 [Online] www.jstor.org/stable/41413611?seq=1 (archived at https://perma.cc/33TH-M72S)

39 Eberhardt, J (2019) *Biased*, William Heinemann, London, pp 103–06

40 Drucker Institute [accessed 2 April 2021] Measurement Myopia [Online] www.drucker.institute/thedx/measurement-myopia/ (archived at https://perma.cc/S6DJ-ADWF)

41 Drucker Institute [accessed 2 April 2021] Measurement Myopia [Online] www.drucker.institute/thedx/measurement-myopia/ (archived at https://perma.cc/S6DJ-ADWF)

42 Buerkli, D [accessed 2 April 2021] What Gets Measured Gets Managed: It's wrong and Drucker never said it, Centre for Public Impact, 8 April 2019 [Online] https://medium.com/centre-for-public-impact/what-gets-measured-gets-managed-its-wrong-and-drucker-never-said-it-fe95886d3df6 (archived at https://perma.cc/NE3H-K387)

43 30% Club [accessed 2 April 2021] Business Leadership: The catalyst for accelerating change [Online] https://30percentclub.org/assets/uploads/2_December_2020_FINAL.pdf (archived at https://perma.cc/U74L-L4DF)

44 Bohnet, I (2016) *What Works*, Harvard University Press, Harvard, USA

45 World Bank [accessed 2 April 2021] Female Population Figure [Online] https://data.worldbank.org/indicator/SP.POP.TOTL.FE.ZS (archived at https://perma.cc/73WF-4KV3)

46 Lewis, H [accessed 2 April 2021] Helena Morrissey: 'If I was doing it for a popularity contest, I probably wouldn't say anything', *The Guardian*, 27 March 2015 [Online] www.theguardian.com/business/2015/mar/27/helena-morrissey-30-percent-club-women-in-ftse100-boardroom (archived at https://perma.cc/M8UG-BPFC)

47 Childs, S and Krook, ML (2008) [accessed 2 April 2021] Critical mass theory and women's political representation, *Political Studies*, **56**, pp 725–36 [Online] http://mlkrook.org/pdf/childs_krook_2008.pdf (archived at https://perma.cc/835J-DHJL)

48 Newton Small, J [accessed 2 April 2021] What Happens When Women Reach a Critical Mass of Influence, *Time*, 20 November 2017 [Online] https://time.com/5016735/when-women-reach-a-critical-mass-of-influence/ (archived at https://perma.cc/VC6T-Z66Y)

49 Salmon, J [accessed 2 April 2021] Named and Shamed: The two FTSE 350 firms that have no women on the board… and the 39 with one 'token' female director, This is Money.co.uk, 12 November 2019 [Online] www.thisismoney.co.uk/money/markets/article-7678673/Named-shamed-FTSE-350-firms-no-women-board.html (archived at https://perma.cc/Z77N-VUYY)

50 Sunstein, CR (1996) Norm entrepreneurs, social norms and social roles, *Columbia Law Review*, **96** (4), pp 903–68

51 Page, SE (2017) *The Diversity Bonus*, Princeton University Press, Princeton, USA, pp 168–71

52 Boston Consulting (2017) [accessed 2 April 2021] The Mix That Matters: Innovation through diversity [Online] www.bcg.com/publications/2017/people-organization-leadership-talent-innovation-through-diversity-mix-that-matters (archived at https://perma.cc/K7N5-UFJF)

53 Botha, A (ed.) (2007) *Chris Brink: Anatomy of a transformer*, Stellenbosch, African Sunmedia [Online] https://scholar.sun.ac.za/handle/10019.1/101778 (archived at https://perma.cc/4PEZ-ZQHG)

54 Farber, M [accessed 2 April 2021] The World's Biggest Mining Company Wants Half Its Workforce to Be Women, *Fortune*, 20 October 2016 [Online] https://fortune.com/2016/10/20/bhp-billiton-hires-more-women/ (archived at https://perma.cc/P8KU-ZDW5)

55 The Engineer [accessed 2 April 2021] Balancing the Scales Between Pay and Gender: Salary survey 2019 [Online] https://theengineer.markallengroup.com/production/content/uploads/2019/06/2019-Salary-Survey.pdf (archived at https://perma.cc/8HCC-WQMP)

56 Sanderson, H [accessed 2 April 2021] BHP on Track to Achieve 50% Female Workforce By 2025, *FT*, 16 October 2018 [Online] www.ft.com/content/063eb6bc-d10f-11e8-a9f2-7574db66bcd5 (archived at https://perma.cc/7XCN-5YM6)

57 Perry, TS [accessed 2 April 2021] The Engineers of the Future Will Not Resemble the Engineers of the Past, IEEE Spectrum, 30 May 2017 [Online] https://spectrum.ieee.org/view-from-the-valley/at-work/education/the-engineers-of-the-future-will-not-resemble-the-engineers-of-the-past (archived at https://perma.cc/P4TL-TWD4)

58 Morrison, K [accessed 2 April 2021] World's Largest Miner Says Workforce Will Be 50% Female By 2025, *The Independent* [Online] www.independent.co.uk/news/business/news/bhp-billiton-worker-half-women-female-2025-gender-equality-mining-a8586696.html (archived at https://perma.cc/LVM7-C7XQ)

59 Goldman Sachs [accessed 2 April 2021] Ajay Banga of MasterCard in 'Talks at Goldman Sachs' [Online] www.goldmansachs.com/insights/talks-at-gs/ajay-banga.html (archived at https://perma.cc/E5CL-MLM8)

60 Mastercard [accessed 2 April 2021] About Mastercard and the Value We Deliver [Online] https://newsroom.mastercard.com/wp-content/uploads/2013/09/MasterStory_Our_Story.pdf (archived at https://perma.cc/J7KK-HZYS)

Chapter 2

1 Staniforth, A and Sampson, F (eds) (2013) *The Routledge Companion to UK Counter-Terrorism*, Routledge, London, p 81

2 Margaret Thatcher [accessed 3 April 2021] Speech to Conservative Party Conference, 12 October 1984 [Online] https://live-thatcher.pantheonsite.io/document/105763 (archived at https://perma.cc/LT9U-LEA7)

3 Building Bridges for Peace [accessed 3 April 2021] Website, http://buildingbridgesforpeace.org/ (archived at https://perma.cc/X3YJ-GBLR)

4 Vernā Myers [accessed 3 April 2021] Twitter, https://twitter.com/vernamyers?lang=en (archived at https://perma.cc/7AEV-VVP4)

5 Sherbin, L and Rashid, R (2017) [accessed 3 April 2021] Diversity doesn't stick without inclusion, *Harvard Business Review* [Online] hbr.org/2017/02/diversity-doesnt-stick-without-inclusion (archived at https://perma.cc/5T2S-WBZM)

6 Gates, HL Jr [accessed 3 April 2021] How Many Slaves Landed in the U.S.? (originally posted on The Root, www.theroot.com/ (archived at https://perma.cc/888J-5HN9)) [Online] www.pbs.org/wnet/african-americans-many-rivers-to-cross/history/how-many-slaves-landed-in-the-us/ (archived at https://perma.cc/6A5D-VF5B)

7 Human Dignity Trust [accessed 3 April 2021] Map of Countries That Criminalise LGBT People [Online] www.humandignitytrust.org/lgbt-the-law/map-of-criminalisation/ (archived at https://perma.cc/597B-F3UX)

8 Malik, K [accessed 3 April 2021]The Rise of White Identity Politics, *Prospect*, 13 July 2020 [Online] www.prospectmagazine.co.uk/magazine/white-identity-politics-black-lives-matter-race-kenan-malik (archived at https://perma.cc/U2FR-EX83)

9 Davis, M [accessed 3 April 2021] Britain at Work: Voices from the workplace 1945–1995 [Online] www.unionhistory.info/britainatwork/narrativedisplay.php?type=womenatwork (archived at https://perma.cc/2Y7D-ASRZ)

10 Kelly, J [accessed 3 April 2021] What Was Behind the Bristol Bus Boycott? *BBC News*, 26 August 2013 [Online] www.bbc.co.uk/news/magazine-23795655 (archived at https://perma.cc/2D3E-LPYM)

11 Norton-Taylor, R [accessed 3 April 2021] Racism: Extremists Led Powell Marches, *The Guardian*, 1 January 1999 [Online] www.theguardian.com/uk/1999/jan/01/richardnortontaylor2 (archived at https://perma.cc/L9CH-X3LP)

12 Yglesias, M [accessed 3 April 2021] Reagan's Race Record, *The Atlantic*, 9 November 2007 [Online] www.theatlantic.com/politics/archive/2007/11/reagans-race-record/46875/ (archived at https://perma.cc/GBX9-ABV6)

13 *Woman's Own* [accessed 3 April 2021] Margaret Thatcher Interview for Woman's Own (no such thing as society) 23 September 1987 [Online] www.margaretthatcher.org/document/106689 (archived at https://perma.cc/ EF4J-VBWV)

14 Margaret Thatcher [accessed 3 April 2021] Speech to Conservative Party Conference, 9 October 1987 [Online] https://live-thatcher.pantheonsite.io/ document/106941 (archived at https://perma.cc/L9PY-PK8C)

15 Erikson, EH (1968) [accessed 3 April 2021] Identity Youth and Crisis 1, WW Norton & Company, London, p 130 (collection of Erik H Erikson's major essays on topics originating in the concept of the adolescent identity crisis) [Online] www.academia.edu/37327712/Erik_H_Erikson_Identity_ Youth_and_Crisis_1_1968_W_W_Norton_and_Company_1_ (archived at https://perma.cc/9UAG-62SX)

16 Moran, M [accessed 3 April 2021] Identity and identity politics: A cultural materialist history, *Historical Materialism* [Online] www.historicalmaterialism. org/articles/identity-and-identity-politics (archived at https://perma.cc/ EK4P-JS29)

17 Friedman, M (2017) *Milton Friedman on Freedom: Selections from the Collected Works of Milton Friedman*, Hoover Institution Press, Stanford, USA

18 Hobart, PJ [accessed 3 April 2021] Consumerism, Capitalism, and Personal Identity, *Prindle*, 8 December 2014 [Online] www.prindlepost.org/2014/12/ consumerism-capitalism-and-personal-identity/ (archived at https://perma.cc/ 2FJT-93LT)

19 Biden, J [accessed 3 April 2021] Joe Biden To Charlamagne: You Ain't Black If You Vote For Trump! 22 May 2020 [Online] www.youtube.com/ watch?v=We6Qr9-dDn8 (archived at https://perma.cc/K8JG-V4CC)

20 Lederman, J [accessed 3 April 2021] New Republic Magazine Pulls Down Homophobic Op-Ed About Pete Buttigieg By an Openly Gay Literary Critic, *NBC News*, 13 July 2019 [Online] www.nbcnews.com/politics/2020-election/ new-republic-removes-homophobic-op-ed-attacking-buttigieg-n1029546 (archived at https://perma.cc/9TZZ-SELF)

21 Keating, S [accessed 3 April 2021] You Wanted Same-Sex Marriage? Now You Have Pete Buttigieg, *Buzzfeed*, 11 December 2019 [Online] www.buzzfeednews.com/article/shannonkeating/pete-buttigieg-marriage-equality-lgbtq-gay-rights (archived at https://perma.cc/ATS3-8XP2)

22 Rutherford, A (2020) *How to Argue With a Racist*, Orion, London, p 59

23 Hughes, L [accessed 3 April 2021] *I Too* [Online] www.poetryfoundation.org/ poems/47558/i-too (archived at https://perma.cc/T2EW-XZE9)

24 Ali, M (1975) *The Greatest: My own story*, Random House, New York

25 Essence [accessed 3 April 2021] Viola Davis Graces the August Issue of ESSENCE [Online] www.essence.com/news/viola-davis-graces-the-august-issue-of-essence/ (archived at https://perma.cc/8RGA-9Y3Z)

26 Rothstein, M [accessed 3 April 2021] Toni Morrison, in Her New Novel, Defends Women, *New York Times*, 26 August 1987 [Online] www.nytimes.com/

1987/08/26/books/toni-morrison-in-her-new-novel-defends-women.html (archived at https://perma.cc/P8YA-NM2G)

27 BLM Mission [accessed 3 April 2021] Website, https://blacklivesmatter.com/about/ (archived at https://perma.cc/L7U6-CY4P)

28 Coates, T-N [accessed 3 April 2021] The Case for Reparations, *The Atlantic*, June 2014 [Online] www.theatlantic.com/magazine/archive/2014/06/the-case-for-reparations/361631/ (archived at https://perma.cc/6MEC-XBL7)

29 Kendi, IX [accessed 3 April 2021] Extract From How To Be an Antiracist, Penguin articles, 9 June 2020 [Online] www.penguin.co.uk/articles/2020/june/ibram-x-kendi-definition-of-antiracist.html (archived at https://perma.cc/K4Z3-DGHT)

30 Ungar-Sargon, B [accessed 3 April 2021] A New Intelligentsia is Pushing Back Against Wokeness, Forward, 20 July 2020 [Online] https://forward.com/opinion/451099/a-new-intelligentsia-is-pushing-back-against-wokeness/ (archived at https://perma.cc/H99D-LJZ7)

31 Ungar-Sargon, B [accessed 3 April 2021] A New Intelligentsia is Pushing Back Against Wokeness, Forward, 20 July 2020 [Online] https://forward.com/opinion/451099/a-new-intelligentsia-is-pushing-back-against-wokeness/ (archived at https://perma.cc/H99D-LJZ7)

32 Reed, A Jr [accessed 3 April 2021] From Jenner to Dolezal: One Trans Good, the Other Not So Much, Common Dreams, 15 June 2015 [Online] www.commondreams.org/views/2015/06/15/jenner-dolezal-one-trans-good-other-not-so-much (archived at https://perma.cc/5H8T-5N3Y)

33 The Equiano Project [accessed 3 April 2021] Website, www.theequianoproject.com/about (archived at https://perma.cc/U6F5-B2S7)

34 McWhorter, J [accessed 3 April 2021] John McWhorter: The Neoracists, Persuasion, 8 February 2021 [Online] www.persuasion.community/p/john-mcwhorter-the-neoracists (archived at https://perma.cc/3MLU-296P)

35 Mounk, Y [accessed 3 April 2021] Stop Firing the Innocent, *The Atlantic*, 27 June 2020 [Online] www.theatlantic.com/ideas/archive/2020/06/stop-firing-innocent/613615/ (archived at https://perma.cc/3A3U-LN98)

36 Wesler, AT [accessed 3 April 2021] Tweet: Come Get Your Boy [Online] https://twitter.com/thereftw/status/1266442248826138624?lang=en (archived at https://perma.cc/QK8Q-X8KK)

37 Mounk, Y [accessed 3 April 2021] Stop Firing the Innocent, *The Atlantic*, 27 June 2020 [Online] www.theatlantic.com/ideas/archive/2020/06/stop-firing-innocent/613615/ (archived at https://perma.cc/3A3U-LN98)

38 Syed, M (2019) *Rebel Ideas: The power of diverse thinking*, John Murray, London, p 184

39 Flaxman, S, Goel, S and Rao, JM (2016) [accessed 3 April 2021] Filter Bubbles, Echo Chambers, and Online News Consumption, *Public Opinion*

Quarterly, 80 (Special Issue), pp 298–320 [Online] https://wisdomofcrowds. stanford.edu/papers/bubbles.pdf (archived at https://perma.cc/D42Y-E64Q)

40   Bail, C *et al* [accessed 3 April 2021] Exposure to Opposing Views on Social Media Can Increase Political Polarization, Proceedings of the National Academy of Sciences of the United States of America, 11 September 2018 [Online] www.ncbi.nlm.nih.gov/pmc/articles/PMC6140520/ (archived at https://perma.cc/UE4Y-ZE3E)

41   UN [accessed 3 April 2021] Declaration on Human Rights [Online] www.un.org/en/universal-declaration-human-rights/ (archived at https://perma.cc/ B9GR-BTYM)

42   Yousafzai, M [accessed 3 April 2021] Website, https://malala.org/malalas-story (archived at https://perma.cc/HY87-AN6J)

43   Matinuddin, K (1999) *The Taliban Phenomenon, Afghanistan 1994–1997*, Oxford University Press, Oxford

44   No Outsiders [accessed 3 April 2021] Website, https://no-outsiders.com/ (archived at https://perma.cc/L6VY-8T37)

45   Ahmed, A [accessed 3 April 2021] Teacher At Centre of LGBT Row in Birmingham Received Death Threat [Online] https://news.sky.com/story/ teacher-at-centre-of-lgbt-lessons-row-in-birmingham-received-death-threat-11688253 (archived at https://perma.cc/K2A5-PRF6)

46   Ahmed, A [accessed 3 April 2021] LGBT Classes Protestor: I Am Not Homophobic, BBC interview [Online] www.bbc.co.uk/news/av/uk-england-birmingham-47631301 (archived at https://perma.cc/4HNV-36HC)

47   Bagwell, M [accessed 3 April 2021] How Protests Over Diversity Lessons in Birmingham Ended in a Win for LGBTQ+ People Everywhere, *Huffington Post*, 28 June 2020 [Online] www.huffingtonpost.co.uk/entry/andrew-moffat-interview-parkfield-school-no-outsiders-protests-one-year-on_ uk_5ef5ecadc5b612083c4c57bf (archived at https://perma.cc/J5LV-HZCM)

48   Moore, M [accessed 3 April 2021] BBC Advises All Staff to Use Trans Friendly Pronouns, *The Times*, 10 July 2020 [Online] www.thetimes.co.uk/ article/8ff3493a-c218-11ea-91bd-3bac3c644e50?shareToken=ca8cb01a96df5e 3168516ef672d9725c (archived at https://perma.cc/QNY8-YPAQ)

49   The Royal Society of Chemists (2019) [accessed 3 April 2021] Is Publishing in the Chemical Sciences Gender Biased? [Online] www.rsc.org/globalassets/04-campaigning-outreach/campaigning/gender-bias/gender-bias-report-final.pdf (archived at https://perma.cc/9U4L-9DZT)

50   Mayer, B [accessed 3 April 2021] The Paradox of Leadership: Cooperating to Compete, Following to Lead, Queens University IRC [Online] https://irc. queensu.ca/sites/default/files/articles/the-paradox-of-leadership-cooperating-to-compete-following-to-lead-by-bernie-mayer.pdf (archived at https://perma.cc/ ZR4G-DA8T)

51 Yoshino, K [accessed 3 April 2021] Uncovering Talent: A New Model of Inclusion [Online] www2.deloitte.com/content/Dam/Deloitte/us/Documents/about-deloitte/us-about-deloitte-uncovering-talent-a-new-model-of-inclusion.pdf (archived at https://perma.cc/ZLC2-6BWQ)

52 Yohn, DL [accessed 3 April 2021] Ban These 5 Words From Your Corporate Values Statement, *Harvard Business Review* [Online] hbr.org/2018/02/ban-these-5-words-from-your-corporate-values-statement (archived at https://perma.cc/G3BF-A9RS)

53 Galunic, C [accessed 3 April 2021] Does Articulating Your Corporate Values Matter? INSEAD, 1 July 2015 [Online] https://knowledge.insead.edu/leadership-organisations/does-articulating-your-corporate-values-matter-4126 (archived at https://perma.cc/W7LW-ZAHU)

54 Heffernan, M [accessed 3 April 2021] Dare to Disagree, TED Global [Online] www.ted.com/talks/margaret_heffernan_dare_to_disagree?language=en (archived at https://perma.cc/LJ77-4TSP)

Chapter 3

1 Mario Savio [accessed 3 April 2021] Speech [Online] www.youtube.com/watch?v=xz7KLSOJaTE (archived at https://perma.cc/8R6Q-YHW8)

2 Johnson, T [accessed 3 April 2021] Freedom Resource Centre Motivational Monday: Ed Roberts Day [Online] www.freedomrc.org/motivational-monday-ed-roberts-day/ (archived at https://perma.cc/W4XZ-XMXC)

3 ENIL [accessed 3 April 2021] European Network on Independent Living, Hall of Fame [Online] https://enil.eu/news/hall-of-fame-ed-roberts/ (archived at https://perma.cc/898G-2AQZ)

4 Dawson, V [accessed 3 April 2021] Ed Roberts' Wheelchair Records a Story of Obstacles Overcome, *Smithsonian Magazine* [Online] www.smithsonianmag.com/smithsonian-institution/ed-roberts-wheelchair-records-story-obstacles-overcome-180954531/ (archived at https://perma.cc/CB5Z-5LBK)

5 Hoover, A [accessed 3 April 2021] Google Doodle Honors Activist Ed Roberts, Pioneer of 'Independent Living' Movement, Christian Science Monitor, 23 January 2017 [Online] www.csmonitor.com/USA/Society/2017/0123/Google-Doodle-honors-activist-Ed-Roberts-pioneer-of-independent-living-movement (archived at https://perma.cc/959Y-TGMX)

6 UC Berkeley [accessed 3 April 2021] Berkeley Disabled Students [Online] https://dsp.berkeley.edu/about (archived at https://perma.cc/JP8Y-Y4DL)

7 UC Berkeley [accessed 3 April 2021] Berkeley Enrolment [Online] https://opa.berkeley.edu/campus-data/uc-berkeley-quick-facts (archived at https://perma.cc/KJV3-WTS9)

8   Dawson, V [accessed 3 April 2021] Ed Roberts' Wheelchair Records a Story of
        Obstacles Overcome, *Smithsonian Magazine* [Online] www.smithsonianmag.com/
        smithsonian-institution/ed-roberts-wheelchair-records-story-obstacles-
        overcome-180954531/ (archived at https://perma.cc/CB5Z-5LBK)

9   MN [accessed 3 April 2021] Ed Roberts 60 Minutes with Harry Reasoner
        [Online] https://mn.gov/mnddc/ed-roberts/sixtyMinutes.html (archived at
        https://perma.cc/YPL9-UX3K)

10 Shirley, S [accessed 3 April 2021] Give and Take, Gresham College Lecture
        2011 [Online] https://vimeo.com/22180733 (archived at https://perma.cc/
        XF4Y-939S)

11 Team Domenica [accessed 3 April 2021] Our Story [Online]
        www.teamdomenica.com/ (archived at https://perma.cc/R774-BVRQ)

12 Flynn, P and Todd, M [accessed 3 April 2021] Velvet Rage, Pride and Prejudice
        for Gay Men, *The Guardian*, 20 February 2011 [Online] www.theguardian.com/
        society/2011/feb/20/gay-men-depression-the-velvet-rage (archived at
        https://perma.cc/Q6N5-5SB8)

13 Criado Perez, C (2020) *Invisible Women: Exposing data bias in a world
        designed for men*, Vintage, London; also Criado Perez, C [accessed 3 April
        2021] Twitter [Online] https://twitter.com/ccriadoperez?lang=en (archived at
        https://perma.cc/SVY2-49S2)

14 Coury, S *et al* [accessed 3 April 2021] Women in the Workplace 2020,
        McKinsey [Online] www.mckinsey.com/featured-insights/diversity-and-
        inclusion/women-in-the-workplace (archived at https://perma.cc/W33J-NNFE)

15 Lutz, K [accessed 3 April 2021] Blog: Women Fast Forward Imagine When XX
        Equals XY, 6 March 2017 [Online] www.managers.org.uk/knowledge-and-
        insights/resource/women-fast-forward-imagine-when-xx-equals-xy/ (archived
        at https://perma.cc/KZ72-VPP6)

16 Urwin, R [accessed 3 April 2021] Why Are Men More Likely to Be Promoted
        Than Women? *Sunday Times*, 18 March 2018 [Online] www.thetimes.co.uk/
        article/why-are-men-more-likely-to-be-promoted-than-women-p7ztwf660
        (archived at https://perma.cc/6DDK-FAA4)

17 Thaves, B [accessed 3 April 2021] From *Frank and Ernest* [Online]
        www.goodreads.com/quotes/192006-sure-he-was-great-but-don-t-forget-that-
        ginger-rogers (archived at https://perma.cc/4HCU-DWVR)

18 Ipsos Mori [accessed 3 April 2021] Men Less Likely Than Women to Need
        Intelligence and Hard Work to Get Ahead, November 2019 [Online]
        www.ipsos.com/ipsos-mori/en-uk/men-less-likely-women-need-intelligence-
        and-hard-work-get-ahead-public-say (archived at https://perma.cc/
        6AXP-WNB9)

19 Office for National Statistics [accessed 3 April 2021] Gender Pay Gap in the
        UK 2020 [Online] www.ons.gov.uk/employmentandlabourmarket/

peopleinwork/earningsandworkinghours/bulletins/genderpaygapintheuk/2020 (archived at https://perma.cc/R472-9QNF)

20 Kumar, A [accessed 3 April 2021] 'Old Boy's Network' Leaves BAME Workers 92% Less Likely to Land Boardroom Job, DiversityQ, 11 November 2019 [Online] https://diversityq.com/old-boys-network-leaves-bame-workers-92-less-likely-to-land-boardroom-job-1508167/ (archived at https://perma.cc/7KPX-Y8KR)

21 Buolamwini, J [accessed 3 April 2021] Gender Shades, MIT thesis [Online] http://gendershades.org/ (archived at https://perma.cc/WH4X-ZHQN)

22 Lohr, S [accessed 3 April 2021] 80% White Facial Recognition Is Accurate, If You're a White Guy, *New York Times*, 9 February 2018 [Online] www.nytimes.com/2018/02/09/technology/facial-recognition-race-artificial-intelligence.html (archived at https://perma.cc/BGL2-B3U6)

23 Gaines, S and Williams, S [accessed 3 April 2021] The Perpetual Line-Up: Unregulated Police Face Recognition in America, *Georgetown Law*, 18 October 2016 [Online] www.perpetuallineup.org/ (archived at https://perma.cc/5UCE-6XNL)

24 Macpherson, W [accessed 3 April 2021] Macpherson Inquiry Chapter 6: Definition Para 6.34 [Online] https://assets.publishing.service.gov.uk/government/uploads/system/uploads/attachment_data/file/277111/4262.pdf (archived at https://perma.cc/J9U5-LHGF)

25 Wilkerson, I [accessed 3 April 2021] America's Enduring Caste System, *New York Times*, 1 July 2020, updated 21 January 2021 [Online] www.nytimes.com/2020/07/31/books/review-caste-isabel-wilkerson-origins-of-our-discontents.html (archived at https://perma.cc/S5EL-N23T)

26 Putnam, RD [accessed 3 April 2021] E Pluribus Unum: Diversity and Community in the Twenty-first Century: The 2006 Johan Skytte Prize Lecture [Online] www.puttingourdifferencestowork.com/pdf/j.1467-9477.2007.00176 (archived at https://perma.cc/B4B5-XGWN) Putnam Diversity.pdf

27 BBC Trending [accessed 3 April 2021] Blog [Online] www.bbc.co.uk/news/blogs-trending-35589621 (archived at https://perma.cc/U7GP-4KBH); also Mahdawi, A [accessed 3 April 2021] Website, http://rentaminority.com/ (archived at https://perma.cc/7EGH-C3QV)

28 Mahdawi, A [accessed 3 April 2021] TED Talk [Online] www.youtube.com/watch?v=mtUlRYXJ0vI (archived at https://perma.cc/4KV9-GEXU)

29 Kew-Armah, K [accessed 3 April 2021] Tweet [Online] https://twitter.com/kwamekweiarmah/status/1213221347691765767?lang=en (archived at https://perma.cc/3GKN-2LVH)

30 Bunglawala, Z [accessed 3 April 2021] Please, Don't Call Me BAME Or BME! 8 July 2019 [Online] https://civilservice.blog.gov.uk/2019/07/08/please-dont-call-me-bame-or-bme/ (archived at https://perma.cc/RC9G-LLEY)

31 Clarke-Binns, O [accessed 3 April 2021] #BAMEOver Live Debate: Snippets from the Speakers [Online] https://soundcloud.com/user-80487003/ozzie-clarke-binns?in=user-80487003/sets/bameover-live-debate-snippets-from-the-speakers (archived at https://perma.cc/4NA2-ZQ8Q)

32 #BAMEOver [accessed 3 April 2021] A Statement for the UK [Online] https://docs.google.com/document/d/e/2PACX-1vQkg5IIoeAqMjMF6VW-eIEtEUEgK3GLudW1meE2DILbJPZYPiP0dO3Qwx6YVxBFxOhI1KEp 5swpok80/pub (archived at https://perma.cc/SBR5-5MKF)

33 Arendt, H (2007) *The Jewish Writings*, Schocken Books, London, p 137

34 Campbell, J [accessed 3 April 2021] Fighting For a Slice, or For a Bigger Cake? The 6th Annual Disability Lecture University of Cambridge, 29 April 2008 [Online] https://disability-studies.leeds.ac.uk/wp-content/uploads/sites/40/library/Campbell-Fighting-for-a-slice-of-the-cake-FINAL-FINAL-29-04-08.pdf (archived at https://perma.cc/3YC7-53EY)

35 Ely, RJ and Padavic, I (2020) [accessed 3 April 2021] What's really holding women back? Harvard Business Review [Online] hbr.org/2020/03/whats-really-holding-women-back (archived at https://perma.cc/ZK3U-2W9Z)

36 Shook, E and Sweet, J (2018) [accessed 3 April 2021] *When She Rises, We All Rise* [Online] www.accenture.com/_acnmedia/pdf-73/accenture-when-she-rises-we-all-rise.pdf (archived at https://perma.cc/UYH8-LUVV)

37 Ford, A [accessed 3 April 2021] Mums Doing Lion's Share of Childcare and Home-Learning During Lockdown Even When Both Parents Work, Sussex University [Online] www.sussex.ac.uk/broadcast/read/52267 (archived at https://perma.cc/Z9A5-WBEH)

38 Gilead [accessed 3 April 2021] FAQs Who are We? [Online] www.gilead.com/news-and-press/press-room/press-faqs (archived at https://perma.cc/XK4P-SVKZ)

39 Gilead [accessed 3 April 2021] Unmet Need [Online] www.gileadgiving.co.uk/ (archived at https://perma.cc/7A8J-BASC)

40 Parker, J [accessed 3 April 2021] Ethnic Diversity Enriching Business Leadership: An update report from The Parker Review, 5 February 2020 [Online] https://assets.ey.com/content/dam/ey-sites/ey-com/en_uk/news/2020/02/ey-parker-review-2020-report-final.pdf (archived at https://perma.cc/SK8Z-2EUW)

41 Green Park [accessed 3 April 2021] Green Park Leadership 10,000 [Online] www.green-park.co.uk/insights/green-park-leadership-10-000-2019/s94929/ (archived at https://perma.cc/H2XR-TZKG)

42 Deaton, A [accessed 3 April 2021] Republic of Unequals, *Prospect*, 4 January 2021 [Online] www.prospectmagazine.co.uk/opinions/us-inequality-wealth-divide (archived at https://perma.cc/D247-7F3U)

43 Sandberg, S (2013) *Lean In: Women, work and the will to lead*, WH Allen, London

44 Page, SE (2017) *The Diversity Bonus*, Princeton University Press, Princeton, USA

45 Criado Perez, C (2020) *Invisible Women: Exposing data bias in a world designed for men*, Vintage, London

46 Brink, C [accessed 3 April 2021] 'Standards Will Drop': Dispelling Fears About the Equality Agenda in Higher Education [Online] https://s3.eu-west-2. amazonaws.com/assets.creode.advancehe-document-manager/documents/ecu/ E_for_E_The_future_of_equality_in_he_1572615485.pdf (archived at https://perma.cc/798P-9F9W)

47 Botha, A (ed.) (2007) [accessed 3 April 2021] Chris Brink: Anatomy of a Transformer, SUN Press [Online] https://scholar.sun.ac.za/ handle/10019.1/101778 (archived at https://perma.cc/4PEZ-ZQHG)

48 Peterson, A [accessed 3 April 2021] What I Am Learning From My White Grandchildren: Truths About Race, TED Antioch [Online] www.youtube.com/ watch?v=u5GCetbP7Fg (archived at https://perma.cc/RCR3-2HF7)

Chapter 4

1 Ellman, R (1988) *Oscar Wilde*, Penguin, London

2 McIntosh, M (1968) The homosexual role, *Social Problems*, **16** (2), pp 182–92

3 Verma, R [accessed 3 April 2021] It Was Standard to See Signs Saying, 'No Blacks, No Dogs, No Irish', Eachother, 29 November 2018 [Online] https://eachother.org.uk/racism-1960s-britain/ (archived at https://perma.cc/ 3WM7-RAWQ)

4 Kelley, N, Khan, O and Sharrock, S [accessed 3 April 2021] British Social Attitudes Survey: Racial prejudice in Britain today [Online] https://natcen.ac.uk/ media/1488132/racial-prejudice-report_v4.pdf (archived at https://perma.cc/ UAD2-JA8Q)

5 Kaur-Ballagan, K [accessed 3 April 2021] Attitudes to Race and Inequality in Great Britain, Ipsos Mori, 15 June 2020 [Online] www.ipsos.com/ipsos-mori/ en-uk/attitudes-race-and-inequality-great-britain (archived at https://perma.cc/ JQ6X-74L7)

6 *Economist* [accessed 3 April 2021] Britain's Mixed-Race Population Blurs the Lines of Identity Politics, 3 October 2020 [Online] www.economist.com/ britain/2020/10/03/britains-mixed-race-population-blurs-the-lines-of-identity-politics (archived at https://perma.cc/5F78-WQNX)

7 Pedley, K and Spielman, D [accessed 3 April 2021] British Attitudes to Moral and Social Issues Have Become Significantly More Liberal in the Last 30 Years, Ipsos Mori, 24 October 2019 [Online] www.ipsos.com/ipsos-mori/en-uk/ british-attitudes-moral-and-social-issues-have-become-significantly-more-liberal-last-30-years (archived at https://perma.cc/D3FY-C3J4)

8 Trau, R, O'Leary, J and Brown, C (2018) [accessed 3 April 2021] 7 myths about coming out at work, *Harvard Business Review* [Online] hbr.org/2018/10/7-myths-about-coming-out-at-work (archived at https://perma.cc/TLY8-Y9D8)

9 NHS England [accessed 3 April 2021] NHS Workforce Race Equality Standard 2019 Data Analysis Report for NHS Trusts [Online] www.england.nhs.uk/wp-content/uploads/2020/01/wres-2019-data-report.pdf (archived at https://perma.cc/GN7G-Y699)

10 McGinn, K and Tempest, N [accessed 3 April 2021] Heidi Rosen, Harvard Business School Case Collection, January 2000, Revised April 2010 [Online] www.hbs.edu/faculty/Pages/item.aspx?num=26880 (archived at https://perma.cc/P2EU-XST3)

11 Greenwald, AG and Banaji, MR (1995) [accessed 3 April 2021] Implicit social cognition: Attitudes, self-esteem, and stereotypes, *Psychological Review*, **102** (1), pp 4–27

12 Project Implicit [accessed 3 April 2021] IAT [Online] https://implicit.harvard.edu/implicit/iatdetails.html (archived at https://perma.cc/696V-EKCC)

13 *New York Magazine* [accessed 3 April 2021] The Creators of the Implicit Association Test Should Get Their Story Straight, 5 December 2017 [Online] https://nymag.com/intelligencer/2017/12/iat-behavior-problem.html (archived at https://perma.cc/P6QL-GTG2)

14 Channel 4 [accessed 3 April 2021] The School That Tried to End Racism [Online] https://nymag.com/intelligencer/2017/12/iat-behavior-problem.html (archived at https://perma.cc/L74J-M2KC)

15 Gov.uk [accessed 3 April 2021] GCSE results ('Attainment 8'), 11 December 2020 [Online] www.ethnicity-facts-figures.service.gov.uk/education-skills-and-training/11-to-16-years-old/gcse-results-attainment-8-for-children-aged-14-to-16-key-stage-4/latest (archived at https://perma.cc/TR7N-P35M)

16 Association for Psychological Science [accessed 3 April 2021] Greenwald's Biography [Online] www.psychologicalscience.org/publications/observer/25at25/anthony-greenwald.html (archived at https://perma.cc/697A-RG3F)

17 Bohnet, I (2016) *What Works*, Harvard University Press, Harvard, USA, p 51

18 Levy Paluck, E and Green, DP (2009) Prejudice reduction: What works? *Annual Review of Psychology*, **60**, p 356

19 Starbucks [accessed 3 April 2021] What 'Race Together' Means for Starbucks Partners and Customers, 16 March 2015 [Online] https://stories.starbucks.com/stories/2015/what-race-together-means-for-starbucks-partners-and-customers/ (archived at https://perma.cc/8LY8-ZAP3)

20 *The Guardian* [accessed 3 April 2021] Black Men Arrested at Philadelphia Starbucks Feared for Their Lives, 19 April 2018 [Online] www.theguardian.com/business/2018/apr/19/starbucks-black-men-feared-for-lives-philadelphia (archived at https://perma.cc/BKP3-KJQX)

21 Winsor, M and McCarthyvia, K [accessed 3 April 2021] Men Arrested at Starbucks Were There For Business Meeting Hoping to Change 'Our Lives': Rashon Nelson and Donte Robinson Came Forward This Morning to Share Their Story, 19 April 2018 [Online] https://abcnews.go.com/GMA/News/men-arrested-starbucks-business-meeting-hoping-change-lives/story?id=54578217 (archived at https://perma.cc/K26T-HBJU)

22 ABC Good Morning America [accessed 3 April 2021] Starbucks CEO Speaks Out After Black Men Arrested, 16 April 2018 [Online] www.goodmorningamerica.com/news/video/starbucks-ceo-speaks-black-men-arrested-54495894 (archived at https://perma.cc/C9D4-H8UX)

23 Hyken, S [accessed 3 April 2021] Starbucks Closes 8,000 Stores For Racial Bias Training: Is It Enough? *Forbes*, 1 June 2018 [Online] www.forbes.com/sites/shephyken/2018/06/01/starbucks-closes-8000-stores-for-racial-bias-training-is-it-enough/?sh=bcceb1c2831a (archived at https://perma.cc/BU94-ANMT)

24 Herzog, K [accessed 3 April 2021] Is Starbucks Implementing Flawed Science in Their Anti-Bias Training? 17 April 2018 [Online] www.thestranger.com/slog/2018/04/17/26052277/is-starbucks-implementing-flawed-science-in-their-anti-bias-training (archived at https://perma.cc/5SA7-RTDA)

25 Santos, C [accessed 3 April 2021] Everybody's Biased, So I Can Be Too: Insights from Melissa C Thomas-Hunt [Online] https://ideas.darden.virginia.edu/everybodys-biased-so-i-can-be-too (archived at https://perma.cc/D42G-9TJU); and Duguid, MM and Thomas-Hunt, MC (2015) Condoning stereotyping? How awareness of stereotyping prevalence impacts expression of stereotypes, *Journal of Applied Psychology*, **100** (2), pp 343–59 [Online] https://psycnet.apa.org/record/2014-43472-001 (archived at https://perma.cc/WB98-AGNS)

26 Bohnet, I (2016) *What Works*, Harvard University Press, Harvard, USA, p 53

27 Dobbin, F, Kalev, A and Kelly, E [accessed 3 April 2021] Diversity Management in Corporate America, 1 November 2007 [Online] https://scholar.harvard.edu/dobbin/files/2007_contexts_dobbin_kalev_kelly.pdf (archived at https://perma.cc/AV6F-72SK)

28 Dobbin, F and Kalev, A (2016) [accessed 3 April 2021] Why diversity programs fail and what works better, *Harvard Business Review* [Online] hbr.org/2016/07/why-diversity-programs-fail (archived at https://perma.cc/8MM3-KULG)

29 Bregman, P [accessed 3 April 2021] Diversity training doesn't work, *Harvard Business Review* [Online] hbr.org/2012/03/diversity-training-doesnt-work (archived at https://perma.cc/9SD6-FSY9)

30 Bertrand, M and Duflo, E [accessed 3 April 2021] Field Experiments on Discrimination [Online] https://economics.mit.edu/files/11449 (archived at https://perma.cc/792M-UQ7B)

31 Kahneman, D and Smith, VL [accessed 3 April 2021] Nobel Citation [Online] www.nobelprize.org/prizes/economic-sciences/2002/kahneman/facts/ (archived at https://perma.cc/PMJ6-PE9H)

32 Kahneman, D [accessed 3 April 2021] Of 2 minds: How fast and slow thinking shape perception and choice, *Scientific American* [Online] www.scientificamerican.com/article/kahneman-excerpt-thinking-fast-and-slow/ (archived at https://perma.cc/99UH-6VHE)

33 Devlin, H [accessed 3 April 2021] Unconscious Bias: What is it and Can it be Eliminated? *The Guardian*, 2 December 2018 [Online] www.theguardian.com/ uk-news/2018/dec/02/unconscious-bias-what-is-it-and-can-it-be-eliminated (archived at https://perma.cc/DQK6-S2FN)

34 Cohen, GL (2012) [accessed 3 April 2021] Identity, Belief, and Bias [Online] https://ed.stanford.edu/sites/default/files/cohen_chap_hanson.pdf (archived at https://perma.cc/2LWU-M5GK)

35 O'Halloran Storgy, J [accessed 3 April 2021] Film Review: I Am Not Your Negro [Online] https://storgy.com/2017/05/06/film-review-i-am-not-your-negro/ (archived at https://perma.cc/DR29-5XD7)

36 Eberhardt, J (2019) Charles White and Samuel George Morton quoted in *Biased*, William Heinemann, London, chapter 6

37 Eberhardt, J (2019) LA Police quotes in *Biased*, William Heinemann, London, chapter 6

38 Flaccus, G [accessed 3 April 2021] GOP Official Apologizes for Obama Chimp Email, *ABC News*, 19 April 2011 [Online] www.nbcnews.com/id/wbna42656911 (archived at https://perma.cc/6R8V-L4MM)

39 Politics Plus [accessed 3 April 2021] Overcoming Republican Insanitea, One Day at a Time [Online] www.politicsplus.org/blog/2019/05/17/friday-fun-plan-b-odds-ends/comment-page-1/ (archived at https://perma.cc/ XEA9-WVEA)

40 Eberhardt, J (2019) Eberhardt & Goff experiment with black names in *Biased*, William Heinemann, London, p 143

41 The Invisible Gorilla [accessed 3 April 2021] Website, www.theinvisiblegorilla.com/ gorilla_experiment.html (archived at https://perma.cc/YPW9-MW76)

42 Improbable [accessed 3 April 2021] Research: Ignoble Prize [Online] www.improbable.com/ig-about/winners/ (archived at https://perma.cc/ SR7D-68BV)

43 The Invisible Gorilla [accessed 3 April 2021] The Invisible Gorilla (featuring Daniel Simons), YouTube, 18 February 2011 [Online] www.youtube.com/ watch?v=hstDjrQNPz4 (archived at https://perma.cc/8FFB-DQGF)

44 Eberhardt, J (2019) *Biased*, William Heinemann, London, chapter 6

45 Edo-Lodge, R [accessed 3 April 2021] Why I'm No Longer Talking to White People About Race, *The Guardian*, 30 May 2017 [Online] www.theguardian.com/

world/2017/may/30/why-im-no-longer-talking-to-white-people-about-race
(archived at https://perma.cc/NFB3-NRJG)

46   IPA [accessed 3 April 2021] Addressing Unconscious Bias in the Workplace
[Online] www.ipa-involve.com/addressing-unconsicous-bias-in-the-workplace
(archived at https://perma.cc/ZAM3-ABAD)

47   Dobbin, F and Kalev, A (2020) [accessed 3 April 2021] Why sexual harassment
programs backfire: And what to do about it, *Harvard Business Review*
[Online] hbr.org/2020/05/why-sexual-harassment-programs-backfire (archived
at https://perma.cc/7CBS-TWQA)

48   University of New Hampshire [accessed 3 April 2021] Evidence Based
Initiatives, Prevention Innovations Research Center [Online] www.unh.edu/
research/prevention-innovations-research-center/evidence-based-initiatives
(archived at https://perma.cc/BY5T-4SUW)

49   Hunt, E [accessed 3 April 2021] That Heineken Ad: Brewer Tackles How
to Talk to Your Political Opposite, *The Guardian*, 28 April 2017 [Online]
www.theguardian.com/media/2017/apr/28/that-heineken-ad-does-it-land-with-
the-audiences-other-beers-cannot-reach (archived at https://perma.cc/
YY2G-M7RH)

50   Brauer, C [accessed 3 April 2021] How Humans Find Common Ground:
And The Science Behind It, *Huffington Post*, 26 April 2017 [Online] www.
huffingtonpost.co.uk/chris-brauer/chris-brauer-common-ground_b_15957494.
html (archived at https://perma.cc/36BQ-T8JX)

51   The Human Library [accessed 3 April 2021] Website, https://humanlibrary.org/
(archived at https://perma.cc/V88X-NLG5)

52   Singal, J [accessed 3 April 2021] The Contact Hypothesis Offers Hope for the
World, The Cut, 10 February 2017 [Online] www.thecut.com/2017/02/
the-contact-hypothesis-offers-hope-for-the-world.html (archived at
https://perma.cc/FM2Z-LLZQ)

53   Pidd, H [accessed 3 April 2021] Bradford Synagogue Saved By City's Muslims,
The Guardian [Online] www.theguardian.com/uk-news/2013/dec/20/bradford-
synagogue-saved-muslims-jews (archived at https://perma.cc/A7CX-UH2Y)

Chapter 5

1   Army Tigers [accessed 3 April 2021] Johnson Beharry Victoria Cross Citation
[Online] www.armytigers.com/persons/johnson-beharry-vc (archived at
https://perma.cc/YJ9M-LJ97)

2   Carlyle, T [accessed 3 April 2021] *On Heroes, Hero-Worship, and the Heroic
in History*, ebook [Online] www.gutenberg.org/files/1091/1091-h/1091-h.htm
(archived at https://perma.cc/4EPF-4N53)

3 Sorensen, DR and Kinser, BE (eds) (2013) *On Heroes, Hero-Worship, and the Heroic in History by Thomas Carlyle*, Yale University Press, Yale, USA [Online] https://quotebanq.com/wp-content/uploads/2018/06/Thomas-Carlyle-On-Heroes-Hero-Worship-and-the-Heroic-in-History.pdf (archived at https://perma.cc/7UTU-22E3)

4 Trevor-Roper, H (1977) *The Goebbels Diaries*, Secker & Warburg, London

5 Collins, J (2001) *From Good to Great*, Random House, London

6 Spector, B [accessed 3 April 2021] Flawed from the 'get-go': Lee Iacocca and the origins of transformational leadership, *Leadership*, **10** (3), pp 361–79

7 Heffernan, M (2014) *A Bigger Prize*, Simon & Schuster, London, p 189

8 Edmondson, AC (2012) *Teaming*, Jossey-Bass, New York, pp 89–113

9 Cross, R, Rebele, R and Grant, A [accessed 3 April 2021] Too much teamwork exhausts employees and saps productivity: Here's how to avoid it, *Harvard Business Review* [Online] hbr.org/2016/01/collaborative-overload (archived at https://perma.cc/8YWB-LSBZ)

10 Page, SE (2017) *The Diversity Bonus*, Princeton University Press, Princeton, USA

11 Wallace-Stephens, F [accessed 3 April 2021] What New Jobs Will Emerge in The 2020s? [Online] www.thersa.org/blog/2020/01/new-jobs-2020s (archived at https://perma.cc/WV7A-HWLX)

12 Phillips, K (2017) *Commentary: The Diversity Bonus*, Princeton University Press, Princeton, USA

13 Dishman, L [accessed 3 April 2021] Diverse teams have a better toolkit. Here's why that matters, *CXO Magazine*, 1 November 2017 [Online] https://medium.com/cxo-magazine/diverse-teams-have-a-better-toolkit-heres-why-that-matters-71ee57705c5 (archived at https://perma.cc/3AR8-3LFC)

14 Phillips, KW, Northcraft, GB and Neale, MA (2006) [accessed 3 April 2021] Surface Level Diversity and Decision Making in Groups: When Does Deep-Level Similarity Help? [Online] https://hal.archives-ouvertes.fr/hal-00571629/document (archived at https://perma.cc/DVY6-RNTB); and Phillips, K [accessed 3 April 2021] How Diversity Makes Us Smarter [Online] www.scientificamerican.com/article/how-diversity-makes-us-smarter/ (archived at https://perma.cc/SJ5X-48KK); and Twenty One Toys [accessed 3 April 2021] Diversity Gives Teams a Significant Advantage [Online] https://twentyonetoys.com/blogs/future-of-work/team-diversity-inclusion (archived at https://perma.cc/CBF4-9AHP)

15 Sommers, SR (2006) [accessed 3 April 2021] On racial diversity and group decision making: Identifying multiple effects of racial composition on jury deliberations, *Journal of Personality and Social Psychology*, **90** (4), pp 597–612 [Online] www.apa.org/pubs/journals/releases/psp-904597.pdf (archived at https://perma.cc/EN7V-XBJT)

16 Criado Perez, C (2019) *Invisible Women*, Penguin, London, pp 151–56

17 Briggs, A (2011) *Secret Days*, Frontline Books, Barnsley, pp 77–79

18 Partington, R [accessed 3 April 2021] 'If it was Lehman Sisters, it would be a
    different world' – Christine Lagarde, *The Guardian*, 5 September 2018
    [Online] www.theguardian.com/business/2018/sep/05/if-it-was-lehman-sisters-
    it-would-be-a-different-world-christine-lagarde (archived at https://perma.cc/
    E7GM-XQ59)

19 Greenhill, S [accessed 3 April 2021] 'It's awful: Why did nobody see it
    coming?': The Queen gives her verdict on global credit crunch, *Daily Mail*,
    6 November 2008 [Online] www.dailymail.co.uk/news/article-1083290/
    Its-awful--Why-did-coming--The-Queen-gives-verdict-global-credit-crunch.html
    (archived at https://perma.cc/86FY-CEQQ)

20 Syed, M (2019) *Rebel Ideas*, John Murray, London, pp 25–33

21 Gov.uk [accessed 3 April 2021] FCA Objectives [Online] www.legislation.gov.uk/
    ukpga/2012/21/section/6/enacted?view=plain (archived at https://perma.cc/
    9JEQ-UAUQ)

22 Kennedy, L [accessed 3 April 2021] Book Review of *The Class Ceiling: Why it
    pays to be privileged* by Sam Friedman and Daniel Laurison, 28 January 2019
    [Online] https://blogs.lse.ac.uk/lsereviewofbooks/2019/01/28/book-review-the-
    class-ceiling-why-it-pays-to-be-privileged-by-sam-friedman-and-daniel-
    laurison/ (archived at https://perma.cc/7DSK-8Y77); also LSE [accessed 3 April
    2021] Book Launch of *The Class Ceiling: Why it pays to be privileged* [Online]
    www.lse.ac.uk/Events/Events-Assets/PDF/2019/01-LT/20190128-Class-Ceiling-
    Book-Launch-to-share.pdf (archived at https://perma.cc/7RZF-ST7W)

23 Linguistic Profiling for Professionals [accessed 3 April 2021] Website,
    www.nottingham.ac.uk/lipp/ (archived at https://perma.cc/9APK-EMVP)

24 The Behavioural Insights Team [accessed 3 April 2021] Promoting Diversity in
    the Police, 24 July 2015 [Online] www.bi.team/blogs/behavioural-insights-and-
    home-affairs/ (archived at https://perma.cc/M7R9-J3NE)

25 Spencer, SJ, Steele CM and Quinn, DM (1999) Stereotype threat and women's
    math performance, *Journal of Experimental Social Psychology*, 35, pp 4–28

26 Bohnet, I (2016) *What Works*, Harvard University Press, Harvard, USA, p 138

27 Neugaard, B [accessed 3 April 2021] Britannica: Psychology [Online] www.
    britannica.com/science/halo-effect (archived at https://perma.cc/5RFC-CDDM)

28 Bertrand, M and Duflo, E [accessed 3 April 2021] Field Experiments on
    Discrimination [Online] https://economics.mit.edu/files/11449 (archived at
    https://perma.cc/792M-UQ7B)

29 Bertrand, M and Duflo, E [accessed 3 April 2021] Field Experiments on
    Discrimination [Online] https://economics.mit.edu/files/11449 (archived at
    https://perma.cc/792M-UQ7B)

30 Bohnet, I (2016) *What Works*, Harvard University Press, Harvard, USA, p 126;
    also Bohnet, I, van Geen, A and Bazerman, B (2017) [accessed 3 April 2021]

When performance trumps gender bias: Joint vs. separate evaluation, *Management Science*, **62** (5) pp 1225–34 [Online] https://ofew.berkeley.edu/sites/default/files/when_performance_trumps_gender_bias_bohnet_et_al.pdf (archived at https://perma.cc/57F8-YBHP)

31 Bohnet, I (2016) *What Works*, Harvard University Press, Harvard, USA, p 135

Chapter 6

1 Gross, T [accessed 3 April 2021] How a Rising Star of White Nationalism Broke Free From the Movement [Online] https://text.npr.org/s.php?sId=651052970 (archived at https://perma.cc/9NQK-TVD6); and Talks at GS [accessed 3 April 2021] Rising Out of Hatred: The Awakening of a Former White Nationalist [Online] www.goldmansachs.com/insights/talks-at-gs/derek-black.html (archived at https://perma.cc/H8GN-3W5E); and Rodriguez, J and Subramaniam, T [accessed 3 April 2021] In First Event After Defection, Former White Nationalist Derek Black Reflects On Racial Climate, *The Hoya*, 27 January 2017 [Online] https://thehoya.com/former-white-nationalist-reflects-on-defection-racial-climate/ (archived at https://perma.cc/KK6G-BE42); and Lorinc, J [accessed 3 April 2021] Former White Supremacist to Share His Story of Transformation, *The Star* [Online] www.thestar.com/news/gta/2019/05/04/former-white-supremacist-to-share-his-story-of-transformation.html (archived at https://perma.cc/9JUB-SGG4)

2 Phillips, K *et al* (2016) The biases that punish racially diverse teams, *Harvard Business Review* [Online] hbr.org/2016/02/the-biases-that-punish-racially-diverse-teams (archived at https://perma.cc/627Y-VPTR); and Lount, RB *et al* (2016) Biased perceptions of racially diverse teams and their consequences for resource support, *Organization Science*, **26** (5), pp 1351–64 [Online] www.researchgate.net/publication/281926547_Biased_Perceptions_of_Racially_Diverse_Teams_and_Their_Consequences_for_Resource_Support (archived at https://perma.cc/3XYN-6ZN2)

3 Fraser, I (2014) *Shredded*, Birlinn, Edinburgh

4 Fraser, I (2014) *Shredded*, Birlinn, Edinburgh

5 Rumsfeld, D [accessed 3 April 2021] Knowns, CNN, 2 December 2002 [Online] www.youtube.com/watch?v=REWeBzGuzCc (archived at https://perma.cc/AB7E-DHBJ)

6 Cooper, M [accessed 3 April 2021] Barenboim Interview: Orchestra That Bridges Mideast Divide Tours a Fractured U.S., *New York Times*, 6 November 2018 [Online] www.nytimes.com/2018/11/06/arts/music/daniel-barenboim-west-eastern-divan-orchestra-tour.html (archived at https://perma.cc/SNS2-JED4)

7 Swed, M [accessed 3 April 2021] How Daniel Barenboim's Orchestra of Israeli and Arab Musicians is Faring in the Current Political Climate, *LA Times*, 8 November 2018 [Online] www.latimes.com/entertainment/arts/la-et-cm-barenboim-berlin-interview-20181108-story.html (archived at https://perma.cc/9N52-E697)

8 Smith, A (1776) [accessed 3 April 2021] *An Inquiry into the Nature and Causes of the Wealth of Nations*, book 1, chapter 10, part 1 'Inequalities arising from the Nature of the Employments Themselves' [Online] https://geolib.com/smith.adam/won1-10.html (archived at https://perma.cc/S82W-B8PB)

9 Kahneman, D (2012) [accessed 3 April 2021] Of 2 minds: How fast and slow thinking shape perception and choice, *Scientific American* [Online] www.scientificamerican.com/article/kahneman-excerpt-thinking-fast-and-slow/ (archived at https://perma.cc/99UH-6VHE)

10 Malmendier, U and Taylor, T (2015) [accessed 3 April 2021] On the verges of overconfidence, *Journal of Economic Perspectives*, **29** (4), pp 3–8 [Online] https://pubs.aeaweb.org/doi/pdfplus/10.1257/jep.29.4.3 (archived at https://perma.cc/DN3E-RNNE)

11 Kingl, A (2020) *Next Generation Leadership*, HarperCollins, London

12 Adkins, A and Rigoni, B [accessed 3 April 2021] Millennials Want Jobs to Be Development Opportunities, Gallup, 30 June 2016 [Online] www.gallup.com/workplace/236438/millennials-jobs-development-opportunities.aspx (archived at https://perma.cc/3BVW-XDM9)

13 Revolution Écologique [accessed 3 April 2021] Website, https://pour-un-reveil-ecologique.org/fr/ (archived at https://perma.cc/7VTN-HW7M); also Ecological Awakening [accessed 3 April 2021] Wake Up Call on the Environment: A Student Manifesto [Online] https://manifeste.pour-un-reveil-ecologique.org/en (archived at https://perma.cc/8L47-EKK2)

14 Hodgson, C and Kuchler, H [accessed 3 April 2021] Google Walkout: Google Employees Across the World Stage Walkouts, FT, 1 November 2018 [Online] www.ft.com/content/7f70c53c-ddcd-11e8-8f50-cbae5495d92b (archived at https://perma.cc/Y64M-6U7X)

15 Fidelity [accessed 3 April 2021] 2016 Fidelity Investments: Evaluate a Job Offer Study [Online] www.fidelity.com/bin-public/060_www_fidelity_com/documents/fidelity-job-offer-fact-sheet.pdf (archived at https://perma.cc/WE4Q-4598)

16 Philip Beeching, P [accessed 3 April 2021] Blog: Why Companies Fail – The Rise and Fall of HMV [Online] www.philipbeeching.com/2012/08/why-companies-fail-rise-and-fall-of-hmv.html (archived at https://perma.cc/8UWN-6BAT)

17   Parker, SK, Knight, C and Keller, A [accessed 3 April 2021] Remote managers
are having trust issues, *Harvard Business Review*, 30 July 2020 [Online]
hbr.org/2020/07/remote-managers-are-having-trust-issues (archived at
https://perma.cc/VKL6-QAFW)

18   Edmondson, AC (2012) *Teaming*, Jossey-Bass, New York, pp 122–48

19   Leonard-Barton, DA (1998) *Wellsprings of Knowledge: Building and
sustaining the sources of innovation*, Harvard Business School Press, Harvard,
USA

20   Davidson, MN (2011) *The End of Diversity As We Know It*, Berrett-Koehler,
San Francisco

21   Gawande, A (2011) *The Checklist Manifesto*, Profile Books, London

22   Thompson, L (2017) [accessed 3 April 2021] How brainwriting can get
better ideas out of your team, *Harvard Business Review* [Online] hbr.org/
sponsored/2017/05/how-brainwriting-can-get-better-ideas-out-of-your-team
(archived at https://perma.cc/7QDA-RNQR)

23   Zack, D (2010) *Networking for People Who Hate Networking: A field guide
for introverts, the overwhelmed, and the underconnected*, Berrett-Koehler,
San Francisco; and Duncan, RD [accessed 3 April 2021] Hate Networking?
Then Change Your Inner Monologue [Online] www.duncanworldwide.com/
hate-networking-change-your-inner-monologue-get-results-you-really-want/
(archived at https://perma.cc/P99Q-6JN6)

24   Low, V [accessed 3 April 2021] Quiet Please! Amazon Meetings Begin in
Silence, *The Times*, 1 May 2018 [Online] www.thetimes.co.uk/article/quiet-
please-amazon-meetings-begin-in-silence-wd0zmhzc0 (archived at
https://perma.cc/CA6E-CR4D)

25   Cooperrider, DL and Whitney, D [accessed 3 April 2021] A Positive Revolution
in Change: Appreciative Inquiry [Online] www.researchgate.net/
publication/237404587_A_Positive_Revolution_in_Change_Appreciative_
Inquiry (archived at https://perma.cc/9SYD-2LMB)

26   Bushe, G [accessed 3 April 2021] What is Appreciative Inquiry? [Online]
www.gervasebushe.ca/appinq.htm (archived at https://perma.cc/N2QP-HLCZ)

27   Cave, N [accessed 3 April 2021] The Red Hand Files, Issue #109, August 2020
[Online] www.theredhandfiles.com/what-is-mercy-for-you/ (archived at
https://perma.cc/6LSM-EZEN)

INDEX